1001 TEXAS PLACE NAMES

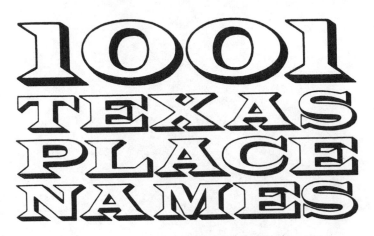

1001 TEXAS PLACE NAMES

BY FRED TARPLEY

Sketches by Sally Blakemore

University of Texas Press
Austin and London

Requests for permission to reproduce material from this
work should be sent to Permissions, University of Texas
Press, Box 7819, Austin, Texas 78712.

Library of Congress Cataloging in Publication Data

Tarpley, Fred.
  1001 Texas place names.
  Includes index.
  1. Texas—Gazetteers.   I. Title.
F384.T28   917.64'00321   80-16828
ISBN 0-292-76015-9
ISBN 0-292-76016-7 (pbk.)

For Jolene,

Ted, Marie, Mark,

names I value above all others.

Contents

Preface

Imprinted on the maps representing the 267,339 square miles of land and water within the boundaries of Texas are place names unsurpassed by those of any other American states for the diversity of their origins and fanciful manipulations of language. The place names mark any geographical spot which Texans or their predecessors have labeled: a city of thousands or a crossroads community with no post office, a major river or a trickling creek, a mountain or a valley, an oil field or a landing strip, a park or a cemetery.

From the research files of the Place Name Survey of Texas, developed during the past twenty years, 1001 place names from the Lone Star State have been selected. In a democratic gesture, each of the 254 counties of Texas is represented by at least two names, but beyond that automatic inclusion the remaining 493 place names compete on the basis of the unique, significant, or appealing stories to be found in their origins. Far more than 1001 names have actually been incorporated into this work, since many of the entries mention names previously used for the same place or for other places in the state sharing the same name.

The components of an entry are listed below:

THE PLACE NAME: *Burkburnett.*

THE COUNTY: *(Wichita).* Where the place is not entirely within one county, all the counties containing it are listed, separated by commas. Where significant information is given about the use of a name for separate places in different counties, the names of the relevant counties are separated by semicolons. (Such lists do not necessarily include all counties in which the name has been used.)

PRONUNCIATION: [bərk bər 'nɛt]: The local pronunciation is recorded in symbols of the phonetic alphabet (see list of symbols below) if there might be any reasonable question about how the name is pronounced. Not even phonetic symbols can represent the melodies of a Texas twang, however. For symbols used, see page xix. In cases of names pronounced differently by local residents of different ethnic and linguistic backgrounds, only the Anglicized versions of the names are given. Research has not been done on how the names are pronounced by non-Anglo residents.

BODY OF ENTRY: In a short narrative, the origin of the name is given and, in many instances, more than one version is reported. An attempt is made to sort out the probable from the improbable origins, but often no hope remains for authenticating the motives of the name-givers, and the folklore might as well be enjoyed. Along with the explanation of the name origin, the narrative includes a generic identification of the map feature bearing the name, historical information, dates, pioneer leaders, earlier names, and the occurrence of the name elsewhere in Texas.

POST OFFICE HISTORY: *PO Sept. 6, 1882 (Gilbert)–May 9, 1891; Mar. 10, 1892–Sept. 15, 1898; Mar. 10, 1902–Oct. 31, 1903; Apr. 18, 1907 (Burkburnett)–*. This information indicates that the first post office to serve the area opened on September 6, 1882, under the name of *Gilbert*, but was discontinued in 1891. The following year a post office was reestablished under the same name and operated for six years before closing. The name was used once again when a post office reopened in 1902, only to close again in 1903. In 1907, the present name was assigned to a new post office, which continues to the present. A few of the postal records are incomplete because of omissions in the federal archives or occasionally because of a blot or crease on a page of old records. Occasionally one or more of the names included in the post office history does not correspond to any of the names discussed in the entry. In such cases, the post office is listed because it served an area including the community listed in the entry and was thus a forerunner of the post office whose history is being traced.

POPULATION: *Pop. 9,829.* The population given is the figure reported by the *Texas Almanac* as the U.S. Census Bureau estimate for 1975.

ELEVATION: For hills or mountains of comparatively significant height in Texas, the elevation reported is that given by the *Texas Almanac,* usually listing altitudes of the U.S. Geological Survey or U.S. Coast and Geodetic Survey, but in some instances figures of highway or railroad engineers.

INCORPORATION: *Inc.* For communities which are incorporated, an indication is given along with a notation if incorporation has taken place since 1970. In some narratives, earlier dates of incorporation are noted.

Origins of these 1001 place names fall rather comfortably into eleven categories devised for a computerized analysis of Texas place names. The subdivisions of these eleven patterns of namegiving are illustrated below by names among the 1001 entries:

1. Names derived from people
   a. Local individuals: *Daingerfield*
   b. Nonlocal individuals: *Tyler*
   c. Local groups: *Kickapoo Creek*
   d. Nonlocal groups: *Tioga*
2. Geographic features
   Cutting across the subdivisions below are both objective descriptions (*Apple Springs*) and subjective descriptions (*Garden of Eden*).
   a. Flora: *Acala*
   b. Fauna: *Antelope Creek*
   c. Minerals: *Alum*
   d. Terrain: *Grand Prairie*
3. Multiple categories
   a. Local name and geographic feature: *Potters Point*
   b. County and person: *Floydada*
   c. Names of disputed origins traced to more than one category of origin: *Sublime*
4. Other places
   a. Nearby places: *New Waverly*
   b. Distant places: *Abilene*
5. Cultural sources
   a. The Bible: *Pisgah*
   b. Religion: *Hardshell Creek*
   c. Literature: *Tarzan*

    d. Mythology: *Amphion*
    e. Radio: *Jot 'Em Down*
    f. Comics: *Mutt and Jeff*
 6. Mode of selection of name
    a. Whim: *Admiral*
    b. Assignment by post office: *Art*
 7. Anecdotes, customs, events
    a. Anecdotes: *Benonine*
    b. Customs: *Ambia*
    c. Events: *Bloody Hollow*
 8. Language alteration
    a. Blends: *Dalhart*
    b. Backward spellings: *Saxet Oil and Gas Field*
    c. Acronyms: *Talco*
    d. Misunderstandings: *Bogata*
 9. Company names and brand names
    a. Company names: *Sugarland*
    b. Brand names: *Wamba*
10. Other sources
    Only a few names would not fit into the nine
    categories above. For example, *Three P* took its
    name from the fact that when three schools
    whose names all began with the letter *P*—Prairie
    Hill, Portland, and Philadelphia—were consoli-
    dated, the new school was called *Three P*. Later
    the surrounding community assumed the name.
11. Unknown origins
    Unfortunately, the reason behind the bestowing of
    some names must be classified as unknown after
    research shows that local stories explaining the
    name are improbable. Such a name in this cate-
    gory is *Algoa*, often attributed to the name of a
    British vessel blown inland to this area during the
    great Galveston hurricane of 1900. The validity of
    this version is shattered by the discovery that the
    post office with this name was established in 1897
    and the name is found on county maps as early as
    1891. The origin must be regarded as unknown
    until plausible explanations can be advanced.

Another significant classification of each place
name may be based on the language in which it originated. Linguistic origins must be considered apart
from the categories of namegiving patterns listed
above, for they cut across divisions of name origins;

nevertheless, the language providing the name casts considerable light on the several waves of immigrants into Texas.

From various North American Indian languages came *Kemah*, *Kiomatia*, and *Tahoka*. Spanish supplied thousands of names, such as *Amarillo*, *Arroyo Colorado*, *Calavaras*, and *Cibolo*, especially in the southern and western portions of the state. French speakers made their presence felt with *La Reunion* and *La Marque*, while Gemans placed *Bergheim* and *Boerne* on the Texas map. Names such as *Hranice*, *Praha*, and *Frydek* lead to Czech settlements, while *Panna Maria* and *Kosciusko* point to Polish-language communities. Speakers of Danish gave their new Texas home the name of *Danevang*. Although speakers of Latin never reached Texas, the influence of this classical language is felt in names such as *Ponta*, *Alto*, and *Aspermont*, while *Walhalla*, *Elysian Fields*, and *Anahuac* indicate a knowledge of Norse, Greek, and Aztec mythology on the part of the residents assigning these names.

It would be a mistake, however, to attempt to link *Italy*, *Tokio*, *Moscow*, or *Roma* to the languages spoken in these international locales. The Texas places bearing the names were assigned not by foreign immigrants but for varying reasons by local residents who had never been outside the country.

Serious research into place names requires the skill, persistence, and inductive powers of the shrewdest detective. Playing a guessing game and deciding that *Cologne* must have been named for the town in Germany or that *Black Cat Thicket* traces its origin to a dark feline lead to the embarrassing revelations that *Cologne* was given ironically for a cattle shipping station that was a "sweet smelling" place and that Black Cat was the name of an Indian chief who hunted in the thicket. Good starting points for research on Texas place names and other topics relating to the state are two encyclopedic authorities: the three-volume *Handbook of Texas* and the *Texas Almanac*, published in alternate years by the *Dallas Morning News*. Two books that deal exclusively with Texas place names are Fred I. Massengill's *Texas Towns*, a 1936 listing of towns with post offices and the origins of their names; and Fred Tarpley's *Place Names of*

Northeast Texas, including 2,600 names in the north-eastern corner of the state. Research then leads to any printed source likely to contain information about Texas map names: county and community histories and archives, newspapers (especially anniversary issues and columns by reporters of name lore such as Frank X. Tolbert of the *Dallas Morning News* and Leon Hale of the *Houston Post*), city directories, telephone directories, birth records, death records, cemetery inventories, postal histories, diaries, letters, old maps, theses, dissertations, magazine articles, abstract records, maps showing land patents, deeds, and family histories.

While continuing to exhaust printed sources, the researcher also obtains information through interviews, telephone conversations, and correspondence with persons familiar with place names: local residents or their descendants, postal officials, county agricultural agents, newspaper editors and reporters, librarians, local historians, church leaders, county clerks, county judges, county tax collectors, teachers, mapmakers, and abstract-office clerks. Often a letter to a smalltown newspaper, listing the names about which information is needed, unlocks the secret of place name origins, for it may elicit responses from persons privy to information which they otherwise would never have put on paper. Radio and television stations are sometimes willing to broadcast appeals to their audiences to send the desperate place names researcher information about specific names. Radio talk shows get immediate responses from listeners who report information on the telephone.

In final desperation, the researcher visits the scene of the namegiving, looking for clues to lead to an inductive conclusion. Do wild onions still grow along *Onion Creek,* or do county records show that an Onion family had reached the area by the time the first maps began to record the name? When viewed from a particular angle, does *Casket Mountain* resemble the shape its name suggests? Does *Star Lake* have five prongs, or did a Star family ever live in the area? Do the earliest tombstones in the *Stewart Cemetery* bear names of the Stewart family, or was there a community nearby named Stewart? On-the-scene investigations and a knock on every door in a community may leave the mystery of the name origins unsolved, causing the onomastic detective to give up until more clues appear.

As an added measure in assuring the accuracy of the information reported in this study, each of these 1001 Texas place names was submitted to postmasters in the immediate locale of the name with the request that postal officials review the entries for accuracy and omissions or pass them on to an authority on local history. Through this process, almost all the entries were returned with the postal officials' approval, recommendations for changes, or comments that the information was accurate as far as anyone could determine. Any corrections that readers can supply will be considered in revisions to be made for future publications on Texas place names.

F.T.

Acknowledgments

The complete enumeration of individuals who have contributed to *1001 Texas Place Names* would be much longer than the list of place names themselves. For most of these names, information has been given by authors, local residents, and student researchers. During the twenty years since the Place Name Survey of Texas began, students at East Texas State University have written term papers, theses, and dissertations and worked as research assistants, with significant achievement by Elizabeth Davis, Dickie Fox, Patsy Gaby, Donald Gill, Jo Anne Gray, Lois Hays, Olga Murley, Bill Riddle, Phillip Rutherford, and Carla Smith Shields, to mention only a few.

Local historians and Texas residents have been generous in sharing their information about map names. The U.S. Geological Survey has made available detailed maps of Texas and has been helpful in offering the resources of its extensive library in Reston, Virginia. Michael McCann of the Texas Land Office provided assistance in supplying maps and names research records from his office.

The James G. Gee Library at East Texas State University, in addition to its excellent collection of Texas historical and onomastic materials, agreed to build a special collection of place names books for its archives division and to bring tons of printed materials through interlibrary loan to the campus for my use. Other collections where research was especially fruitful were the Dallas, Fort Worth, Houston, San Antonio, Abilene, and Austin public libraries; the old Main and new Perry-Castañeda libraries and the Barker Texas History Center at the University of Texas at Austin; the Texas State Library; the New York Public Library; and the Library of Congress.

Research for the study of Texas place names was made possible in part by two grants through Organized Research at East Texas State University, an educational research program directed by Dr. H. M. Lafferty, and I am most appreciative of this support, which included statistical analysis of materials by the computer center at East Texas State University. I am also endebted to Nina Smith and Una Harris for their assistance in the preparation of this manuscript, to Margaret Roberts for her perceptive editing, and to George M. Stokes of Baylor University for permission to use material from his *Guide to the Pronunciation of Texas Towns*.

Special acknowledgement is made to the encouragement given by the American Name Society through its Place Name Survey of the United States and through its annual meetings, which have served as a forum for scholars interested in place names research and other branches of onomastics. Among the American Name Society members who have exerted strong influence on my work are Margaret M. Bryant, Lurline Coltharp, Frederic G. Cassidy, E. C. Ehrensperger, Byrd Granger, Kelsie Harder, W. F. H. Nicolaisen, Donald J. Orth, Allen Walker Read, Elsdon Smith, and George R. Stewart. To the many other unnamed persons who have aided in Texas place names research, including scholars who come to Commerce each June for the South Central Names Institute and members of my family, I express my gratitude for their support.

F.T.

Phonetic Symbols

Vowels	Key Words
i	b<u>ee</u>, s<u>ea</u>
ɪ	p<u>i</u>ty, s<u>i</u>t
e	r<u>a</u>te, b<u>ai</u>t
ɛ	y<u>e</u>t, p<u>e</u>t
æ	m<u>a</u>t, s<u>a</u>t
a	<u>ah</u>
ɔ	j<u>aw</u>, <u>a</u>ll
o	n<u>o</u>, b<u>oa</u>t
ʊ	f<u>u</u>ll, w<u>oo</u>d
u	b<u>oo</u>t, r<u>u</u>le
ə	<u>a</u>bove, ag<u>e</u>nt, penc<u>i</u>l, <u>o</u>ccur, circ<u>u</u>s

Diphthongs	Key Words
aɪ	b<u>i</u>te, wh<u>i</u>le
aʊ	h<u>ow</u>, l<u>ou</u>d
ɔɪ	t<u>oy</u>, b<u>oi</u>l

Consonants	Key Words
p	<u>p</u>ipe, li<u>p</u>
b	<u>b</u>ee, <u>bib</u>
t	<u>t</u>ot, pi<u>t</u>
d	<u>d</u>i<u>d</u>, la<u>dd</u>er
k	<u>k</u>eep, coo<u>k</u>
g	<u>g</u>o, bi<u>g</u>

f	full, enough
v	vivid, of
θ	thin, ether
ð	then, either
s	source, less
z	zone, is
š	shy, machine
ž	vision, measure
h	hat, ahead
č	church, watch
ǰ	judge, gem
m	mum, dim
n	no, noon
ṇ	cotton, button, with n forming its own syllable
ŋ	sing, ink
l	level, pool
w	walk, we
hw	which, as pronounced by those who do not give it the same pronunciation as witch
y.	young, first sound of union
r	rarity, red

Other Symbols	Meaning
ˈ	primary or strong secondary stress in syllable following symbol [a la ˈsan]
ˌ	secondary or weaker stress in syllable following symbol [ə ˌræn zəs ˈpæs]
[ ]	enclosure for phonetic symbols

1001 TEXAS PLACE NAMES

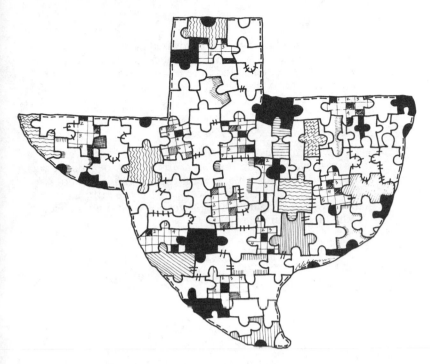

Abe *(Houston)*

The first postmaster in the community was Abraham B. Thomas. His nickname of *Abe* was submitted to Washington when the post office was established.
PO Dec. 16, 1887–Oct. 24, 1888.

Aberdeen *(Collingsworth)*

The community is named for the Earl of Aberdeen from Aberdeen, Scotland, who owned the Rocking Chair Ranch before 1900. Aberdeen was a division headquarters for the ranch.
PO Dec. 28, 1889–Mar. 14, 1942.

Abilene *(Jones, Taylor)* ['æb ə lin]

The town was established on March 15, 1881, when the Texas and Pacific Railway completed track to the townsite and an auction sale of lots was held. The founders, John Simpson and Colonel C. W. Merchant, believed that their Texas venture would become an even more important city than the Kansas cattle-shipping point after which it was named.
PO Feb. 14, 1881–; Pop. 107,000; Inc. 1883.

Acala *(Hudspeth)* [ə 'ke lə]

The name of the town refers to Acala cotton, a type of long-staple cotton which originated in Acala, Mexico. W. T. Young, who settled here in 1921, was a grower of Acala cotton.
Pop. 25.

Acampo *(Shackelford)* [ə 'kæm po]

This whistle stop on the Missouri, Kansas, and Texas Railroad was once called *Reynolds Switch* because it was the location of loading pens on the Reynolds Ranch. Spanish-speaking laborers working for the railroad lived in converted boxcars called *acampos*, and the railroad soon adopted the name.

Acton *(Hood)* ['æk tən]

Formerly *Comanche Peak*, for a hill used as a Comanche lookout post, the town became *Acton*, either for a Miss Acton, sweetheart of a Mr. Hollis, the first merchant in town, or because the large stands of oak trees suggested the old English name of *Acton*, meaning "oak town."
PO Mar. 16, 1868–Sept. 15, 1906; Pop. 130.

Addran *(Hopkins)* ['æd 'ræn]

The community was named by Ulysses Aguier, a minister who settled there in 1857 after attending Add-Ran

College in Hood County, now Texas Christian University in Fort Worth. The original name of the college came from its founders, Addison and Randolph Clark.
PO Dec. 8, 1890–Oct. 31, 1906.

Admiral *(Callahan)*

The German founder, Henry L. Buchen, seems to have been very fond of military tradition.
PO Sept. 21, 1897–Aug. 31, 1929; Pop. 18.

Adsul *(Newton)* ['æd səl]

A combination of the names *Adams* and *Sullivan* gave the community its name, referring to the Adams-Sullivan Lumber Company, which built a sawmill here in 1906.

Afton *(Dickens)* ['æf tən]

Seeking something more poetic than a name referring to the West Texas cottonwood tree, citizens chose a name suggested by the song, "Flow Gently, Sweet Afton." *Beckton*, the name chosen for the first postmaster, Francis E. Beck, had become *Cottonwood*, for the school on Cottonwood Creek, when the teacher, Myra Kelley, was asked to choose a new post office name. Her first choice of *Acton* was rejected because of duplication, but a one-letter alternation produced *Afton* and a pleasing reference to the well-known song.
PO Feb. 19, 1891 (Beckton)–July 10, 1893; May 5, 1894–Sept. 17, 1895; Apr. 24, 1900 (Afton)–; Pop. 100.

Alamo *(Hidalgo)* ['æl ə mo]

The Alamo Land and Sugar Company established the town in 1909. It was first called *Ebenezer*; later the name became *Swallow*, but residents did not like either name. Promoters decided that *Alamo* should be the name, honoring the shrine of Texas liberty in San Antonio. Despite frowns from postal authorities, *Alamo*, the Spanish word for "cottonwood tree," finally won approval. Another post office named *Alamo* had operated in Reeves County from November 3, 1903 to May 16, 1905.
PO Aug. 29, 1919 (Forum)–Oct. 30, 1919 (Alamo)–; Pop. 5,564; Inc.

Alazan Bay *(Kleberg)* [a la 'san] [a lə 'zan]

The name is taken from El Alazán, the Spanish grant of Vicente de Ynojosa, which bordered the bay on the northwest. The name is Spanish meaning "sorrell" or "sandy" and may have been applied to either wild horses, cattle, or the color of the soil.

Algoa *(Galveston)* [æl 'go ə]

Tradition and several printed sources have attributed the name to a British vessel, the *Algoa*, blown inland to this area during the great hurricane and flood of September 1900. The ship remained here for sixteen months and was remembered when the town later needed a name for its post office. The fallacy of this tradition is exposed by two facts: the post office was named three years before the storm, and the name *Algoa* appears on a map of the county as early as 1891.
PO Oct. 14, 1897–July 31, 1959; Pop. 135.

Allenreed or Alanreed *(Gray)*

After surviving the names of *Spring Tank* or *Springtown*, for a large tank of water fed by springs; *Prairie Dog Town*, for the rodents of the plains; and *Gouge Eye*, for a

saloon fight, the town was given a new name. It honors the owners of a contracting firm, Allen and Reed, active when the Rock Island Line came in 1901.
PO Mar. 20, 1886 (Eldridge)–Oct. 5, 1893; Apr. 17, 1894– Apr. 24, 1902 (Alanreed)–discontinued by 1924.

Allentown *(Angelina)*

So many members of the Allen family lived in the community which began as *Allen's Gin* that the town became *Allentown* with the demise of cotton farming.

Allred *(Yoakum)* ['ɔl rɛd]

The town was established in 1938 as James V. Allred was completing his term as thirtieth governor of Texas. A Mr. Young and associates founded the town in December 1937.
PO May 17, 1938–Mar. 14, 1957.

Alpine *(Brewster)* ['æl paɪn]

When the Southern Pacific Railroad came in 1882, T. C. Murphy owned Kokernot Springs, the only water in the area. He bargained with the railroad to supply its water if the station would be named *Murphyville*. While the railroad did not object to the name, some of the townspeople did. One day C. E. Way, Walter Garnett, and others were talking in the back of the drug store when the subject of the town name came up. Garnett picked up a post office directory and began thumbing through it, stopping at the name of Alpine, Alabama. That name seemed suitable for their town, situated in the mountains at an altitude of 4,481 feet. A petition was circulated asking the government to change the name to Alpine, and on February 3, 1888, an election in which ninety-two votes were cast made the new name official.
PO Dec. 14, 1883 (Murphyville)–Feb. 3, 1888 (Alpine)–; Pop. 6,171; Inc.; El. 4,481.

Altair *(Colorado)* [ɔl 'tær]

Conflict with *Stafford* in Fort Bend County caused the name of Stafford Ranch to be changed to *Altair* for the largest star in the Alpha Aquilae constellation. Curly Jones is credited with suggesting the new name. A minority voice reports that the name actually refers to cowboys who were "all on a tear."
PO Oct. 5, 1888 (Stafford Ranch)–Sept. 19, 1890 (Altair)–; Pop. 80.

Alto *(Cherokee)* ['æl to]

In Latin and Spanish, *alto* means "high," alluding to the location on a high divide between the Neches and Angelina rivers. Captain Henry Berryman is said to have originated the name when the original townsite was planned in 1849. Those who believe the name came from the Spanish word for "stop" contend that the town was to be the first stop for stage coaches on the way from Nacogdoches to San Antonio.
PO Dec. 12, 1850 (Branchtown)–May 27, 1851 (Fort Lacy)–June 30, 1852 (Alto)–; Pop. 1,058; Inc.

Altoga *(Collin)* [æl 'to gə]

Dock Owensby, who has been called a Gay 90s advocate of "togetherness," wanted the postal authorities to accept *All Together*, Texas, but the policy in Washington at the time was to reject imaginative titles, especially those in phrase form. A compromise produced *Altoga* as a suggestion of the citizens' cooperative spirit. *Pop. 348.*

Alum *(Wilson)*

The alum content of the water in a nearby creek gave the stream a bitter taste as well as its name, which was transferred to the community developing along its banks.

Alward *(Howard)*

Citizens took the first syllable from Albert Fisher's name and the last from his brother Edward's to share the naming honors of this community, which is now extinct.

Amarillo *(Potter, Randall)* [æm ə 'rɪl o] [æm ə 'rɪl ə]

Amarillo is a Spanish word meaning "yellow." In 1887, Henry B. Sanborn laid out a townsite near Amarillo Lake, named by Spanish-speaking herders because of the yellow color of its banks and the yellow flowers that abounded there. Sanborn first called his townsite *Oneida,* but changed it to *Amarillo* when it was designated county seat in an election in which cowboys of the three major ranches of the area served as principal voters. Some sources trace the yellow reference to houses in the area that were painted yellow.
PO Nov. 23, 1887–; Pop. 156,000; Inc.

Ambia *(Lamar)* ['æm bɪə] ['æm bi]

The word was coined by a justice of the peace in nearby Roxton to describe the amber jets of tobacco juice expectorated by men congregating at the village store.
PO June 17, 1886–Apr. 29, 1905; Pop. 20.

Amphion *(Atascosa)* ['æm fi ən]

In Greek mythology Amphion, one of the sons of Zeus and Antiope, built the walls of Thebes by charming the stones into place with a lyre.
PO Aug. 27, 1886–Sept. 15, 1916.

Anacacho Mountains *(Kinney)* [æn ə 'ka čo]

One account says the name was derived from a ceremonial rite honoring an Indian god, but the Indian name for the mountain was *Decate*. Another more believable explanation traces the name to Ana Cacho, wife of an early Spanish rancher in the area.

Anahuac *(Chambers)* ['æn ə wæk]

The town is well described in its Aztec name meaning "plain near the water." An earlier name was *Chambersia*, given when a post office was established in 1859. Chambersia, often spelled *Chambersea*, was the plantation home of Thomas Jefferson Chambers, for whom the county was named. Between 1821 and 1825, the place had been called *Perry's Point*, for Henry Perry.
PO May 22, 1846 (Anahuac)–Aug. 15, 1846 (Chambersia)–Apr. 11, 1849 (Anahuac)–June 28, 1853; Oct. 9, 1855 (Chambersia)–Aug. 17, 186?; June 13, 1870 (Anahuac)–; Pop. 1,936; Inc.

Anarene *(Archer)* ['æn ə rin]

The name honors Anna Laurene Graham, using *Ana-* from her first name and *-rene* from her second name.
PO Mar. 6, 1909–Feb. 28, 1955.

Anchor *(Brazoria)*

When the railroad built a line from Velasco to connect with the International–Great Northern in the early 1900s, the site became known as *Chenango Junction*, the Spanish meaning "short and shady." It was about this time that Jacob Whistler arrived from Anchor, Illinois, and built a hotel to accommodate passengers who changed trains here. He honored his hometown by suggesting the name change. Another story attributes the name to the cattle brand from a nearby ranch.
PO Apr. 28, 1897–June 15, 1920.

Anchorage *(Atascosa)*

A Scottish seaman named Thomas Whittet declared when the settlement gained permission for a post office: "I don't know, but I've anchored here, so I think I'll call it *Anchorage*."
PO Jan. 2, 1889–1920s.

Andrews *(Andrews)*

The first man to fall in the Texas Revolution, at the Battle of Concepción, was Richard Andrews, for whom the county and its seat of government were named. The town's population grew from 611 in 1940 to 3,309 in 1950 as oil and livestock expanded. By 1965, the county of 15,000 served by this one post office had produced its billionth barrel of oil.
PO Jan. 20, 1909–; Pop. 9,915; Inc.

Angel City *(Goliad)*

Only an abandoned schoolhouse remains in the community named ironically because of the rowdy residents associated with the area years ago. Infamous fights often accompanied the regular weekend dances held here.

Angelina River *(Angelina, Cherokee, Jasper, Nacogdoches, Rusk, San Augustine)* [æn jə ˈli nə]

According to an old Spanish legend, an Indian girl who helped the early Spanish missionaries among the Tejas Indians in 1690 was given the pet name of *Angelina*, "little angel." Historical accounts tell of a Hainai Indian girl who, because of her unusual promise, was taken to the mission of San Juan Bautista on the Rio Grande, where she was baptized. Before 1713 she returned to her people and became a fluent interpreter, befriending both Spanish and French in the area. The river and the county took their name from the Indian girl.

Antelope Creek *(Throckmorton)*

The large herds of antelope at play in the area suggested the name of the creek. At least nine other Antelope creeks flow in Texas.

Anthony *(El Paso)* [ˈæn θə ni]

When the Santa Fe Railroad built its line in 1881, the station was placed on the Texas side and named *La Tuna*, Spanish for "prickly pear cactus." A Spanish-speaking woman named Sabrina, who had a chapel on the New Mexico side dedicated to Saint Anthony of Padua, insisted on the name *Anthony* rather than *La Tuna* for the new town. The name is shared by communities in Fannin and Bexar counties.
PO Mar. 17, 1884–Apr. 1, 1884; reestablished on Texas–New Mexico border–; Pop. 2,299; Inc.

Apolonia *(Grimes)* [æ pə 'lo ni ə]

Nineteenth-century Polish Catholic settlers took the name of their town from Saint Apollonia, dropping one *l*. It was established about 1835 as a lumbering center.
PO Aug. 14, 1889–Dec. 31, 1907.

Apple Springs *(Trinity)*

Apple Springs was originally named May Apple Springs because of the abundance of May apples growing near the springs. Later the name was shortened.
PO June 23, 1884–; Pop. 130.

Aransas Pass *(Aransas, Nueces, San Patricio)*
[ə ˌræn zəs 'pæs]

When the town was laid out in 1885, it was called *Aransas Harbor*; it was changed to *Aransas Pass* in 1892. The name was taken from that of the pass between Mustang and St. Joseph's islands. The origin of the name *Aranzazu* is not clear. It could have come from the name of a castle in Spain or from the Karankawa language. The name was used by Joaquín de Oribio Basterra in 1746 when he explored and mapped the Gulf Coast.
PO Aug. 27, 1890 (Aransas Harbor)–Aug. 26, 1892 (Aransas Pass)–; Pop. 6,417; Inc.

Ariola *(Hardin)*

The present name honors Eduardo and Francisco Ariola, on whose leagues part of the town was first built in 1889. The original name of *Sharon* was later changed to *Hooks Switch*, for George W. Hook, in 1886, and the town was later known locally as *Chance* for a local family.
PO Nov. 6, 1888 (Hooks Switch)—Feb. 21, 1901 (Ariola)—Oct. 15, 1907.

Arrow Oil Field *(Gaines)*

The name of the field was coined to suggest the Amarado and Rowing Drilling Company.

Arroyo Colorado *(Cameron)* [ə 'rɔ yo 'ka lə ra do]

Throughout the state these two Spanish words are often found separately in place names. *Arroyo* is "a creek bed," and *colorado* is "reddish." The Cameron County stream was named for its reddish waters, and the name was transferred to the nearby settlement in the 1860s. The water course is an old bed of the Rio Grande.
PO Aug. 22, 1887—Dec. 31, 1907.

Arroyo River *(Hudspeth)* [ə 'rɔ yo]

While no one would ever think of tolerating *Creek River* or *Mountain Hill* as place names, such combinations are possible if the meaning of one of the names is obscured by a foreign language. Such is the case of *arroyo*, Spanish for "wash" or "creek," combined with English *river*. Other instances of such repetitive meanings are *Rio Grande River*, *River Avon*, and *River Thames*.

Art *(Mason)*

When a post office was assigned, the town was called *Plehweville* for Otto Plehwe, the first postmaster and general store keeper. In December 1920, the town was told by the postal authorities that *Plehweville* was out, not only because of its troublesome spelling but because so much mail intended for the town was being sent to Pflugerville. When Ely W. Deckart, the postmaster, wrote to Washington asking for ideas, *Art* was suggested, from the last three letters of his name. The first recorded name for the area was Willow Creek.
PO Mar. 29, 1886 (Plehweville)—Dec. 6, 1920 (Art)—; Pop. 30.

Aspermont *(Stonewall)* ['æs pər mant]

In Latin *asper* means "rough" and *mont* is "mountain," giving this town the name of "rough mountain." It was known as *Sunflower Flat* to ranchers in the 1880s, but when A. L. Rhomberg donated the townsite in 1889 he chose the new name, perhaps influenced by nearby Snake Mountain, with snakes suggesting *asper*, or perhaps as a Latin translation of his German name.
PO Sept. 9, 1889–; Pop. 1,072; Inc.

Athens *(Henderson)*

First known as *Alvin*, Athens received its present name from Mrs. Dull Averitt in 1850. She thought it would be the cultural center of East Texas, and not until twenty-five years later was it noticed that Athens, Texas, like Athens, Greece, was built on seven hills. The name of the first post office in the area was *Alfred*, for Alfred F. Mallard, postmaster, but it was used as the post office name for only two years. There are those who contend that *Athens* was given by Mrs. Ducenia Thomas for her former home in Athens, Georgia.
PO June 13, 1848 (Alfred)–Mar. 11, 1850; Apr. 15, 1850 (Athens)–; Pop. 9,020; Inc.

Atlas *(Lamar)*

A rock quarry in the community was given a name alluding to Atlas, the Greek mythological character con-

demned to act as a stone pillar and support the sky on his shoulders. The name is attributed to Colonel E. H. R. Green, owner of the Texas Midland Railroad.
PO Feb. 13, 1884–Apr. 30, 1943; Pop. 30

Aubrey *(Denton)* ['ɔ brɪ]

Until the Missouri, Kansas, and Texas railroad and the Pacific railroad came, the community had been called *Ornego* for some unknown reason. When the post office was established, *Aubrey* was the name drawn from a hat containing three proposed names for the new town. Some believe the name drawn was that of a girlfriend of one of the men participating in the drawing. Local historians dismiss as unfactual a yarn that a wagon master was coaxing a team of mules down main street when he became annoyed because the mules were braying. He shouted, "Aw bray, you blankety-blanks." The incident, the listener is asked to believe, caused the town to be called *AwBray*, later evolving into *Aubrey*.
PO June 27, 1881–; Pop. 838; Inc. 1924.

Auburn *(Johnson)* ['ɔ bərn]

In 1850 the first settlers arrived in the autumn of the year and decided to name their new home *Autumn*. Later they decided that *Auburn*, suggested by the older name, would be more appropriate. A shift in the county line moved Auburn from Ellis to Johnson County in 1881.
PO Aug. 27, 1887–Oct. 31, 1906; Pop. 12.

Austonio *(Houston)* [ɔs 'to nɪ o]

The original name of *Pearville* was changed to *Creek* and then *Austonio*, suggested by a Miss Isbell. Stephen F. Austin, founder of the first Anglo community in the state, and the old San Antonio Trail, the oldest road in Texas, provided the two ingredients of this blended name.
PO Feb. 17, 1888 (Creek)–June 1, 1933 (Austonio)–June 1, 1936; Pop. 37.

Austwell *(Refugio)* ['ɔs wɛl]

The name consolidates the surname of the first two settlers in the area, Preston R. Austin and Jesse C. McDowell, founders of the community. Mrs. W. H. Dunson is credited with suggesting the blend of the two surnames.
PO Oct. 26, 1912–; Pop. 272; Inc.

Avoca *(Jones)* [ə ˈvo kə]

In the early 1870s when buffalo hunters, bone haulers, and cattlemen passed through on their way to market, the area was called the *Spring Creek Community*. With the coming of the Texas Central Railroad, J. L. Crostwaite moved his general store to the railroad from a location three miles away called *Avo*. He added *-ca* to *Avo* for the name of the new location.
PO Sept. 29, 1893 (Avo); Mar. 26, 1900 (Avoca)–; Pop. 121.

Avon *(Wichita)* [ˈe van]

A post office operated here from 1879 to 1881 in the community named for the English river. *Avon*, in Celtic, means "river."
PO Aug. 26, 1879–June 8, 1881.

Baby Head *(Llano)*

At the end of an Indian attack, the head of a baby belonging to one of the slain settlers was placed on a pole. The name was also given to a nearby mountain and to a creek.
PO Mar. 21, 1879–Aug. 31, 1918; Pop. 20.

Bachelor Peak *(Burnet)*

Two stories tell how unmarried men gave the mountain its name. One account describes five pioneer bachelors spending the night gambling and feasting on the highest point in the area. Another claims that Alexander Brown and six other bachelors from Burnet had a picnic here.

Bacontown *(Jackson)*

The smell of bacon cooking at breakfast time in this Black community had nothing to do with its naming. The title honors one of the original settlers, Wash Bacon.

Bagdad *(Williamson)* [ˈbæg dæd]

After Charles Babcock surveyed the town in 1854, name-givers began looking for something that sounded historic and romantic. They found it in the name of the old city of Iraq. In 1882, the community merged with Leander, named for Leander Brown, an official of the A&NW Railroad.
PO May 8, 1855–Oct. 6, 1882 (merger with Leander).

Bald Prairie *(Robertson)*

The open land is located on a rise between Duck and
Steele creeks, and its appearance suggested the name.
This childhood home of novelist Jewel Gibson inspired
parts of *Joshua Beene and God.*
*PO Sept. 29, 1875–Oct. 16, 1878; Dec. 20, 1878–July 31,
1950; Pop. 31.*

Balmorhea *(Reeves)* [bæl mə 're]

The land promoters who established the town were Bal-
colm, Morrow, and Rhea. Someone figured out a method
of honoring all three by combining the first three or four
letters of their surnames.
PO Aug. 4, 1908–; Pop. 651; Inc.

Balsora *(Wise)* [bæl 'zor ə]

The community was called *Wild Horse Prairie* until a
post office was established, and the postal department
assigned *Balzora* as the name. A resident living there
then petitioned that the spelling be changed to *Balsora*
because he could not make a *z.*
*PO Apr. 14, 1894–Feb. 8, 1896; Apr. 12, 1900–Oct. 15,
1924; Pop. 50.*

Bandera Pass *(Bandera)* [bæn 'dɛ rə]

The most probable source of the name is General Bandera, sent by the king of Spain to San Antonio to protect

the colony from Apaches. The general is known to have fought battles at the pass. Attempts have been made to relate the name to its Spanish meaning of "flag." One story says that after pursuing Indians to the pass, Spaniards left flags planted on the mountain to warn them of punishment if they resumed raids. Another says a flag was placed on the mountain top as a sign of treaty between the Spanish and Indians.

Bankersmith *(Gillespie, Kendall)*

Although his official name was Temple D. Smith, the president of the first bank established in Fredericksburg was generally known as Banker Smith. Since *Smithville, Smithton,* and the like were no doubt already claimed as Texas town names, *Bankersmith* provided a distinctive possibility for incorporating *Smith* into a place name. *PO Sept. 28, 1915–;*

Barbarosa *(Guadalupe)* [bar bə 'ro sə]

The most probable version of the naming traces it to a German immigrant who settled in the area. His name was Frederick Barbarosas, whose surname means "of the red beard." During the middle ages, the emperor Frederick Barbarossa founded the first reich of Germany. *PO July 6, 1900–Oct. 16, 1900; Pop. 25.*

Bare Butte *(Wichita)* [bær 'byut]

The name is not descriptive of the hill, which is covered with a thick growth of grass; instead the name comes from a Mr. Barre, who settled in the southeast part of the county in the 1850s while leading a copper mining expedition. *El. 1,070.*

Barilla *(Reeves)* [bə 'rɪ lə] [bə 'ri yə]

In attempting to trace the name to Spanish, one source reports it is a word for "impure soda," often applied to a mineral alkali extracted from plants. Thus the salt brush plant growing in the area has given its name to mountains and to a creek.

Barnum *(Polk)* ['bar nəm]

The name is traced to two different men–Phineas T. Barnum, the legendary circus promoter and a friend of W. T. Carter, who established a sawmill here; or a Mr.

Barnum who owned a sawmill in Groveton, Texas.
*PO May 20, 1899 (Deaton)—Mar. 7, 1902 (Barnum)—;
Pop. 29.*

Barwise *(Floyd)*

Imaginations run wild on the background of this designation until it is established that the name honors the Joseph Hodson Barwise family of Wichita Falls. That name replaced *String,* used earlier as a tribute to J. W. Stringer.
Pop. 30.

Bass Hollow *(Stephens)* ['bæs ha lə]

Sam Bass and his gang, notorious for their daring train and bank holdups during the 1870s, once made their outlaw camp here.

Battle Creek *(Henderson)*

In 1838 in a battle between Whites and Indians, Chief Bowles, leading war chief of the Caddo Confederation, was killed along the stream by soldiers commanded by Sul Ross. *Battle Creek* also is found as a name in Armstrong, Callahan, and Shackelford counties.

Battle Ridge *(Cherokee)*

The battle referred to is a fuss caused by disagreement over the naming of the town. Finally an acceptable name emerged from the dispute itself. An earlier name of *Silas* had been selected for Silas Baines, the first merchant in the town.
PO Apr. 11, 1892 (Silas)—Mar. 15, 1907.

Baytown *(Harris)*

The present Baytown was born on January 24, 1951, from Goose Creek, Pelly, and Baytown. In the beginning Baytown developed around a sawmill and a store located near Galveston Bay. Pelly took its name from a leading citizen, F. T. Pelly. When the communities merged and took the name of *Baytown, Goose Creek* was retained as the name of the school district for the area.
PO Mar. 12, 1859 (Baytown)—Jan. 23, 1867; Aug. 12, 1924—; Pop. 48,191; Inc.

Beans Creek *(Cherokee)*

People, not vegetables, inspired the name. Chief Little Bean of the Cherokee Indians is one influence frequently mentioned in the name selection. Several families named Bean were among the first settlers in the county; prominent among them was Peter Ellis Bean, who settled on the stream about 1830.

Beans Place *(Jasper)*

Ira S. Bean built a store here in 1903 and established a post office named *Horger* for James M. Horger, president of the W. H. Ford Male and Female College at nearby Newton from 1893 to 1897. Confusion caused by the similarity of *Horger* with *Borger* and *Spurger* caused the postal department to request a change. The choice was *Beans Place.*
PO Sept. 2, 1903 (Horger)–Aug. 1, 1929 (Beans Place)–closed by 1933.

Bear Grass *(Leon)*

Native bear grass once provided good grazing for livestock. A new wave of settlers began to arrive in the early

20

1900s to develop a mining town, which declined after the soft coal was exhausted by 1930.
PO July 12, 1861–Dec. 5, 1863; Mar. 21, 1865–closed by 1904.

Beaumont *(Jefferson)* ['bo mant]

First called *Tevis Bluff* for Noah Tevis, who came to Texas in 1826, and then *Cow Bayou, Jefferson City*, and other names, the seat of Jefferson County received its present name according to some sources from Jefferson Beaumont and according to other sources from the French words meaning "beautiful hill," referring to a slight elevation along the coastal plain. On October 26, 1835, the *Telegraph and Texas Register*, published in San Felipe de Austin, stated: "It has received the name of Beaumont which, from the description of the place, strikes our fancy as very appropriate."
PO May 22, 1846–; Pop. 113,696; Inc.

Bebe *(Gonzales)* [beb]

Just as the town was looking for a name, a salesman promoting Beebee baking powder plastered signs in the community, and the town became known as Bebe. The

actual choice of the name is attributed to W. G. Bair, a grocer and the first postmaster.
PO Aug. 10, 1900–; Pop. 52.

Becerra Creek *(Webb)*

The Spanish name alludes to flood waters, which were controlled along the unruly creek when two dams were built in 1837.

Beef Head Creek *(Liberty)*

The name of this famous watering place in the early years of the area informed cattlemen that there was water in the creek for their herds.

Beeville *(Bee)*

First called *Maryville* for Mary Hefferman, only surviving heir of James Hefferman, who was killed by the Indians here in 1835, the town became *Beeville on the Poesta* (to differentiate from *Beeville on the Medio*) when another Maryville was discovered. The source of the latter name was General Barnard E. Bee, who founded the Texas army and later served as secretary of war and secretary of the treasury for the Republic of Texas.
PO Oct. 31, 1857 (Medio Hill)–May 6, 1859 (Beeville)–; Pop. 13,682; Inc.

Belgrade *(Newton)* ['bel gred]

The Serbian capital, also a river port, is believed to have been the source of the community's name. An earlier designation was *Biloxi*, given by Indians who might have recalled a visit to Biloxi, Mississippi, or who might have been from the Biloxi tribe themselves.
PO Dec. 17, 1847 (Biloxi)–Sept. 24, 1852; Dec. 13, 1853–Sept. 1, 1860 (Belgrade)–Nov. 5, 1866; Oct. 27, 1879–Apr. 14, 1906; Jan. 13, 1910–1936.

Belle Plain *(Callahan)*

Because the town was at one time connected by a cattle trail with Belle Plaine, Kansas, the name seemed appropriate. The name was also used for a post office in Moore County, 1929–1930.
PO Feb. 26, 1877 (Callahan)–June 18, 1878 (Belle Plain)–Oct. 12, 1888 (Belle Plaine)–June 25, 1894; Jan. 24, 1908 (Belle Plain)–Oct. 30, 1909.

Bells *(Grayson)*

The original name was *Gospel Ridge* because of the many churches, but when the Texas and Pacific Railroad opened in 1873 the church bells rang so loudly the citizens decided to adopt *Bells* as a new name.
PO June 12, 1871 (Dugansville)–Sept. 11, 1871; July 7, 1873–Sept. 8, 1879 (Bell)–June 20, 1893 (Bells)–; Pop. 629; Inc.

Ben Bolt *(Jim Wells)*

Some settlers had names so short that their first names and surnames could both be used in designating a town, as in *Tom Bean, Tomball, Ed Couch,* and *Burkburnett.* In this case, Ben Bolt was an early settler who was honored. Tom Collins laid out the townsite and, thinking of the ballad about "Ben Bolt and Sweet Alice," decided that *Ben Bolt* was most appropriate as a name for the community only seven miles from the town of Alice.
PO Dec. 4, 1906 (Nueces County)–Nov. 19, 1914 (Jim Wells County)–; Pop. 110.

Benhur *(Limestone)* [bɪn ˈhər]

A. T. Derden, impressed by Lew Wallace's epic novel *Ben Hur,* gave the name to the community.
PO May 3, 1895–Nov. 30, 1906; Pop. 200.

Benonine *(Wheeler)* [bɪn ə ˈnaɪn]

It is much easier to believe the town was named for the Benonine Oil and Gas Company than it is to accept the following tall tale. While a few men were gambling one night, one of the cards from the deck was lost–number nine. A card was named and used for the number, and the gambling continued almost all night. One man kept

winning, so much so that he was accused of winning because he had the marked card. He replied, "Well, it's been a nine all night."
PO Oct. 6, 1909–May 14, 1918.

Berclair *(Goliad)* [bər 'klær]

General agreement traces the name to the combination of syllables from the names of Bert and Clair Lucas, owners of a nearby ranch. Nevertheless, there is also a tradition that the name refers to the ancestral home of a Major Temple, a railroad surveyor, in Virginia.
PO Dec. 2, 1889–; Pop. 61.

Bergheim *(Kendall)* ['bərg haɪm]

The term is German, meaning "home of the hills," and refers to the hills in the area. Andreas Engel suggested the name when he and F. Hofheim settled the area in 1887.
PO May 17, 1901–Dec. 30, 1965.

Berlin *(Washington)* [bər 'lɪn]

All that remains of the town established in 1864 by German immigrants is the cemetery. Between 1881 and 1902, the community was called *Pesch* for a family operating a general store. Another community named *Berlin* was the site of a post office in Erath County from 1887 until 1905.
PO Nov. 26, 1860–Jan. 20, 1881 (Berlin); Jan. 25, 1881 (Pesch)–Feb. 15, 1899; Aug. 7, 1899 (Pesch)–Feb. 28, 1902.

Bessmay *(Jasper)*

After J. H. Kirby built a small sawmill here in 1900, his lumber business began to boom. When the time came to name the settlement, he gave it the name of his daughter *Bessmay*.
PO Sept. 16, 1903–; Pop. 1,669.

Best *(Reagan)*

Tom Best was a stockholder in the Kansas City, Missouri, and Ohio Railroad when this model oil camp was established during the boom days of the Big Lake Oil Field. The town came to be known as the one with the "best name and worst reputation." Hays County also had a Best community.
PO Aug. 26, 1924–; Pop. 25.

Big Foot *(Frio)*

The famous scout and Indian fighter, William A. (Big Foot) Wallace, 1817–1899, is remembered in the name of this town. The area was settled about 1854 and called *Connally's Store* for Bob Connally, who applied for a post office to be named *Big Foot* since Wallace was a resident in the community at that time.
PO Feb. 7, 1883–; Pop.75.

Big Fossil Creek *(Tarrant)*

The first fossil formations discovered on this waterway were found by John Boone, a descendant of Daniel. He was one of the first settlers on the creek near Birdville.

Big Spring *(Howard)*

Captain R. B. Marcy described *Big Spring* in Sulphur Draw in 1849 as the area's "abundant mesquite springs, surrounded by limestone rock, situated in a basin." It was also called the *Baptizing Hole*, the *Swimming Hole*, and the *Drowning Hole*. Herds of buffaloes, coyotes, lobos, antelopes, and wild mustangs used the watering place. The spring was a point of contention between Comanche and Shawnee Indians, and it provided a camping site for early explorations into the western area of Texas.
PO Oct. 2, 1882–; Pop. 29,134; Inc.

Birome *(Hill)* [baɪ 'rom]

R. L. Cartwright, an early settler, had two grandsons, Bickam and Jerome. Instead of choosing between them to give the town a name, he took the first two letters from *Bickam* and the last four letters from *Jerome*. When the post office was established, both *Cartwright* and *Birome* were submitted, but the postal department chose the latter.
PO Aug. 29, 1912–; Pop. 31.

Bi-Stone Oil Field *(Freestone, Limestone)*

The oil field is situated on the border between Freestone and Limestone counties.

Black Ankle *(Caldwell; San Augustine)*

The San Augustine County town was so named after a local belle tore her silk stocking at the ankle before a dance and concealed the rip by painting her exposed skin black with soot. In Caldwell County, the deep, black, waxy soil literally created some black ankles after heavy rains.

Black Cat Thicket *(Hunt)*

This region, once covered with thick undergrowth, was named for an Indian Chief, *Black Cat*, who settled with his tribe in the area before the coming of White settlers.

Black Monk *(Fannin)*

The Blacks and the Monks were leading families wishing to be honored when the post office was acquired in the 1880s. The name chosen recognized both clans.

Black Spring *(Bowie)*

The unusually dark color of the spring was given by its mineral content. When Uncle Andrew Dodge of Simms died at 110, friends said he had drunk from the spring every night to keep him "frocky."

Blanket *(Brown)*

While working in the eastern section of the county in
1852, a group of surveyors came upon the blankets of
Tonkawa Indians who had been hunting buffalo in Coleman County. Caught in a downpour of rain, the Indians
had spread their blankets on the sumac bushes near a
creek. When the bewildered surveyors saw this sight,
they found an obvious name for the creek. The name was
later transferred to the community that developed along
its banks.
PO June 10, 1875–; Pop. 453; Inc.

Bledsoe Creek *(Liberty)*

Names honoring Sam Houston were plentiful throughout
the state, but this creek name pays homage to Antoinette
Bledsoe, the sister-in-law of Sam Houston. Post offices
were given the name of *Bledsoe* in Cochran County
(1926–) and in Lubbock County (1918–1942).

Blessing *(Matagorda)*

Jonathan Edwards Pierce was so elated over the arrival of
the Southern Pacific Railroad as a boon to ranchers that
he wanted to name the town *Thank God*. The railroad
refused such a name, and *Blessing* was settled upon as a
less enthusiastic statement of appreciation for the rail
service. The earliest post office operated as *Deming's
Bridge*, named for E. A. Deming, the postmaster.
*PO June 22, 1858 (Deming's Bridge)–Nov. 5, 1866; Feb.
28, 1872–Mar. 3, 1899 (Hawley)–Aug. 17, 1903
(Blessing)–; Pop. 571.*

Bloodweed Island *(Palo Pinto)*

This island in Possum Kingdom Lake was named for the tall, red-snapped weed that grows here.

Bloody Hollow *(Delta)*

A serious disagreement between Mose Alexander and Tom Younger at a brush arbor meeting (an outdoor religious gathering under a log or timber frame with a brush canopy) resulted in a bitter feud, bloodshed, and a name for the community.

Bluetown *(Cameron)*

In war games for troops from Fort Brown in Brownsville and from Fort Ringgold in Rio Grande City, the "blue" forces and the "red" forces practiced their tactics along the Rio Grande. A favorite spot for the "blue" team developed into the little community that was given the name of *Bluetown*. A less likely explanation is the report that even before national prohibition, many people in the area objected to drinking so strongly that their neighbors called them "bluenoses" who resided in Bluetown.
PO Apr. 18, 1893–Sept. 21, 1898; Pop. 40.

Board *(Navarro)*

The name comes from the burr oak trees used for lumber in building the community of Board.
PO Jan. 27, 1886–Feb. 5, 1889; May 29, 1899–Dec. 15, 1904.

Bobo *(Shelby)* ['bo 'bo]

The name came from the owner of a local mill. In 1903, Emmett Burns from Teneha enlisted with other young men from the area in the National Guard. While stationed in Timpson, they would chant the names of their home towns while marching: "Teneha, Timpson, Bobo, and Blair." The chant was taken up as a marching song, and later the words added, "Let me off just any ole where." Bobo has since been absorbed into the area now known as *Meldrum*, honoring the president of the East and West Texas Railroad, which was built in 1885.
PO Apr. 18, 1893–Sept. 21, 1898.

Boerne *(Kendall)* ['bər nɪ]

Ludwig Boerne, the German writer and poet who had become a political refugee in West Texas, was honored by

German settlers in Kendall County. The community grew out of a town called *Tusculum*, laid out in 1849 but abandoned in 1851.
PO June 18, 1856–; Pop. 3,213; Inc.

Bogata *(Red River)* [bə ˈgo də]

J. E. Horner's handwriting on the post office application was intended as *Bogota*, for Bogotá, Colombia, but the flourishes were interpreted as *Bogata*. Although the name was recorded officially as *Bogata*, it was pronounced by citizens as if it were *Bogota*, with the stress on the second syllable. This community, thought to be the earliest Anglo-American settlement in North Texas, was begun by William Humphries as *Maple Springs* on Mustang Creek. During the 1880s, John Nance Garner, later vice president of the United States, attended a school that served Bogata and Rosalie.
PO Feb. 7, 1881–; Pop 1,258; Inc.

Bolsa Rancho *(Hidalgo)* [ˈbol sə ˈræn čo]

In Spanish, the name means "Ranch of the Purse." The settlement area was so named because the ranch which once existed in the area was the bandit lair of the notorious Juan Cortina, who brought his purse here.

Bone Hill *(Shelby)*

An entire herd of cattle waited for the return of Don Torbellino, cattle baron from Mexico, until all were dead. Their bodies were found in windrows around the rim of the hill, and later their bones bleached in the hot sun, suggesting the name for the summit. In Ellis County,

Bone Branch takes its name from huge bones, presumably those of dinosaurs, found along the creek.

Bones Chapel *(Grayson)*

A Presbyterian minister named Bone founded the chapel. The name was extended to the surrounding community.

Bono *(Johnson)* ['bo no]

The town leaders' search for a good name for such a good community ended when someone proved with a Latin dictionary that the word for "good" was *bono*. An earlier name for the area had been *Billingsley*, for James Billingsley. A post office named *Bono* operates in Wharton County.

Bon Wier *(Newton)* [ban 'wir]

B. R. Bonner and R. W. Wier were officials of the Kirby Lumber Company, an important industry for the region. *PO Dec. 1, 1906–; Pop. 475.*

Booker T. Washington Park *(Limestone)*

The land was set aside by deed in 1899 to be a permanent site for celebrating Juneteenth, the anniversary of the Texas announcement of the Emanicipation Proclamation. News of the signing of the proclamation on January 1, 1863, did not reach the Lone Star State until June 19. Slaves in the area first heard their freedom announced two miles south of the site named for the Black leader.

Boonville *(Brazos)*

Daniel Boone's distant relative, Mordecai, lent his name to the first county seat of Brazos County. The town tract was surveyed in 1841 after Boone came seeking a plantation site on the Brazos River. When the railroad was built through Bryan in 1866, missing Boonville by three miles, Bryan became the county seat.
PO May 22, 1846–Dec. 1, 1866.

Boracho Peak *(Jeff Davis)* [bə 'ra čo]

To explain the Spanish name meaning "drunk," the story is told of a man from Fort Davis who would become drunk in town. Being terribly afraid of his wife, he would ride his mule up this particular mountain and wait until

he was sober before returning home. *Borracho* can also
mean "violet colored," and this meaning is also reported
as the source of the name.
PO Dec. 7, 1908–Mar. 15, 1912; El. 5,661.

Bovina *(Parmer)* [bo 'vi nə]

Because the Santa Fe railroad workers often had to dis-
mount their trains to chase cattle from the XIT Ranch off
the tracks to be able to get through town, the area was
identified as *Bull Town*. The name was dignified as
Bovina when the post office was established, but the
new name retained the reference to the troublesome
cattle.
PO Jan. 31, 1899–.

Box Car Center *(Limestone)*
Because the first settlers used an abandoned railroad car
for living quarters and a store, the surrounding community took that name.

Brandy Creek *(Hood)*

A prohibited beverage was sometimes produced along
this stream.

Britamer *(Baylor)* ['brɪ tə mər]

The area developed its name from an abbreviated compounding of the British-American Oil Company. To ship oil to Canada, the company built a pipeline from its oil field to the railroad, and a loading dock called *Britamer* was built. When the station was abandoned in World War II, oil was then shipped to the Shell Pipeline Station.

Bronco *(Yoakum)* ['bran ko]

The location of the town in stock country and the delight of the cowboys in busting broncos led to the name. In Spanish, *bronco* means "wild, untamed horse."
PO Nov. 21, 1903–Aug. 26, 1966; Pop. 30.

Bronte *(Coke)* [brant]

The name of *Oso* (Spanish for "bear") was changed to *Bronco*. Then in 1890, it was changed again to honor the English novelist Charlotte Brontë (1816–1855). Some sources say the name is a tribute to the two Brontë sisters Charlotte and Emily.
PO Sept. 19, 1890–; Pop. 1,056; Inc.

Browndell *(Jasper)* [braun 'dɛl]

John Wilcox Brown, president of the Maryland Trust Company, lent his last name and the first name of his wife, Dell, to the naming of the town established in 1903 by the Kirby Lumber Company. The town declined after a fire destroyed the sawmill in 1925.
PO Aug. 14, 1903–May 31, 1928; Pop. 252; Inc. after 1970.

Buckeye *(Matagorda)*

Ohio is known as the Buckeye State for the tree native to the region. J. W. Stoddard and Dr. A. A. Plotner of Dayton, Ohio, both important landowners, named the place for their native state.
PO July 23, 1907–; Pop. 25.

Buckhorn Creek *(Atascosa)*

Although not a unique name for Texas streams, in this case it comes from a pair of interlocking bucks' horns found on the creek before 1900. The bucks had locked horns while fighting, so that they could not disengage themselves and later died beside the creek.

Buck Naked *(Parker)* [bək 'ne kɪd] [bək 'nɛ kɪd]

Buck Naked is a place name looking for a new home. The three-acre community near Weatherford was opened and closed during the 1970s by mayor-owner Johnny Logo, who promises to reestablish Buck Naked as a camping and amusement park somewhere along Interstate 20. "The name came to me as a fresh idea for humor," Mayor Logo says. "The possibilites are unlimited. For instance you can say to a friend, 'The next time you come through Buck Naked, be sure to stop for a visit.' " Mayor Logo has no interest in nudist camps, he must often explain to those who find that suggestion in the name.

Bucksnag Creek *(Colorado)*

No one snagged or bagged a buck along this stream; the name honors a German pioneer family of that name.

Buda *(Hays)* ['byu də]

An earlier name of *Do Pray* or *Du Pree* developed because the people were praying for a railroad. The present

name is said to have been inspired by a widow (Spanish *viuda*) who operated a hotel in the early days of the settlement. Another version is that around 1889 a traveler arrived and asked a Spanish-speaking citizen the name of the place. "Señor, this is the City of Widows," was the reply. The legend continues that this response caused the city officials to give the settlement the name of *Buda*, their spelling of *Viuda*.
PO Aug. 25, 1887–; Pop. 553; Inc.

Buffalo Bayou *(Harris)*

The bayou on which Houston was built has inspired stories about its naming involving herds of buffaloes, but the more likely explanation is that it was named for buffalo fish. Sig Byrd, a prominent newsman in Houston, recalled that his friend Fred Morris often told of the days of his youth when Buffalo Bayou was so full of buffalo fish that seiners had to dump half their catch to keep it light enough to handle.

Buggy Whip Creek *(Hopkins)*

The switch cane that grew along the creek made excellent buggy whips, often needed to encourage horses to make the deep crossing.

Bug Tussle *(Fannin)* ['bəg ˌtə səl]

One of Texas' most famous place names identifies a small community in an area once popular with Sunday school classes for picnics. One anecdote describes how swarms of bugs attracted to an ice cream social ruined the party. Another tradition maintains that after the Sunday school picnics, there was nothing to do but watch the tumblebugs tussle. Stories generally agree, however, that the area was a favorite gathering place for both bugs and Sunday school outings. The name has inspired bumper stickers, and the highway department has given up placing road signs at the crossroads because they became such a prized trophy for dormitory rooms and fraternity houses.
Pop. 30.

Bula *(Bailey)* ['byu lə]

In 1924, W. B. and Tom Newsome subdivided their Bailey County ranch, designating a townsite that was known as Newsome until a post office was requested. Because *Newsome* duplicated the name of another Texas post of-

fice, the name of the daughter of the Reverend Oaks, a Newsome real estate agent, was submitted.
PO May 8, 1925–; Pop. 105.

Bull Creek *(Coleman; Travis)*

At least six Texas creeks have this name. In Coleman County, the name Bull Creek came from a bull seen floating down the stream during a severe flood. In Travis County, longhorn cattle which roamed wild in the area gave the creek its name.

Bull Head Creek *(Edwards)*

This tributary of the Nueces River was named for the bull-shaped head of a mountain that lies between the forks of Bullhead and Hackberry creeks.

Bullhide Creek *(McLennan)*

J. Frank Dobie tells a story in *Straight Texas* of how a hunter hung a bullhide in a tree. When the hide dried, it remained clinging to the tree for many years, suggesting a name for the nearby creek.

Bull Hide Slough *(Gregg)*

During the flooding season, the backwater from the Sabine River once got so high that cattle lodged in trees. The victims were left there when the water receded, and as the cattle decayed their hides were left hanging in the trees.

Bull Run Creek *(Irion)*

By taking the name of the Civil War Battle of Bull Run and assigning it to the creek, the namegiver created a coincidental duplication in that *run* means "creek."

Buncombe *(Panola)* [ˈbəŋ kəm]

Sometimes spelled as *Bunkom*, the community tells a story crediting an Indian with naming the spot where he bunked.
PO Oct. 26, 1891–Aug. 8, 1893; Pop. 87.

Burkburnett *(Wichita)* [bərk bər ˈnɛt]

The area was settled about 1867, and in 1879 a post office was named *Gilbert* in honor of Mabel Gilbert, earliest settler. After the townsite moved one mile to the railroad in 1907, the name was changed to *Burkburnett*, reputedly after personal intercession with the postal department by Theodore Roosevelt. In 1905 the president had met Burk Burnett, owner of the 6666 Ranch, on whose land the town is located, and had been his guest for a wolf hunt in the Big Pasture. The president believed the town should bear the full name of its benefactor and not be reduced to *Burk* or *Burnett* as rumor had indicated it might be.
PO Sept. 6, 1882 (Gilbert)–May 9, 1891; Mar. 10, 1892–Sept. 15, 1898; Mar. 10, 1902–Oct. 31, 1903; Apr. 18, 1907 (Burkburnett)–; Pop. 9,829; Inc.

Burks *(La Salle)*

The name of the settlement is taken from the ranch formerly owned and operated by Amanda Burks, "Queen of the Trail Drivers."

Bushland *(Potter)* [ˈbəš lənd]

The name alludes not to the bushes of the plains, which are plentiful, but to W. H. Bush of Chicago, the landowner who gave the townsite. Because Charles B. Bush was the first postmaster and William Henry Bush owned ranch land surrounding the town, the community was very much a Bush land in its early days. The ranch owner, a widower, took a new wife in 1908; she decided that *Bushland* would be a more attractive name than *Bush* painted on the red clapboard station. When it came time to repaint the building, she directed that the new name be used.
PO Jan. 14, 1909–; Pop. 130.

Buttermilk Hill *(McLennan)*

A milky gypsum fluid that oozed from sinkholes gave the Buttermilk Hill area its name.

Byspot *(San Jacinto)* ['baɪ spat]

When the area was settled in 1898, it was known as *Teddy*. A new name was given by J. O. H. Bennett of Conroe, who spelled his wife's name (*Topsy*) backward and used the first letter in the name *Bennett* to create *Byspot*. *PO Sept. 8, 1899 (Teddy)–May 5, 1911 (Byspot)–Sept. 30, 1922.*

Cactus *(Moore)*

The only living thing in sight—cactus—gave New York engineers their inspiration for naming the Cactus Ordinance Works. When a post office was established, the name was transferred. Early residents remember how cactus and other prickly plants had to be cleared before the first housing units could be built in Cactus. Webb County also claimed a Cactus post office from 1884 to 1916. *PO Jan. 26, 1948–; Pop. 658; Inc.*

Cadiz *(Bee)* ['keɪ ˌdiz]

Ohio and Spain compete as the source of this community name. Some say W. V. Howard, store owner in 1897, was

remembering his former home of Cadiz, Ohio; others say the early Spanish settlers were longing for Cadiz, Spain.
PO Oct. 31, 1892 – discontinued during 1940s; Pop. 15.

Caesar *(Bee)*

Of all the names copied from the Bible for a list submitted by R. L. Peevy in requesting a post office, the postal authorities rendered unto Caesar. An earlier name was *Wolfe's Neighborhood,* because P. W. Wolfe lived here before 1876.
PO Dec. 8, 1903 – discontinued between Jan. 1, 1933, and June 1, 1936.

Calallen *(Nueces)* [kæl 'æl ɪn] [kæl 'æl ən]

Calvin J. Allen donated land for the St. Louis, Brownsville, and Mexico Railroad when it was built through here in 1905.
Pop. 70.

Calamity Creek *(Brewster)*

The calamity referred to by the name of the stream is the drowning of a man and his wife who made their camp in

the dry bed of the creek, only to be washed away during the night as a result of a cloudburst.

Calaveras *(Wilson)* [kæl ə 'vɛr əs]

An earlier name was *Wright*, dating to the settlement of the area in the 1860s. The later name came from a nearby creek, so called because a human skull was found along the stream. In Spanish, *calaveras* means "skulls." Another possibility is that the name is a corruption of *Calvillo*, the name of a family who owned ranch land in the area before 1830.
PO Mar. 24, 1882 (Wright)–Dec. 15, 1882 (Calaveras)– Nov. 14, 1925; Pop. 70.

California Creek *(Val Verde)*

What is a person to believe? Did the name come from the report that workmen laying rails for the Southern Pacific commented that the creek was probably as close to California as they would ever get, or did it originate because some people who camped on its banks were traveling to El Paso and California?

Camp Ruby *(Polk)*

One camp believes the town was named for Ruby Caton, daughter of A. B. Caton, the first foreman for a nearby lumber mill. Another camp is convinced that a more romantic naming circumstance occurred: When a name was needed for the post office, the manager of the logging camp said he would submit the name of the first girl who came along. In walked Ruby Moore, who was fifteen at the time.
Pop. 35.

Cannonsnap Creek *(Milam)*

In 1837 a company of soldiers was collected to repel an invasion of Indians and Mexicans. While camping along the stream, a tenderfoot hearing a twig snap aroused the sleeping camp, saying he heard a Mexican cannon snap. One version of the story says he actually fired at the imaginary foe.

Can't 'Cha Get Over Creek *(Kaufman)* [kænt čə gɪt 'o vər krik]

This tributary of a large creek in the area blocked the route of travelers because it flooded the road after the smallest rains.

Canton *(Van Zandt)* ['kænt n̩]

Two stories relate the origin of the name of the county seat. The French word *canton* designating a geographical division of a territory was appropriate because Van Zandt County had been created from a portion of the Nacogdoches Territory. Another explanation recalls a horse race in which a pony named *Canter* outdistanced all others. By changing the last two letters of *Canter*, citizens formed *Canton* and assigned the name to the new town. Canton is known widely for its First Monday trade day, which encourages casual bargaining and swapping of dogs, antiques, junk, and donkeys.
PO Apr. 7, 1852–; Pop. 2,496; Inc.

Canvasback Lake *(Bexar)*

The lake was named for the canvasback ducks that flocked to the area.

Caradan *(Mills)* ['kær ə dæn]

A combination of the names of two early settlers produced *Caradan*. S. L. Caraway lent the first syllables of his surname to the compound, and Dan T. Bush gave his first name.
PO July 3, 1889–; Pop. 15.

Carey *(Childress)* ['ke rɪ]

If a school teacher had owned the railroad, the town might still be named for her, but *Tallulah*, honoring Tallulah Collier, teacher in the first school in 1888, received a new name at the direction of the railroad. Don Carey, who had filed on land in the vicinity, was a railroad contractor, and the name was changed as a tribute to him.
PO July 7, 1896 (Tallulah)–May 5, 1898 (Carey)–; Pop. 57.

Carthage *(Panola)* ['kar ɵɪj]

Mr. Major Holland had his native state in mind when he transferred the name of Carthage, Mississippi, to the East Texas community.
PO July 31, 1849–; Pop. 5,274; Inc.

Cash *(Hunt)*

The president of the Texas Midland Railroad, E. H. R. Green, wanted to name the town in honor of J. A. Money,

a storeowner who worked for the extension of the railroad. The modest Mr. Money declined the honor, but agreed to the synonymous name of *Cash*.
PO Dec. 3, 1875–Feb. 28, 1954; Pop. 56.

Casket Mountain *(Jeff Davis)*

From a distance the mountain appears to a person with a lively imagination to resemble a closed coffin.
El. 6,860.

Cat Claw Creek *(Taylor)*

The source of the name is the cat claw plant which grows in abundance here. The thistlelike plant reaches a height of less than one foot and feels like a cat clawing on the leg of anyone walking through a patch of it. Nearby Abilene, Texas, is often distinguished from Abilene, Kansas (its namesake), by being called *Abilene on the Cat Claw*.

Caverns of Sonora *(Sutton)* [sə 'no rə]

The caverns take their name from their proximity to the town of Sonora, named for the state in Mexico. In Spanish, *sonoro* means "sonorous," suggesting "great" or "grandiloquent." The *-a* ending was used because of a belief that place names should be of feminine gender.

Cayote *(Bosque)* ['ke ot]

The presence of the coyote and the misspelling of the word when it was recorded as the post office name created the designation of the predominantly German-speaking community.
PO Dec. 29, 1879–Sept. 30, 1909; Pop. 75.

Cayuga *(Anderson)* [ke 'yu gə]

Immigrants from Tennessee and Alabama settled in a community known as *Tennessee Colony* in 1837. When a later post office was established in 1894, W. A. Davenport, the postmaster, honored his home in New York, named for the Cayuga Indians, one of the five nations of the Iroquois, who lived along the shores of Cayuga Lake. The discovery of oil in 1933 caused a temporary boom.
PO Mar. 24, 1852 (Tennessee Colony)–Nov. 5, 1866; June 10, 1867–Aug. 14, 1871; Sept. 22, 1875–?; May 7, 1894 (Cayuga)–1960s; Pop. 58.

Cee Vee *(Cottle)* [si 'vi]

Will Newson submitted the name in 1928 and served as postmaster until the 1940s. He intended the name to be *CV* for the CV Ranch, but the postal department spelled out the initials.
PO Nov. 22, 1928–; Pop. 71.

Celery Creek *(Menard)*

Wild celery grew in profusion here. An earlier Spanish name was *Arroyo de Juan Lorenzo,* "Creek of Juan Lorenzo."

Celotex *(Fisher)* ['sɛ lo tɛks]

The source of the name has not been established firmly, although some folk have a feeling it combines the Spanish word for "sky," *cielo,* with the abbreviation of *Texas.*

Centennial *(Coleman)*

The community grew up around a school constructed during the 1936 Texas Centennial celebrating independence from Mexico and foundation of the Republic of Texas in 1836.

Center City *(Mills)*

The town is said to occupy the geographical center of the state of Texas.
PO June 4, 1877–; Pop. 75.

Chalk Bluff *(Borden)*

Those who make educated guesses about the origins of place names without research will get stung on this

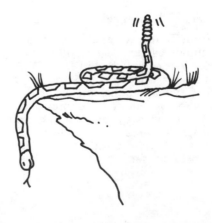

name. Logically, it would describe the chalk exposed in the bluff. Actually, it was named for Bud Chalk, who had a camp on this site. His small daughter was fatally bitten by a rattlesnake and buried near the foot of this bluff. Because of white chalk formations at the bluff, the role of Bud Chalk is seldom recognized in the naming process.

Chaparrosa Creek *(Zavala)* [ˈčæ pə ˌro zə]

The Spanish word *chaparro* meaning "scrub oak" refers to the thick growth of shrubs in the area. Earlier names of the stream were *Ona*, an Indian word meaning "salty"; *Rio San Isidro Labrado*, given by Spaniards; *Guanapaci*, the Indian name recorded by Father Damian Massanet when he crossed the stream near its mouth in 1691; and *Arroyo de San Lucas*, the replacement name given by Father Massanet.

Charco *(Goliad)*

The name has been traced to both Spanish and American Indian languages. In Spanish, the word means "little puddle" or "little mud hole," referring to the location of the community in a very low place where water stands for days following a rain. As a corruption of an Indian word, it is said to have referred to a water hole on the Lincoln Ranch. Those who think the word is English in origin say it refers to a petrified tree stump that marked a water hole. *PO Dec. 13, 1855–Nov. 5, 1866; June 11, 1878–June 30, 1954; Pop. 61.*

Chatt *(Hill)*

When railroaders passed through, they always saw people standing around chatting. How the double *t* appeared in the name has not been explained.

Cheapside *(Gonzales)* [ˈčip saɪd]

Some of the early settlers from London, England, remembered the ancient and famous street Cheapside. The request that this name be given came from Dr. J. Henry, who had studied in England. *PO June 5, 1882–; Pop. 31.*

Cherry Point Gully *(Chambers)*

The gully has local historians arguing about whether its name refers to Aaron Cherry, an early landowner, or to the wild cherry trees which once grew in the area.

Chester *(Tyler)*

The community moved in 1883 from Peach Tree Village, one mile north, to become the namesake of Chester A. Arthur, president of the United States, 1881–1885. U. G. Feagin founded the town on land conveyed to him by the Trinity and Sabine Timber Company.
PO Aug. 22, 1876–; Pop. 391; Inc.

Chicken Creek *(Walker)*

The last wild chicken was seen in the area in 1912, but reports of a large population of fowls in earlier days provided the name.

Chigger Creek *(Brazoria)*

The chiggers, or redbugs, infesting the banks of the creek caused enough scratching to inspire the name of the stream.

Chillicothe *(Hardeman)* [čɪ lɪ 'ka ɵɪ]

Chillicothe, Missouri, was the former home of Will and Ed Jones, early men in the town. In Shawnee, the word means "the big town where we live."
PO Oct. 17, 1883–; Pop. 1,038; Inc.

China Grove *(Van Zandt)*

A grove of chinaberry trees once grew near the church around which the community developed. The same name has been used for communities in Brazoria, Gonzales, Jefferson, and Trinity counties.

Chinquapin *(San Augustine)* [ˈčin kə pın]

The name is derived from the location of the settlement on Chinquapin Creek and from the chinquapins or dwarf chestnuts growing there. The stream is also known as *Egg-Nog Branch*, named when a group of men returned to their wives after the Fredonian Rebellion on Christmas Day and were served repeated rounds of egg nog. A town by the name of *Chinquapin* in San Jacinto County had a post office from 1888 to 1890.

Chocolate Bay *(Calhoun)*

Who would ever confuse pepper and chocolate? A corruption of the pronunciation of *chiltipiquín*, an Indian name for a small pepper grown locally, resulted in *Chocolate Bay*, designating a coastal inlet.

Choice *(Shelby)*

Indecision over which name to choose from a list of three suggestions by the post office department caused town leaders to return the list with a note: "Pick your choice." And *Choice* it was, rather than any of the three original names. Another explanation is that E. A. Cammack, an early settler, considered this community a "choice place in which to live."
PO May 10, 1904–Feb. 15, 1954; Pop. 21.

Christmas Mountain *(Brewster)*

In the eyes of some beholders, the mountains were shaped like Christmas trees.
El. 5,735.

Christoval *(Tom Green)* [krıs ˈto vəl]

The name was formed by taking the name of an early settler, Christopher Columbus Doty, and adding to the first two syllables of his given name the Spanish word *val*. Some residents trace the name to *Cristóbal*, the Spanish version of Christopher, or to a shortening of *Christ's Valley*.
PO Jan. 21, 1889–; Pop. 216.

Cibolo *(Guadalupe)* ['sɪ bə lo]

The Indian and Spanish name of the buffalo is given to Cibolo Creek and to the community that developed nearby. A story is told that because the creek has high, steep bluff banks along much of its course, it was a favorite hunting ground of the Indians, who drove herds of buffalo toward the creek, causing them to fall over the high banks and break their necks. Earlier names for the settlement were *Fromme's Store*, for Charles Fromme, and *Cibolo Valley*.
PO June 4, 1877 (Cibolo Valley)—Oct. 31, 1882; Dec. 12, 1883 (Cibolo)—; Pop. 478; Inc.

Circleville *(Williamson)*

The town was settled about 1846 by D. H. McFadin and laid out in a circular pattern. At one time, its industries included a pewter factory and weaving looms.
PO Mar. 13, 1857—Apr. 15, 1915; Pop. 42.

Cistern *(Fayette)*

This community was first called *Whiteside Prairie*, then *Cockrell Hill* for M. Cockrell, a banking and wholesale merchandiser. It became *Cistern* when each family had to build an underground water reservoir because the well water contained too much iron and sulphur.
PO Mar. 31, 1861—1940s.

Citrus City *(Hidalgo)*

A man named Judd developed large areas of citrus groves which gave their name to the town, sometimes called *Judd City* as well.

Clabber Creek *(Coryell)*

The proximity of the stream to Buttermilk Creek, named for buttermilk weeds, probably led to its related name.

Clara *(Bee; Wichita)*

Behind the name of the railroad switch and stockpens in Bee County lies the story of the "Saviour of the Alamo"—Clara Driscoll. She was the granddaughter of E. O. Driscoll, who gave the right-of-way to the San Antonio and Aransas Pass Railroad in 1886. In 1903 Clara provided the personal check credited with preventing the

sale and destruction of the fortress church in San Antonio, now regarded as the shrine of Texas liberty. Clara in Wichita County was named for the wife of Herman Specht.
(Bee Co.) Pop. 23. (Wichita Co.) Pop. 100.

Clarendon *(Donley)* ['klær ɪn dən]

Both the wife of a Methodist minister and an English lord are cited as the sources of the town name. The original town was established in 1878 by Lewis Henry Carhard, a Methodist minister who located six miles north of the present site and named the town for his wife, Clara. A change in the railroad survey in the late 1880s moved the townsite to the Fort Worth and Denver Railroad. Then the older settlement was known as *Old Clarendon* or *Saints Roost,* for its religious origins. The claim is also made that the source of the name is Lord Clarendon of England, since some immigrants from England are known to have settled in the area.
PO Sept. 25, 1878–; Pop. 2,222; Inc.

Clayton *(Panola)*

The present name is the third given the town. In 1880, Jacob Cariker settled here and applied for a post office. Although the community had originally been called *Cariker,* he requested that the name be *Clayborne,* for one of his faithful slaves. Because *Clayborne* was in use, the name was modified to *Clayton,* suggesting the slave's name and also honoring *Clayton,* Alabama.
PO June 25, 1874–Feb. 24, 1879; June 16, 1879–; Pop. 79.

Cleveland *(Delta; Liberty)*

Citizens of Delta County wished to pay tribute to the twenty-second and twenty-fourth president of the United States, Grover Cleveland. Cleveland in Liberty County was named for W. D. Cleveland, a Houston cotton broker.

Coahoma *(Howard)* [kə 'ho mə]

James B. Frazier, a local historian, translates the Indian term as "favored or good place to live," but the traditional meaning is "signal," referring to a small hill nearby called *Signal Mountain.*
PO Oct. 24, 1891–Apr. 3, 1895; June 15, 1901–; Pop. 1,135; Inc.

Cobb Jones Creek *(Franklin)*

An early settler along the creek earned the nickname of "Cobb" Jones because he raised corn and corked whiskey bottles with corn cobs.

Coffeeville *(Upshur)*

A camping ground in the eastern part of Upshur County near the Big Cypress Creek was a day's journey by wagon from Jefferson and a favorite stopping place for travelers. Here they would camp, build a fire, and brew coffee. Before the Civil War, the smell of coffee in the camp area provided the name. A widely circulated anecdote about the name, which is discounted by county historians, says that during the Civil War when coffee was scarce this community was one of the few places in East Texas where the commodity could be bought.
Pop. 50.

Coldspring *(San Jacinto)*

The original name of *Coonskin* was short-lived after it was given to a post office on January 18, 1847, for on

March 8 of the same year it became *Firemen's Hill*.
Three years later, the name changed to *Cold Spring*, for
the pure, clear spring here, and in 1894 the spelling be-
came *Coldspring*.
PO *Jan. 18, 1847 (Coonskin)—Mar. 8, 1847 (Firemen's
Hill)—Oct. 30, 1850 (Cold Spring)—Dec. 31, 1894
(Coldspring)—.*

Coleto Creek *(De Witt)* [kə 'lɛ to]

Four streams originally bore this name, which is possibly
a corruption of the diminutive of *cola*, the Spanish word
for "tail." These small creeks converge to form a pattern
resembling a maze of little tails. Later the Coleto creeks
came to be referred to as the mile creeks, stating the
distance from Clinton, the county seat—*Three-Mile
Coleto, Five-Mile Coleto, Twelve-Mile Coleto*, etc.

College Station *(Brazos)*

The town grew up around the railroad station for Texas
Agricultural & Mechanical College. An unsuccessful at
tempt was made to change the name in 1967, since there
was no longer a railroad station and the school had become a university.
PO *Feb. 7, 1877—; Pop. 45,000; Inc.*

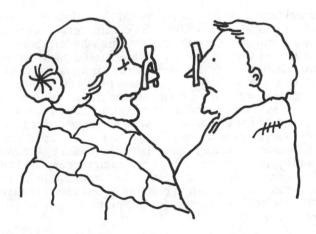

Cologne *(Goliad)* [kə 'lon]

An educated guess that the community was named for
the German city underestimates the sense of humor behind the naming process in Texas. The settlement was

built around a cattle slaughter and shipping center, including a hog rendering plant, and the name was chosen ironically because it was such a "pleasant" smelling place—like cologne.
PO Apr. 8, 1898–July 15, 1915; Feb. 16, 1917–June 15, 1925; Pop. 35.

Comal *(Comal)* ['ko mæl]

The place has been variously called *Comal, Comal Creek, Comal Settlement, Comal Ranche, Comal Town,* and *Old Comal Town.* The Spanish word means "basin" or "flat, earthenware pan for cooking maize cake." The name most likely describes the valley through which the Comal River flows.
PO Oct. 19, 1861 (Comal Ranche)–discontinued by 1900; Pop. 40.

Cometa *(Zavala)* [kə 'mɛ tə]

This settlement, dating to the 1860s, became the headquarters for the T. A. Coleman ranch about 1900. Because the ranch brand was a comet, the Spanish-speaking hands called it *cometa,* a name adopted by farmers and ranchers for the community.

Comfort *(Kendall)* ['kəm fərt]

Local historians have constructed the following account of the naming of Comfort: The community was settled by a group of free-thinking Germans who left their homeland with no church beliefs. After a hard journey from Indianola, Texas, some of the immigrants stopped at what is now Round Top; others proceeded to New Braunfels, while some continued to the area that is now Comfort. As they reached the confluence of Cypress Creek and the Guadalupe River, they agreed that this was a great "gemütlicher Platzt" to settle. *Gemütlich* translates as "comfortable," later shortened to *Comfort.* Some printed sources offer a contradictory explanation, stating that the original settlers had in mind their firm belief in "the everlasting comfort to be found in heaven," but few residents accept this account.
PO July 12, 1856–; Pop. 1,460.

Commerce *(Hunt)*

As early as 1857, a settlement known as *Jackson's Store* had grown up around a business owned by Si Jackson on the backbone of a divide between the South and Middle

Sulphur rivers. Later settlers built their homes nearby in an area between the rivers known as Cow Hill because cattle gathered there on high ground when the rivers flooded. When a post office was requested, the name of *Ashland*, suggested by the many ash trees in the area, was submitted. When the railroad was built just north of Ashland, a new point of settlement was established near the station. An early storekeeper, William Jernigan, was asked by a supplier where to ship goods, and Jernigan replied, "Commerce," hoping that a new community transected by several trade routes would indeed become a commercial center.

PO Jan. 13, 1873 (Ashland)–Dec. 27, 1880 (Commerce)–; Pop. 10,800; Inc.

Concan *(Uvalde; Real)* ['kan kæn]

A Mexican gambling game known as coon can, derived from Spanish *conquian*, supplied the name of *Concan* in Uvalde County. The first post office was given this name by E. P. Hale in 1881. The same Spanish source is given for the community in Real County written as *Con Can*. *(Uvalde Co.) PO 1881–1894; 1900–; Pop. 71.*

Concord *(Anderson; Cherokee; Hardin; Hunt; Jefferson; Leon; McLennan; Rusk; Upshur)* ['kan 'kɔrd]

Originally named *Fitzgerald* for the Fitzgerald family who were original settlers, the Anderson County community was renamed *Concord* in 1871 because the Kelleys, Funderburks, and Lunsfords had come from Concord in Union Parish, Louisiana. In Cherokee County, the distant hometown of some of the first settlers was Concord, Massachusetts. The same source is given for the Concord community in Leon County, but the harmonious relations within communities provided the name in Hardin, Harrison, Hunt, Jefferson, McLennan, Rusk, and Upshur counties.

Content *(Runnels)* [kən 'tɪnt]

Daniel W. Hale came from Kentucky in 1879 and moved his store into a new building in the valley. He chose the name for the contentment he found here. From 1905 to 1916, the name of *Tokeen* replaced *Content*, but the earlier name was restored after the Tokeen post office was discontinued.

PO Apr. 21, 1883 (Content)–Jan. 10, 1905 (Tokeen)–?.

Contrary Creek *(Gillespie; Hood; Kimble)* [kən 'trer ɪ]

One Hood County story has it that the name stems from the way the creek twists and turns contrarily as it makes its way to the Brazos River. A more colorful explanation traces it to a church located on the banks of the stream. Some members were rather positive about their position on certain matters in the church. Those with opposing views held just as firmly. Both groups called each other *contrary* and passed the epithet on to the creek. In Gillespie and Kimble counties, Contrary Creek is a tributary of the South Llano River, taking its name from its many meanderings before it makes confluence with the Llano.

Coon Hollow *(Roberts)*

A Black man known as Nigger Bill lived in this hollow, and the name is presumed to have been derived from a derogatory name for Blacks.

Copperas Creek *(Comanche)* ['kap rəs]

When the water dried out, a seepage came to the surface that looked like copperas, a sulfate of various crystalized metals.

Cost *(Gonzales)*

When *Oso*, meaning "bear" in Spanish, was rejected because another Texas post office had claimed the name, local citizens made alterations to create an acceptable

name. They added a *C* and replaced the final *o* with a *t*, and then submitted *Cost* to the postal deparment.
PO Sept. 22, 1897–; Pop. 62.

County Line *(Cochran)*

The community was named for its proximity to the Cochran-Hockley boundary. Throughout the state, communities, churches, and businesses bear the name of *County Line*, a handy locational designation. Post offices named *County Line* existed at different times in Anderson, Cook, and Rains counties.

Cowhouse Creek *(Bell, Coryell, Hamilton, Mills)*

Cattle found natural shelters formed by limestone bluffs with overhangings along the banks of the creek.

Cowskin Creek *(Hunt)*

Two colorful explanations are given: (1) an early joke developed that the brush was so thick along the creek that it would skin a cow; (2) cattle rustlers once took stolen cattle here to skin them and sell the hides.

Cow Trap Lake *(Brazoria)*

After several cattle bogged down in the lake and became trapped here, area residents had no problem thinking of a name for the body of water.

Cranell *(Refugio)* ['kre nɛl]

The namesake of the town is Nell Crane, wife of Jeff N. Miller, a railroad vice president. A reversed combination of her names provided the town designation.

Crawar Oil Field *(Crane)* ['kre war]

The oil field was named for its position near the Crane-Ward county line.

Crawfish Creek *(Crosby)* ['krɔ fɪš]

Game fish in the stream were not worth noting in the name, but the abundance of crawfish was.

Creedmoor *(Travis)* ['krid mor]

A strict religious group first settled here and chose a name as an expression of their faith: *Creed* for "belief"

and *moor*, meaning "to fix firmly." When the town moved several miles from its original location to its present site, it was known for a time as *Willow Springs*, for a nearby water source shaded by willow trees.
PO Jan. 19, 1880–Sept. 30, 1954; Pop. 75.

Crockett Oil Field *(Upton)*

The oil field in Upton County was named for Crockett County, which forms the border to the south. Crockett County in turn was named for Davy Crockett, hero of the Alamo.

Cross Cut *(Brown)*

When local people were trying to find a name for their new post office, it was suggested that it be named *Cross Out* because it was across the county and out of the way of usual travel. When the name was submitted for approval, the second *o* was mistaken for a *c*, and the name remained. In McMullen County, a community was given the name of *Cross Out* for its location on a ranch road that cut across the area.
PO Apr. 9, 1879–June 30, 1958; Pop. 45.

Crush *(McLennan)*

A head-on collision between two locomotives was staged on September 15, 1896, as a publicity stunt conceived by

William G. Crush, Missouri, Kansas, and Texas Railroad passenger agent, for whom the area was named. More than 30,000 spectators watched the two trains speeding toward each other and, contrary to the assurances of mechanics, the steam boilers exploded on impact, killing two persons and injuring others who were struck by pieces of metal blown into the crowd. The event inspired Texarkana-born ragtime composer Scott Joplin to write "The Crash at Crush."

Cryer Creek *(Navarro)*

The stream was so called because the settlers near the creek thought the water sounded like a woman crying as it passed over the falls. A community close by was first settled in 1845 by William Melton, and it took the name of the creek.
PO Feb. 24, 1879–Jan. 2, 1907; Pop. 15.

Crystal City *(Zavala)*

Many flowing wells were found in the southern section of the county in the early days, with water said to be as clear as crystals. When a town was founded, it was given the name of *Crystal City* in 1907. It became the county seat in 1928. As "Spinach Capital of the World," it erected a statue of spinach-loving Popeye in 1937.
PO Jan. 10, 1908–; Pop. 7,693; Inc. 1910.

Cuero *(De Witt)* ['kwɛr o]

Indians called the creek *Skin Creek* in reference to the hides of animals killed on the banks. The Spanish translated the Indian name and placed *Cuero Creek* on maps in 1745. The nearby town of Cuero was named for the stream.
PO listed for the Republic of Texas as Quairo, *1840; May 22, 1846 (Cuero)–Mar. 17, 1859; Feb. 17, 1860–Oct. 16, 1860; Feb. 24, 1873–; Pop. 6,989; Inc.*

Culleoka *(Collin)* [kə lɪ 'o kə]

When settlers from Culleoka in Maury County, Tennessee, moved to Collin County, they transferred the name to their new home.
PO May 29, 1883–Sept. 27, 1906.

Custer *(Cooke)*

An earlier name for the town, now extinct, was *Centennial City*, because it was established in 1876. Despite

sources which claim the name alludes to General George Custer, the Indian fighter, the source is a trotting horse that had a winning record about the time the settlement was named.
PO Nov. 19, 1877–Jan. 31, 1902.

Cut and Shoot *(Montgomery)*

Most of the stories agree that there was once a preacher who was much too popular with the women. When charges were made at a church meeting, the men ran to wagons and buggies to get knives and rifles to cut and shoot. Another explanation is that cutting and shooting developed from an argument over the design of a new church steeple.
Pop. 791; Inc. since 1970

Cuthand *(Red River)*

The community was called *Enterprise* from its settlement before 1850 until 1867, when its new name was taken from Cuthand Creek, which flows nearby. The creek was named in honor of a famous Delaware Indian scout called "Cut Hand" because he lost one of his hands to a British saber while fighting in the Battle of Tippecanoe. This popular explanation of the name is disputed by those who believe it honors Chief Cuthand, an Indian who was instrumental in arranging a major treaty with unfriendly tribes of Indians. Others know a story about a cowboy who cut his hand severely during a roundup in the creek bottoms.
PO Jan. 11, 1867–Sept. 30, 1953; Pop. 32.

Dad's Corner *(Archer)*

The veteran oil wildcatter C. M. "Dad" Joiner gave his name to this crossroads community in Archer County as well as to a town in Gregg County—Joinerville—during the oil boom of the 1920s.

Dads Creek *(Trinity)*

The stream was named *Mason* originally, but Mr. Mason's sons called it *Dads Creek*.

Daingerfield *(Morris)* ['den jər ,fild]

Captain London Daingerfield was killed during a fight with Indians in the area, and the scene of the battle was

named in honor of the soldier. Homeseekers began to move into Daingerfield between 1840 and 1845.
PO May 9, 1876–; Pop. 2,624; Inc.

Daisetta *(Liberty)* [de 'zɛt ə]

The blending of the first names of Daisy Barrett and Etta White was suggested by Newt Farris, a local store owner. Settlers began arriving in the area as early as 1850, but a town did not develop until after oil was discovered in 1917.
PO Feb. 16, 1921–; Pop. 1,117; Inc.

Dalhart *(Dallam, Hartley)* ['dæl hart]

Rancher Ora D. Atkinson named the town from parts of the names of Dallam and Hartley counties for the location near the county line. Earlier names were *Twist, Twist Junction*, and *Denrock* combining the names of the Fort Worth and Denver and Rock Island railroads. When the post office department objected to *Denrock*, the present name was submitted.
PO Apr. 29, 1901 , Pop. 7,792, Inc.

Dallas *(Dallas)*

Although the origin is routinely reported as an honor for George Mifflin Dallas, vice president of the United States under John Tyler, 1845–1849, the only reason given for the selection by John Neely Bryan, town founder in 1841, was that it was chosen "for my friend Dallas." Historians who find it unlikely that the "friend" was the vice president trace the name to several men named Dallas, among them Joseph Dallas, an old Arkansas friend who settled at Cedar Springs near Dallas in 1843.
PO May 22, 1846–; Pop. 822,451; Inc.

Dancl *(Johnson)* ['dæn səl]

Once upon a time, a saloon in the region was called "Dancing Lillian," and the surrounding community came to be known by that name. It shortened to *Dancl* in a more appropriate designation for the town as it grew and sought respectability.

Danevang *(Wharton)* ['dæn væŋ]

In the spring of 1894, immigrants belonging to the Danish Folk Society of America moved onto twenty-four thousand acres of Wharton County. *Danevang* means "Danish meadow."
PO July 23, 1895–; Pop. 61.

Darco *(Harrison)*

A carbon products plant and coal mine are located in the community. *Darco* is a brand name referring to the dark color of the lignite coal products manufactured by the Atlas Powder Company.
Pop. 85.

Dawn *(Deaf Smith)* [dɔn]

The community developed around a store established by J. H. Parrish on his ranch in 1887 and named the "Dawn of Civilization" or "Dawn of a New Country." Another version reports that H. H. Parrish, who had bought a section of the T. Anchor Ranch from Jim Moore, exclaimed upon seeing the land and dugout for the first time, "This is the dawn of a new day."
PO Dec. 2, 1889–Nov. 26, 1894; Jan. 23, 1895–July 28, 1899; Nov. 3, 1914–; Pop. 94.

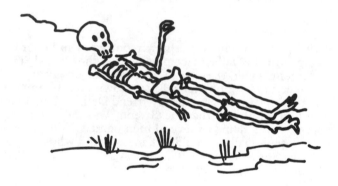

Deadman Creek *(Callahan)*

A dead man was found on the banks of the stream. It was never determined whether he had died of thirst or at the hands of Indians. The same name was given to streams in Knox and Val Verde counties.

Dead Man's Well *(Burnet)*

No figurative meaning can be assigned to this name, once its grisly background is known. Beginning about 1860, an elm tree growing over the well opening was used as a hanging tree, with the convenience of a seemingly bottomless well to receive the bodies when

they were cut loose. Later cattlemen found the well a convenient disposal system for rustlers they captured. The name was transferred to the surrounding community.

Deadwood *(Panola)*

Established in 1837 as *Linus,* the community took the new name of *Deadwood* in 1882 as a result of a joke on those who were trying to get a post office closer to the Sabine River. During a meeting to discuss establishing the post office, someone said, "We've got the Deadwood on them now."
PO Feb. 9, 1882–July 14, 1917; Pop. 106.

Deal *(Carson)*

Attempts have been made to relate the name to land deals, poker deals, and the like, but it is derived from a prominent family named Deahl, the spelling of which was Americanized over the years.
PO Oct. 23, 1926–Oct. 31, 1928.

Delmita *(Starr)* [del ˈmit ə]

Niceforo G. Peña, an early settler, had seven sons he involved in the selection of the post office name. He permitted each son to draw a letter of the alphabet. N. C. drew *d;* E. P. drew *e;* Fred drew *l;* S. R. drew *m;* Joe drew *i;* G. C. drew *t;* and A. G. drew *a*—hence the name. The letters were combined to form *Delmita,* rather than

Meltida, Deltima, or the like. The naming process suggests the one used by the publisher of a newspaper in Jefferson, Marion County, Texas, who dropped randomly selected pieces of type on a table and juggled them around until they spelled *Jimplecute,* the name still carried today by the weekly newspaper.
PO Sept. 12, 1925 (Zaragoza)—May 1, 1931 (Delmita)—;
Pop. 99.

Democrat *(Comanche)*

Two theories explain the name in Comanche County. The influence of a Mr. Hill, the first postmaster and a fervent Democrat, is said to have been the source. The other theory is that during an election in 1882, a voting box was located in the store in the community, and citizens voted solidly Democratic. The name is also found in Mills County.
(Comanche Co.) PO Aug. 10, 1893—Jan. 31, 1919.

Denver City *(Yoakum)*

The Wasson post office, located on the Wasson Ranch, was moved in 1938 to Denver City, following what was declared the second largest known oil discovery in the world. Surveyed in June 1938, Denver City was developed by Ben Eggink and C. S. Ameen. Its first name was *Denver,* for the Denver Production and Royalty Company, one of the principal developers of the new oil field, but confusion with the Colorado capital led to the change to *Denver City.* The population grew to five thousand during the first year, and the town was incorporated within six months.
PO June 28, 1938 (Wasson); Apr. 1, 1939 (Denver City)—;
Pop. 4,308; Inc. 1938.

Derby Town *(Frio)* ['dər bɪ]

Derby, England, was the former home of John Bennett's English bride. He bought several thousand acres of land, served as postmaster, and operated a gin in the community he named.
PO Apr. 12, 1882 (Lenore)—Jan. 7, 1884 (Derby)—; Pop.
50.

Desert *(Collin)* ['dɛz ərt]

In 1846 while Will Warden looked for land to settle, his cook ran from the Indians and deserted the campsite.

Although his action provided a name for the community which developed here, it is no longer remembered: The name is pronounced as if it were the noun *desert*, rather than the verb.
PO Jan. 7, 1893–Dec. 15, 1904; Pop. 25.

Devils Back Bone *(Comal)*

The geographical area takes its name from a high ridge with devilishly deep valleys on each side. The same name is applied in Hays and Montague counties.

Devil's River *(Crockett, Schleicher, Sutton, Val Verde)*

Captain John Hays of the Texas Rangers, after riding across a barren, rough strip of country, came to a formidable gorge, at the bottom of which he could see water. When he asked the name of the stream, a Mexican told him it was *San Pedro's*. Hays supposedly replied, "St. Peter's, hell! It looks like the Devil's River to me." A post office by this name operated intermittently in Val Verde County between 1886 and 1914. It is believed that the river was the stream called *Laxas*, Spanish for "slack or feeble," a name given by Gaspar Castaño de Sosa in 1590.

Devil's Sinkhole *(Edwards)*

On a divide near Rocksprings, a sunken cavern was discovered in 1875 by Amon Billings. It is the home of millions of bats, and an underground river passes through it. The forbidding nature of the cavern suggested its name.

Dew *(Freestone)* [dyu]

Persons inquiring about the naming of the town are given two accounts: (1) a resident named Drew was honored by having his name sent to postal authorities, but it was misread and recorded as *Dew*; (2) of seventy-five names picked at random and submitted, *Dew* was the only name not already being used at that time. An earlier name was *Avant Prairie*, for M. S. Avant, who came here in the 1850s. The name was shortened to *Avant* when a post office was first established.
PO Jan. 22, 1853 (Avant)–Nov. 21, 1853; Jan. 7, 1884; Jan. 16, 1885; Dec. 30, 1885 (Dew)–Feb. 15, 1909; Pop. 71.

Dexter *(Cooke)*

In the same county where a trotting horse named Custer lent its name to a town, Jesse Morris decided that his community should be called *Dexter*, for another famous trotter.
PO Mar. 31, 1873–April 30, 1955; Pop. 70.

Diablo Mountains *(Culberson)*

The rugged, jagged nature of the mountains suggested the Spanish word for "devil."

Dicey *(Parker)*

First called *Power* for Parson Power, an early settler, it was later called *Dicey* in honor of the wife of another pioneer, W. G. Puryear.
PO Apr. 23, 1888 (Power)–July 17, 1890; Mar. 26, 1891 (Dicey)–July 31, 1929.

Diddy Waw Diddy or Ditty Waw Ditty *(Brazoria)*
['dɪ dɪ 'wɔ 'dɪ dɪ]

The significance of the name given by Black residents of the area lies somewhere between heaven and hell. One explanation is that it was a conception of heaven, a place of no work or worry for "man or beast," thought up by nineteenth-century slaves. Diddy Waw Diddy wasn't nearly so stern and formal as the White folks' heaven, however. Another version claims Diddy Waw Diddy was the last depot stop on the railroad to hell. Youngsters who did not walk the straight and narrow were told by

elders that they were headed for Diddy Waw Diddy if they didn't mend their ways.

Dido *(Tarrant)* [ˈdaɪ do]

Classical mythology or a frisky mare could be the source of this town name. One story is told of a penmanship teacher at the school who frequently told his students about ancient myths. He was especially fond of giving accounts about Dido, queen and founder of Carthage. Another story tells how the grandmother of the lad who was to become Major K. M. Van Zandt gave him a young mare for school graduation. The horse cut such didos in the pasture that the town name was inspired by her antics. The same name was given a post office in Walker County, 1900–1909.

Dilley *(Frio)* [ˈdɪ lɪ]

This dilly of a town owes its name to George M. Dilley of Palestine, who was an official of the International and Great Northern Railroad. The previous name of *Darlington* had honored a local ranch owner from 1891–1892. *PO Feb. 13, 1885 (Dilley)–July 13, 1891 (Darlington)– May 24, 1892 (Dilley)–; Pop. 2,586; Inc.*

Dime Box *(Lee)*

The name perpetuates the memory of a time when there was a community mail box, erected by citizens, where teamsters and freighters passing that way carried mail to the residents, asking a service charge of ten cents for each article delivered. Mail arrived in this way from Bryan, Brenham, and Houston. When a nearby post office was planned, efforts were made to call it *Brown's Mill*, for the proposed postmaster, but confusion with *Brownsville* made the citizens decide to reestablish it as *Dime Box*. National publicity came in 1943, when Dime Box was the first U.S. town to "contribute 100 percent" to the March of Dimes.
PO June 6, 1877 (Brown's Mill)–Oct 12, 1883; May 16, 1884 (Dime Box)–; Pop. 313.

Dinero *(Live Oak)* [dɪ ˈnɛ ro]

The settlement was first called *Barlow's Ferry*, for E. Barlow, until application was made for a post office and

citizens were informed that another town had that name. Postal supervisors suggested the name *Dinero* ("money" in Spanish) because during the Texas-Mexican War General Santa Anna sent pay for his soldiers by forty-mule teams, and, when attacked by Texas soldiers, the teamsters buried the gold and fled. For many years, people searched for the gold in this region. None was found, although black gold was struck here in 1918.
PO Nov. 4, 1885–; Pop. 35.

Ding Dong *(Bell)*

I. V. and Z. O. Bell, first cousins, established a store here in 1923, and John Hoover, a nearby farmer who was also an artist, historian, and sign painter, offered to paint them a sign for free—"if you'll let me do it the way I want to." The Bells agreed, and Hoover came up with a three-by-four-foot sign which was a pictorial pun. At each end were pictures of bells—one with initials *I. V.* on it and the with *Z. O.* Between the two bells, Hoover painted *Ding Dong*. The community took its name from the sign. A few years ago the tiny community of perhaps a half-dozen people got its first real bell when the honorary mayor of Ding Dong, Charlie Hold, was given a bell on behalf of the Santa Fe Railroad by Raymond Shelton of Chicago, who was acting vice president at the time.

Dinkins *(Brazos)* [ˈdɪŋ kɪnz]

Through a post office mistake, the name originally submitted as *Dunlap*, for G. W. Dunlap, went into the records and on subsequent post marks as *Dinkins*. A part of Stephen F. Austin's original colony, the settlement began to attract residents in the 1850s.
PO Feb. 27, 1913–July 15, 1931.

Dinner Creek *(Briscoe)*

Cowboys on the J. A. Ranch tried to make it to this stream by dinner time.

Direct *(Lamar)* [ˈdaɪ rɛkt]

An early revivalist told the people they were going "direct to hell" in the community where Indians came from across the river "direct for whiskey." Tradition has it that the local church was built with money donated by a converted saloon keeper.
PO Sept. 3, 1887–Jan. 1, 1954–; Pop. 70.

Divot *(Frio)* ['dɪv ət]

Because the settlement was located at crossroads, the name *Pivot* seemed appropriate. However, the *P* was mistaken for a *D*, and the postal department recorded the name as *Divot*. The original name was *Kingsville*, for J. J. King, who established a store at the site in 1908, but the duplicative name had to be relinquished.
PO July 12, 1912 (Divot)–?. Pop. 28.

Dixie *(Grayson)*

Confederate veterans maintained loyalty to the South when the community was founded soon after the Civil War. The same name was chosen in other counties, including Jackson, Lamar, Panola, and Young.
Pop. 25.

Doctors Creek *(Delta)*

Two stories explain the creek name: One recalls that Indians gathered herbs on the creek bank and brewed them in the dry creek bed to heal their sick. The other recounts that a doctor's horse and buggy got bogged down while he was attempting to cross the creek.

Dodge *(Walker)*

The name honors G. C. Dodge of Dodge-Phelps Construction Company, which built the railroad through the area. Another railroad-related version claims that citizens of Huntsville declined to assist a line being built through their city; therefore, officials decided to bypass Huntsville and establish another town—dodging the county seat but providing a new town and its name.
PO July 7, 1881–; Pop. 150.

Dollarhide *(Andrews; Angelina; Atascosa)*

Although some Andrews County residents insist that a Mr. Dollarhide was the town namesake, a more popular story involves a drought that killed off most of the cattle. Hides were sold for one dollar each at the site of a windmill where the community began to develop. In Atascosa County the name is traced to the days of cattle drives, when steers would kill themselves by drinking waste oil deposited in the water; one dollar per hide was the price received for each animal, alive or dead. Another version claims that the Atascosa County town was once a way station for cattle drives. Cattle reaching this point were

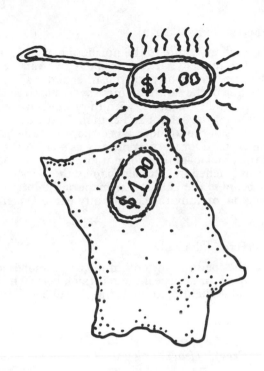

usually very weak and thin, thus lowering their price to one dollar per steer or a dollar a hide. In Angelina County, Dollarhide Lake traces its name to Cornelius Dollarhide, who was born in Kentucky in 1803 and who came to Angelina County in the 1840s.

Dollar Point *(Galveston)*

One of the surviving stories from the days of Pirate Jean Lafitte is that he buried his treasure here at Dollar Point.

Donie *(Freestone)* ['do nɪ]

The name is a mistake, but disagreement surrounds explanations offered for the intended name. Some say it was to have been *Dovie*, for Edward L. Dovie, a prominent rancher, but that when the post office was petitioned, the name was recorded as *Donie*. Others say the intended name was *Douie Prairie*, misinterpreted and shortened to *Donie*. The town developed when the Trinity and Brazos Valley Railroad was surveyed through the area.
PO Dec. 9, 1898–; Pop. 206.

Dougherty *(Rains)* ['dar tɪ]

R. N. Dougherty came to the northern part of Rains
County before the Civil War. He built two vats near Lake
Fork bottom, where he tanned leather and made shoes.
The spelling of the family name wavered between
Daugherty and *Dougherty,* with the *Daugherty* spelling
being used for the school and church. In the early 1970s
descendants of the founder asked that the *Dougherty*
spelling be used for the community as well. A decision
about the official spelling for purposes of maps and road
signs was reached in October 1979 by the domestic
names board of the U.S. Department of the Interior in
Washington, making the community name *Dougherty.*
Pop. 76.

Douro *(Ector)* ['dyur o]

Despite the spelling, the community was supposedly
named by a Spanish-speaking rail-track layer who found
the ground unyielding to pick and shovel. He described it
as *duro,* Spanish for "hard." It was established in 1880 as
a station on the Texas and Pacific Railroad.

Dragoo Creek *(Titus)* ['dræ gu]

The name probably developed from the word *dragoon,*
referring to Civil War infantrymen from Titus County.

Drop *(Denton)*

Three different tales about the naming of the town have
been reported by Frank X. Tolbert, *Dallas Morning News*
columnist. People along Denton Creek wanted to name
it *Dewdrop,* but postal officials rejected the name, and
Drop was chosen as a compromise. Or, John Russell of
Dallas claimed his Uncle Hardy Holmes, replying to a
compliment paid the town, said, "Oh, this town is just a
drop in the bucket." Or, a Drop resident said, "The Indians never stayed long in the camping places. Early
settlers said the Indians just dropped in and dropped out,
a practice that caused the town to earn its name."
PO Jan. 6, 1886–Sept. 30, 1905.

Drunkards Branch *(Tyler)*

Temperance societies would approve of this name because it refers to a place where pioneers on horseback
stopped to drink water from this stream.

Dryburg *(Jasper)*

The reputation for being the driest spot in the county
according to rainfall records earned a name for the community. Its earlier name of *Harrisburg*, used from its
settlement in 1840, honored a pioneer family. The new
name of *Dryburg* was necessitated because *Harrisburg*
duplicated a post office name. After the Dryburg post
office closed, the place was once again called *Harrisburg*.
*PO Feb. 7, 1912–discontinued between June 1, 1933, and
June 1, 1936.*

Dry Duck Creek *(Kent)*

It isn't the duck that is dry, but the Duck Creek that
holds no water most of the time. This example of a common name that takes on interesting possibilities when a
modifier is added can be found throughout the state, in
North Cow Creek, Little Red Mud Creek, and the like.

Duffau *(Erath)* [ˈdəf o]

Attempts to explain the name have traced it to Old
Duffo, a popular Indian chief of the 1870s who died while
on a hunt and was buried near this place. Dr. Francis
Dauffau, a friend of Sam Houston who arrived two days
late to fight for Texas independence at San Jacinto, and a

district surveyor named Duffau also received credit for the name.

PO Feb. 13, 1860–Oct. 31, 1867; Dec. 17, 1867–Aug. 22, 1870; Dec. 19, 1870–Nov. 30, 1906; Aug. 29, 1912–;Pop.76.

Dull *(La Salle)*

This lively community owes its name to A. J. and J. J. Dull of Harrisburg, Pennsylvania, who were given a large amount of land by the state of Texas in exchange for steel to build railroads. They had established their holdings in the 1870s and 1880s before the town was founded in 1912. O'Henry worked on the Dull Ranch after he came to Texas from North Carolina to improve his frail health.

PO June 24, 1879 (Waughs Rancho)–Feb. 1, 1889 (Dull's Ranch)–Jan. 31, 1909; June 20, 1913 (Dull)–Dec. 21, 1915.

Duplex *(Fannin)* ['dyu plɛks]

The community was named not for a single family, but for two families settling here in the early 1850s. The names of the two families referred to in the dual name are not recalled.

PO Jan. 8, 1889–Apr. 30, 1909; Pop. 25.

Durango *(Falls)* [də 'ræŋ go]

Formerly called *West Falls*, the settlement grew up around the store built by J. B. Fuller. The name was changed to *Durango* when a drunken cowboy who had recently returned from Mexico insisted that he was in Durango, Mexico.

PO Sept. 29, 1871 (West Falls)–Jan. 8, 1883 (Durango)–Nov. 30, 1906; Pop. 54.

Duster *(Comanche)*

Citizens met in the 1880s to choose a name for their community. When inspiration was slow in coming, one of the men picked up a sheet of paper covered with dust and said, "Let's call her *Duster*."

PO Apr. 28, 1891–Sept. 30, 1927.

Dutchman *(Motley)*

Stories agree that Dutch people camped along the stream for which the town was named. Whether they were a Dutchman and his wife or Dutchmen who hunted buffalo is in dispute.

Eagle Lake *(Colorado)*

If an old Karankawa Indian legend is to be believed, two suitors for the hand of an Indian princess had a contest to determine which one could be first to swim the lake, climb a cliff, and bring back a young eagle. One brave drowned in the lake; the other won the hand of the squaw. The legend provided the name for a lake in eastern Colorado County and for the town which developed nearby.

PO June 19, 1849–Oct. 18, 1869; Feb. 18, 1879–; Pop. 3,515; Inc.

Earth *(Lamb)*

A sandstorm seems to have had something to do with the naming. One report claims that a storm came along about the time patrons were trying to decide on a name in 1925, and the airborne earth caused Earth to be placed on a list sent to the postal department. Another account tells how Mr. Reeves, who was to become the postmaster, described a sandstorm in a letter to the postal

people, who wrote back, "The Earth seems to move in your county. You will call the post office Earth." The name is also appropriate because residents remarked, "There wasn't a single tree in sight. All you could see was earth." *Fairleen*, an earlier name, was rejected along with *Tulsa* when the post office application was made.
PO May 25, 1925–; Pop. 1,128.

Ebony *(Mills)*

First called *Buffalo*, until the name was rejected for a post office because of duplication, the community offered the names of Ennis and Edna, children of Mrs. Griffin, the first postmaster, but these names had already been claimed by Texas post offices. Finally a new name was given for Ebony Shaw, a local cowboy and mail carrier. Some sources trace the name to ebony trees which are said to have grown in the area in the early days of settlement. That explanation is suspect since most of the ebony trees in Texas are limited to the southern tip of the state, some two hundred miles south.
PO Jan. 5, 1891–discontinued before 1945.

Echo *(Coleman)*

In 1881, Captain William Dibrell bought acreage here and named it *Echo Ranch*, for the echo resounding from a nearby cliff. The town took its name from the ranch.
PO Dec. 2, 1910–Feb. 28, 1914; Pop. 16.

Ecleto *(Karnes)* [ɪ 'kli to]

The town was first *Cleto*, said to be an Indian name. Then the Spaniards settled in the area and prefixed it with the masculine article to become *El Cleto*. Anglo ranchers later shortened the name to *Ecleto*.
Pop. 22.

Edenville *(Hale)*

To travel-weary settlers, this new flat land for farming looked as beautiful as the Garden of Eden, hence *Edenville*.
PO Aug. 7, 1908–July 31, 1909.

Edhube *(Fannin)* [ɛd 'hyu bɪ]

The community was first named *Bentonville* in honor of Edmond Hugh Benton, an early settler. Because of another post office of that name in the state, a new name

was created by taking the first two letters from each of Benton's names to form *Edhube*.
PO May 18, 1894–Apr. 14, 1906.

Edna *(Jackson)*

Previously, the town was called *Macaroni Station* because it was a commissary for Italian-speaking laborers on the Texas and New Orleans Railroad, built through this area in the 1880s by Italian Count Joseph Telfener. The count did not take kindly to the *Macaroni* label, alluding to the favorite food of the laborers, and he changed it to *Ednaville* in honor of his daughter, a name shortened to *Edna* four years later.
PO Dec. 12, 1882 (Ednaville)–Feb. 12, 1886 (Edna)–; Pop. 5,458; Inc.

Edroy *(San Patricio)*

The town honors Ed Cubage and Roy Miller, who laid out the townsite in 1910.
PO Oct. 22, 1914 Nov. 30, 1917, Aug. 16, 1950–; Pop. 200.

Egypt *(Wharton)*

The community felt kinship to biblical Egypt because farmers from all around came during droughts to buy grain just as had been done in the Bible. The area was settled around 1830 by Captain W. J. E. Heard. A post office by this name also operated in Kaufman County, 1876–1879 and 1880–1888.
PO Oct. 24, 1855–May 1, 1870; July 1, 1870–Feb. 15, 1871; June 12, 1871–discontinued before 1878; May 6, 1902–; Pop. 26.

Eight Mile Canyon *(Terrell)*

The name indicates the distance of the canyon eight miles from the county seat of Anderson. Throughout Texas, names of landmarks were often given names to designate the number of miles from an important point, often the county seat.

Elbow *(Howard)*

While there has been the suggestion in jest that Elbow may have been titled from the elbow-bending which the British Earl of Aylesford enjoyed while he was ranching in Howard County, the community was actually named for the bend in the north fork of the Concho River which is nearby.

El Capitan *(Culberson)* [ɛl kæp ə 'tæn]

The term, Spanish for "captain," suggests the command-ing majesty of the sharply profiled peak visible from the highway.
El. 8,078.

Eldorado *(Schleicher)* [ɛl də 're də]

When early settlers first arrived in the area, they were so proud of their "rich" location that an appropriate name seemed to be *El Dorado*, Spanish for "place of gold."
W. B. Simmiman gave the name in 1895 when he formed a company with W. L. Gray and M. H. Murchison to establish the first store in town. An earlier name for the area was *Verand*, given by a company of Vermonters in 1884 in reference to their home state. *Eldorado* was also the name of a Wise County community, later changed to *Paradise*.
PO June 4, 1892 (Verand)—Apr. 15, 1895; July 20, 1895 (Eldorado)—; Pop. 1,617; Inc.

Electra *(Wichita)* [ɪ 'lɛk trə]

The town was given the name *Electra* in honor of the only daughter of the cattle and oil baron W. T. Waggoner when the first post office was established there. It is said that the Electrajet plane was also named for her. The town then took the name of *Beaver*, already given to a nearby post office, when the Fort Worth and Denver Rail-road came. Confusion between the load pens and depot named *Waggoner Switch* and the post office named *Beaver* led citizens to petition in 1902 that the town be renamed in honor of Waggoner's daughter.
PO June 13, 1893 (Electra)—Oct. 21, 1895 (discontinued to merge with Beaver PO established Aug. 14, 1889)— May 1, 1902 (Electra name restored)—; Pop. 3,597; Inc.

Elgin *(Bastrop)* ['ɛl gɪn]

In April 1869, after unprecedented flood waters rose sixty feet above the low-water mark along the Colorado River and washed away surveyors' stakes, a substitute route for a Houston-to-Austin railroad was laid through an area that was to become Elgin. The name given for the station followed the railroad custom of honoring an official or individual who helped to promote the road. In this case, the honor went to Robert Morris Elgin, who resigned his position with the Texas State Land Office in 1865 to be-come land commissioner for the Houston and Texas

Central Railroad. Later, mob violence in the community caused train conductors to have their porters shout as they approached the Elgin station, "Hell-again; a half-mile to Hades," combining a humorous corruption of the name *Elgin* and its reputation for lawless events.
PO May 13, 1873–; Pop. 3,893; Inc.

Eli *(Hall)* [ˈi laɪ]

The area was known as *Twin Buttes* because of small hills nearby until the post office was established as *Eli*, honoring Eli Melton Dennis, an early community leader. A year after the Eli post office was discontinued, a new one was formed by adding *-te* to *Eli* to create the new name of *Elite*. After the *Elite* post office closed, the name of the area reverted to *Eli*.
PO June 29, 1906 (Eli)–Dec. 31, 1914; Nov. 17, 1915 (Elite)–Aug. 15, 1919.

Elkhart *(Anderson)*

A pioneer family traveling through the area abandoned their wagon after it broke down. The head of an elk was carved on the back of the wagon. Other settlers moving into the area found the elk cart, which became *Elkhart*.

An alternate story traces the name to an Indian chief named Elkhart who was friendly with early settlers.
PO Mar. 19, 1850 (Elkheart)–Dec. 28, 1851; Jan. 22, 1874 (Elkhart)–; Pop. 1,261; Inc.

Elmaton *(Matagorda)* [ɛl 'met n̩]

The Spanish name meaning "the killer" was bestowed on the community by the Missouri Pacific Railroad. Some say it was because a group of men got into an argument and began a fight at the spot where the railroad crosses FM 1095, with several members of the group dying in the fracas. Others believe the name involves a railroad accident in which a worker was accidentally killed in 1905 when his foot got caught on a rail and a handcar ran over him. Still others say that the killing refers to a slaughter house once located in the area.
PO Nov. 23, 1915–Mar. 15, 1921; Jan. 4, 1927–; Pop. 165.

El Paso *(El Paso)*

Located on the Rio Grande at a site named *El Paso del Norte,* "the pass of the north," by sixteenth-century conquistadores searching for the fabled seven cities of gold, El Paso has grown out of earlier settlements called *Magoffinsville,* for James Wiley Magoffin, owner of a

trading post in 1849; *Franklin*, for Franklin Coons, postmaster in 1852; and *Concordia*.
PO July 26, 1852–; Pop. 385,691; Inc. 1873; El. 3,762.

Elwood Lake *(Camp)*

The name was originally *Elmwood*, referring to the elm trees surrounding the lake, but it was altered to *Elwood*.

Elysian Fields *(Harrison)* [ə ˌli žən ˈfildz]

In 1818 Captain Edward Smith and other Virginians came on horseback to Texas and returned home via New Orleans. While recounting experiences to friends in Louisiana, the captain described a beautiful Texas village with large trees and gushing springs. Someone hearing his vivid description exclaimed, "You found the Elysian Fields." Smith returned to Harrison County with his family in 1834, settled here, and named the town for the Greek paradise.
PO June 15, 1848–Jan. 23, 1867; Nov. 16, 1871–; Pop. 300.

Embar *(Andrews)*

The brand for the Frank Cowden Ranch was the M—(M Bar), which was respelled to provide a name for the settlement.

Emhouse *(Navarro)* [ˈɪm haus]

Emhouse was named for Colonel E. M. House, superintendent of the Trinity and Brazos Railroad and advisor to President Woodrow Wilson. The town was originally called *Lyford* and was formed from the communities of Kelm, named for T. R. Kelm, who began a plantation here in 1854, and of King Willow.
PO Apr. 28, 1894 (Kelm)–Jan. 15, 1907; June 12, 1894 (King Willow)–June 15, 1906; Nov. 18, 1908 (Emhouse)– Feb. 29, 1960; Pop. 157; Inc.

Eminence *(Chambers)*

Wanting their town to be of wide renown, the people of the settlement found the most eminent name possible.

Enchanted Rock *(Llano)*

The 640-acre granite outcropping, the largest in the Southwest, received its name because the Comanche Indians living nearby believed the rock was haunted. The

sounds they heard coming from it were actually caused by the rock's contracting as it cooled at night.
El. 1,824.

Encino *(Brooks)* [ɪn 'si no]

A Mexican land grant made to Manuel and Luciano Chapa in 1831–1834 was given the name of *La Encantada y Encina del Pozo*, "The Enchanted Place and Live Oak in a Hole." It was said that the live oak tree which gave the grant part of its name was large enough to be seen for miles; constant trampling of the soil around the tree by horses seeking its shade and wind erosion created a large circular hole. The community took its name from the tree in the hole, and the name was later shortened to *Encino*.
PO July 11, 1914–; Pop. 110.

Energy *(Comanche)*

Although the name sounds quite contemporary, it was suggested in 1903 by William and Charlie Baxter, managers of the first store. They thought the group of men who gathered at their store were unusually energetic. Later, the town lent its name most appropriately to the nearby Energy Gas Field. In June 1979, Virginia Harris, postmaster, reports that although the community has dwindled to only one store, the residents are still full of energy.
PO Nov. 23, 1897–; Pop. 65.

Enon *(Upshur)* ['i nan]

The oldest church in the county and the surrounding community were probably named for Aenon in the Bible (John 3:23) because a nearby brook reminded settlers of the spot associated with John the Baptist. An explanation sometimes given for the name is that the letters were taken from the last names of four prominent settlers: Eason, McNight, Oliver, and Norris. A study of family names in the community cemetery by local historians lends no support to this explanation.

Eola *(Concho)* [i 'o lə]

The name has been traced to the Latin Aeolus, "god of the winds," and to the Indian word *eola*, meaning "good return from the blowing wind."
PO Oct. 31, 1901 (Jordan)—Aug. 1, 1902 (Eola)—; Pop. 218.

Eskota *(Fisher)* [ɛs 'ko tə]

The community was named by mistake when a Texas and Pacific Railroad crew accidentally threw out a station marker with *Eskota* written on it instead of the one with *Trent*, as intended. Some say *Eskota* is derived from an Indian word.
PO July 17, 1888—May 18, 1918; Dec. 3, 1918—Jan. 31, 1954.

Espantosa Lake *(Dimmit)* [ɛs pən 'to sə]

The Spanish name means "ghost" or "frightful, dreadful, fearful," alluding to superstitions about the body of water. Supply trains for Spanish missions stopped at the lake, and so many legends of horror grew up around it that travelers for years avoided stopping here overnight, even though doing so often caused them to make a dry camp.

Espiritu Santo Bay *(Calhoun)* [es 'pɪ rə tu 'sæn to]

Religious influence is seen in the naming of the bay for the Holy Ghost as expressed in Spanish. The name was applied to several locations on the Gulf Coast, but it is generally used here in the Matagorda Bay area.

Espuela *(Dickens)* [ɛs 'pwe lə]

From 1870 to 1910 the Espuela Land and Cattle Company operated a large ranch, which provided the name of the nearby community, the first county seat of Dickens County. The Spanish name translates as "spur" in En-

glish. Earlier names were *Dockham, Dockham Ranch,* and *Dockum Ranch,* for *Dockum Creek,* named for Warren C. Dockum, noted buffalo hunter and store owner.
PO Sept. 24, 1879 (Dockham Ranch)–Aug. 19, 1885 (Dockum Ranch)–July 8, 1891 (Espuela)–Jan. 15, 1910.

Estacado *(Crosby)* [ɛs tə ˈka do]

The Spanish word suggesting the Llano Estacado, "Staked Plain," replaced *Marietta,* a name given in honor of Mary Cox, wife of the leader of a colony of English Quakers who reached the county in 1879. *Marietta* was refused as a post office name because of duplication. The town served as the first county seat from 1886 until the government moved to Emma in 1891. Crosbyton, founded in 1899 within five miles of the center of the county, became the county seat in 1911.
PO Oct. 31, 1881 (Estacaddo)–Jan. 25, 1884 (Estacado)–Oct. 15, 1918.

Etoile *(Nacogdoches)* [ɪ ˈtoɪl]

An early French settler contributed the name, which means "star."
PO June 25, 1886–Sept. 14, 1901; Feb. 24, 1902–; Pop. 1,100.

Eureka *(Delta; Navarro)* [yu ˈri kə]

A grange meeting of the settlers in Navarro County brought up the need for a new post office, and the name *Eureka* was selected for its implication of finding the ideal place. In Delta County, a one-store community with a limited supply of merchandise was known as *Needmore* until a larger selection made the name *Eureka,* meaning "I have found it," seem more appropriate. The name was also used by communities in Collin and Kaufman counties.
(Navarro Co.) Pop. 75.

Excell *(Moore, Potter)*

The community is located at the site of a large U.S. government helium plant. The name comes from the cattle brand of Lee T. Bivins's ranch, "XL."

Fairfield *(Freestone)*

After being called *Mount Prairie* and *Mount Pleasant* for a time, the town was designated as county seat and was

to have a new name selected by a committee of eight. Mrs. Dunbar Bragg suggested *Fairfield*, for the former home of some of the settlers in Fairfield, Alabama. That name won over *Camden* and *Sumter*, names familiar to families from Alabama and South Carolina.
PO Nov. 17, 1851–; Pop. 2,560; Inc.

Fair Play *(Panola)*

Travelers were impressed by the fair rates and hospitality received at John Allson's general store, boarding house, and blacksmith shop. He also served as county judge in 1846 when the county was organized.
PO Mar. 22, 1851 (Fair Play)–Jan. 23, 1867; June 21, 1874–June 6, 1894 (Fairplay)–Apr. 14, 1904; Pop. 80.

Fairy *(Hamilton)*

Originally *Martin's Gap*, for an Indian fighter killed and buried in the gap of the mountain, the community was named in 1886 as a compliment to Miss Fairy Fort, so small she weighed only forty pounds and stood a little over three feet when she died in 1938 at age seventy-three. Her father was a Confederate captain, Battle Fort, who came to the area about 1873.
PO Mar. 17, 1884–June 14, 1957; Pop. 31.

Falcon Reservoir *(Zapata)* ['fæl kn̩]

Land on which the reservoir is located was granted in 1767 to José Clemente Ramírez, who married Rita Falcon in 1780. The town named *Falcon* in her honor was one of the communities covered by water of the Falcon Reservoir.
PO July 18, 1911–discontinued between 1930 and 1933.

Falfurrias *(Brooks)* [fæl 'fyu rɪ əs]

Robert Rice, an early postmaster, is quoted as tracing the name to a sheep herder who wore a leather apron resembling a skirt and called *falda* in Spanish. Rice claimed that the wearer of such a skirt is a *falduras* and that *Falfurrias* grew out of *Falduras*. Citizens can give several other Spanish and French words that might have provided the name of the town, but the attitude is that no one really knows the origin. Those who believe the word came from Indian origins tell of a Lipan chieftan seeking new hunting ground. Upon viewing this region, he exclaimed, "Falfurrias," which in his language supposedly meant "the land of the heart's delight." Other translations are "ragged man" or "Indian heaven."
PO Dec. 13, 1898–; Pop. 6,201; Inc.

Fashing *(Atascosa)* ['fæ šɪŋ]

A town meeting at the local store was called to select the name. The merchant, casting an eye over his stock, noted some Fashion Tobacco and suggested the name. A misreading in the postal department produced *Fashing*.
PO May 12, 1920–; Pop. 50; Inc.

Fastrill *(Cherokee)* ['fæs trɪl]

The community started as a lumber camp of the Southern Pine Lumber Company and blended its name from portions of the names of F. F. Farrington, F. H. Strauss, and Will Hill.
PO Dec. 11, 1922–discontinued before 1940.

Fate *(Rockwell)*

It is agreed that *Fate* is an abbreviation of *Lafayette*, but whether the name came from Lafayette Peyton, owner of a gin, of Lafayette Brown, a popular sheriff, is still debated.
PO July 13, 1880–; Pop. 275; Inc. 1908.

Fieldton *(Lamb)*

Since the town is halfway between Littlefield and Olton, citizens thought that a combination of the names of the two towns would be appropriate. The townsite was developed in 1924.
PO Dec. 6, 1930–; Pop. 126.

Fife *(McCulloch)*

Agnes Blythe Finlay, who came from Fifeshire, Scotland, recalled the town of her birth in naming the Texas community.
PO Sept. 11, 1902–; Pop. 32.

Fig Ridge *(Chambers)*

A fig canning plant which suggested the name was destroyed by a hurricane in 1915.

Fincastle *(Henderson)*

The abundance of fish in the vicinity of the community inspired the name given by Daniel R. McRae, a Scotch settler of the early 1850s.
PO Mar. 6, 1855 (Finecastle, spelling corrected to Fincastle *by 1856)–July 20, 1871; Aug. 7, 1881–Feb. 28, 1907.*

Fink *(Grayson)*

Fred Finke was a popular leader among early settlers. In recent years, after the name assumed humorous connotations, Finkites discussed changing the name to *Georgetown*, an earlier designation, but a post office of that name exists in Williamson County. In the 1960s, the citizens decided to capitalize upon the name by staging national Fink Day on the weekend closest to June 15 and inviting all persons named Fink to come to the community for the celebration.
PO Sept. 16, 1897–Dec. 31, 1903.

First, Second, Third, Fourth, Fifth creeks *(Lipscomb)*

The five parallel streams flow southward into Wolf Creek and lie west of Lipscomb, the county seat. Starting at the Ochiltree County line, they are numbered consecutively first through fifth. Next come Dugout Creek and Skunk Creek, indicating that the numerical system constitutes only a partial pattern for naming streams in the county.

Five Mile *(De Witt)*

College graduates from Germany settled here in 1849 and, as professional men who had studied Latin, they called the community *Latin Settlement* or *Lateiner,* later *Five Mile* because it was along Five Mile Creek, measuring that distance from the courthouse door in Clinton.

Five Notch *(Harrison)*

Two traditions account for the name of the road leading southeasterly from Marshall. One story attributes it to a resident who boasted five notches on his gun. Another version suggests that the road once had five offshoot trails or notches.

Flag Creek *(Bosque, Erath, Gillespie, Llano)*

Flat rocks, known as flagstones, lie in the creek bed and provide the name.

Flagg *(Castro)*

The town was named for the Flagg Ranch, which was called thus because the land area was in the shape of a flag. The town was located near the center of the fifty-three-section ranch owned by C. T. Herring until it was cut into 160-acre blocks and sold as farms in 1925.

Flomot *(Motley)* ['flo mat]

The town is located so near the Floyd County line that it took the first three letters in the name of both counties to form *Flomot.*
PO Jan. 27, 1902–; Pop. 181.

Flour Bluff *(Nueces)*

Looking south from Corpus Christi Bay, the namegivers could see sand dunes resembling high piles of flour. Flour Bluff served as a port for shipping cotton down the Laguna Madre into Mexico during the Civil War.
PO Mar. 3, 1909–June 30, 1913.

Flowella *(Brooks)* ['flo ɛl ə]

Founded in 1909 by Burton and Danforth, the town was planned by promoters so that its street would form diamonds as in Washington, D.C., with the center of the community at a flowing well.
PO Dec. 8, 1910–Nov. 15, 1923.

Flower Mound *(Denton)*

In 1854 the settlement received its name from a large
mound west of the first homesites, where an unusual
array of flowers grew after heavy rains. In the 1970s, after
the opening of the Dallas–Fort Worth regional airport,
the name gained prominence as part of the Flower
Mound New Town model community project which
ended in bankruptcy.
Pop. 1,577; Inc.

Floydada *(Floyd)* [flɔɪ ˈde də]

Dolphin Floyd, who was killed at the Alamo, provided
the name for the county and for the original name of the
county seat, Floyd City. When a post office was applied
for, a duplication was found, and T. W. Price, a rancher,
coined *Floydada*, combining the name of the county and
of his mother, Ada Price.
PO Aug. 4, 1980–; Pop. 4,032; Inc.

Fluvanna *(Scurry)* [flu ˈvæn ə]

The name was taken from the county of the same name
in Virginia where W. J. Jones, promoter of the townsite,

was reared. A man named Cunningham, who surveyed the townsite, is also said to have come from the same county and to have seconded the motion for the name. *PO June 26, 1899 (Light)–Jan. 7, 1908 (Fluvanna)–; Pop. 104.*

Fly Gap *(Mason)*

When a group of settlers left their horses in a thicket while they laid an ambush for Indians, they returned to find that flies had made a bloody mess of their mounts. The name *Fly Gap* was given to the spot and to the community later located in the same area.
PO Oct. 7, 1884–Nov. 18, 1898.

Fodice *(Houston)* ['fo dɪs]

The victory cry of "Fo' dice!" was heard at a dice game behind the post office when someone made a point of four, thus naming this town settled in the late 1880s. The source provides some embarrassment to the citizens today, and it has been suggested that the name might have actually come from a misspelling of Fordyce, Arkansas, home of one of the founders.
PO May 13, 1902–Sept. 30, 1966.

Fool Creek *(Glasscock)*

Because the creek runs in a direction which appears to be contrary to the natural drainage, it earned a descriptive name.

Forest *(Cherokee)*

Although East Texas forest surrounds the community, trees had nothing to do with the naming. Settled in the 1880s with the coming of the railroad, the area has a tradition that a traveler who stopped under a tree was asked why he stopped. "For rest," he replied, explaining his action and providing a name at the same time.
PO Mar. 17, 1879–Mar. 25, 1887; Dec. 2, 1887–; Pop. 85.

Forsan *(Howard)* ['for sæn]

Four oil-producing sands were believed to be present in the oil field discovered in 1928. Reference to the four sands was reduced to *Forsan* when a post office was established.
PO Jan. 30, 1929–; Pop. 303; Inc.

Four Notch *(Walker)*

In the early 1800s, a trail passing through the county toward the Trinity River was designated by four notches cut in trees at intervals along the way. The name was transferred to the surrounding settlement.

Four Way *(Moore)*

The spot where the highway connecting Dumas and Masterson crosses the road from Channing to Border is called *Four Way*.

Francitas *(Jackson)* [fræn 'si təs]

The Spanish word meaning "Little France" was applied to the community where a single French family resided as early as the 1890s.
PO Jan. 27, 1911–; Pop. 30.

Frankell *(Stephens)* [fræŋ 'kɛl]

The townsite was opened by Frank Kell, president of the Wichita Falls and Southern Railroad. The town became a station on the railroad after the Ranger oil boom of 1916.
PO July 8, 1920–June 30, 1955.

Franklin Mountains *(El Paso)*

A common explanation for the name is that a profile on the mountain is said to be that of Benjamin Franklin. A more reasonable explanation is that the mountain was

named for Franklin Coons, who also gave the city of El
Paso an earlier name, *Franklin*.
El. 7,100.

Fredericksburg *(Gillespie)*

Prince Frederick of Prussia was honored by German set-
tlers who established the town in 1846 when John O.
Meusebach led a wagon train of immigrants from New
Braunfels. On early maps the spelling was recorded as
Friedrichsburg.
PO Dec. 7, 1848–; Pop. 5,536; Inc.

Freeport *(Brazoria)*

The original intention of creating a free port, with no
charge being made for entry by boats, is recollected in
the name.
*PO Apr. 4, 1898–Aug. 24, 1898; Sept. 6, 1912–; Pop.
11,724; Inc. 1917.*

French John Creek *(Llano)*

The creek was named for an Englishman named John,
but because the settlers thought he was French it was
called *French John Creek*.

Frenstat *(Burleson)*

The European home of many of the early settlers was
Frenstat, Moravia.
PO Mar. 7, 1891–Mar. 31, 1908.

Fresno *(Fort Bend)* ['frez no]

The climate and geography of the area reminded a settler from Fresno, California, of his former home. A post office with this name operated in Dimmit County for five months in 1905.
PO May 31, 1910–; Pop. 3,000.

Friday *(Trinity)*

With Fred Friday as the first postmaster and Murray M. Friday as the second postmaster, addressing mail to *Friday* seemed the natural thing to do.
PO June 3, 1903–Dec. 31, 1904; Oct. 26, 1909–Oct. 31, 1955; Pop. 41.

Friendship *(Franklin)*

The first families who settled the area enjoyed each other's company so much that they decided upon the name *Friendship* to cement good relations. The popular name is also found in communities in Denton, Harrison, Milam, Williamson, and Wise counties.

Friendswood *(Galveston)*

A Quaker colony led by Francis J. Brown arrived from Halstead, Kansas, in 1895 and settled in a live oak wood along Clear Creek. The town was named for the wood and for the Society of Friends.
PO Dec. 15, 1899–; Pop. 12,037; Inc.

Frijole *(Culberson)* [fri 'ho li]

When the postmaster conducted a contest to select a name for the town, *frijole*, Spanish for "bean," was the most popular entry.
PO Aug. 30, 1916–discontinued before 1968.

Frio *(McMullen)* ['fri o]

The Spanish word for "cold" was first given to the Frio River which flows through the county and then transferred to the town. The name is shared with communities in Castro, Frio, and Parmer counties.
PO July 21, 1859–June 18, 1860.

Friona *(Parmer)* [fri 'o nə]

Because the average January temperature is thirty-five degrees, the inhabitants showed their distaste for the cold

weather by altering the Spanish word *frio,* meaning "cold." Frio Draw, running just south of town, was another influence in the name selection.
PO Mar. 16, 1907–; Pop. 3,166; Inc.

Frognot *(Collin)*

Three conflicting anecdotes tell how the community was named. (1) In the early days when the community was known as *Dixon School,* a name honoring a prominent family, boys often took frogs to class. Whenever the principal discovered the frogs, he whipped the owners. Soon this antifrog policy caused the community to acquire its name. (2) Soon after the community was founded, the overabundance of frogs forced the inhabitants to go on a frog-killing campaign. Within a short time, there were no frogs left, and the community assumed the name of *Frognot.* A frog sitting on a toadstool was painted on the municipal water tank as a community emblem. (3) Railroad men maintain the name refers to the fact that citizens asked that a frog—or track connection—not be put in the railroad tracks where they passed through the town.

Frydek *(Austin)* [fraɪ 'dɛk]

The Czech name was given by early settlers from Czechoslovakia in 1895.
PO June 22, 1901–Feb. 13, 1906.

Garden City *(Glasscock)*

In the early days of the settlement, William Gardner operated a small store and was first postmaster here. Settlers chose the name *Gardner City* when application was made for a post office. Through error or bad penmanship, the name was misread and returned as *Garden City.* The original site was abandoned for a higher location two and one-half miles away. With the move came the name of *New California,* but it was soon changed again to *Garden City.*
PO July 28, 1886–; Pop. 293.

Garden of Eden *(Tarrant)*

The truck farming community of two thousand acres took irrigation water out of the Clear Fork of the Trinity River with such success that prospects were good for a vegetable paradise.

Gasoline (Briscoe)

A cotton gin with a gasoline engine was installed here in 1907, a time when such a power source was a great novelty in the state.
PO Oct. 1, 1907–Dec. 15, 1948.

Gay Assembly (Marion)

A folk etymology of the unfamiliar sound sequence Gethsemane produced a more appropriate name for the community, where joyous citizens gathered for religious meetings. The church community named *Gethsemane* came to be called *Gay Assembly* by those who associated the place with lively revivals rather than with the biblical reference.

Gay Hill (Washington)

In 1836, two brothers, Thomas and James Gay, went around naming hills and villages for themselves. Tom Gay shared billing with William Carroll Jackson Hill in the titling of this town. The other Gay Hills in Texas are in Milam and Fayette counties and are only ghost towns today.
PO May 1, 1850–Sept. 9, 1868; Aug. 23, 1872–; Pop. 145.

Gem (Hemphill)

The jewel is not a precious stone, but Gem Hubbard Moody, wife of the founder.
PO June 19, 1909–Mar. 31, 1954.

Geneva *(Sabine)*

Before becoming a post office in 1885, the town was
known as *Jim Town*. Then Jim Wells changed the name
because he liked the name *Geneva*.
PO July 23, 1884–; Pop. 100.

Genoa *(Harris)* [jɪ 'no ə]

Similarities of climate between Harris County and
Genoa, Italy, led Colonel J. H. Burnett, founder and area
rancher, to name the town he established south of
Houston for the Italian city.
*PO July 27, 1892–Mar. 15, 1907; May 13, 1907–Sept. 14,
1962.*

Geronimo *(Guadalupe)* [jə 'ra nə mo]

The Indian chief Geronimo lent his name to the creek
and to the nearby town which was named for the stream.
The Apache Indian chief lived in this section and led his
band on many raids. He was originally named Goyahkla,
meaning "one who yawns." He surrendered in 1886, became a Christian, rode in Theodore Roosevelt's inaugural

parade in 1905, and died in the Fort Sill, Oklahoma, hospital on February 17, 1909, of pneumonia.
PO Nov. 20, 1889–; Pop. 150.

Gettysburg Peak *(Presidio)*

The town of Gettysburg, Pennsylvania, site of the Civil War battle and Lincoln's great address, provided a name for the mountain.

Gewhitt *(Hutchinson)* ['ji 'hwɪt]

A combination of the names of George Whittenburg became *Gewhitt*. Another town that had been named *Whittenburg* to honor the pioneer cattleman became *Phillips* in 1938 because so many of the citizens worked for Phillips Petroleum Company, and they called it Phillips's town.

Ginger *(Rains)*

In 1900 Arch Willis opened a lignite coal mine and persuaded the Katy (Missouri, Kansas, and Texas) Railroad to lay a spur track to Grand Saline. Willis wanted to name the mining community *Coyd* for one of his sons, but railroad officials thought it would be confused with *Hoyt*, also on the Katy line. Then Willis suggested *Spicer* because the Spicer Tie Yard was located near the mine. *Spicer* was also rejected because the tie yard's spur track would be confused with the mine track. A secretary in the Katy office commented that if Willis wanted a "spicy" name, he should choose *Ginger*. That name was adopted, and *Ginger* became very appropriate after the establishment of a factory which produced brick with the texture of old-fashioned gingerbread.
PO May 1, 1900–discontinued during the 1930s; Pop. 96.

Ginville *(Jackson)*

Cotton, a principal crop of the area, was taken to this community to be ginned.

Girard *(Kent)* [jɪ 'rard]

The Girard Trust Company of Philadelphia created the townsite from its holdings on the Spur Ranch. The company purchased 430,000 acres here in 1907 after its parent company, Swenson Land and Cattle Company, had sponsored the building of the railroad through the area.
PO Dec. 24, 1909–; Pop. 125.

Given Creek *(Throckmorton)*

When Colonel Newton C. Givens was stationed in Throckmorton, he enlisted his soldiers to build a rock house. The rocks and stones used in the construction came from a small stream later known as *Given Creek*.

Glenfawn *(Rusk)*

Glen Garland, a farm owner, killed a fawn here. When the post office was established, the incident involving Glen and the fawn was remembered.
PO Aug. 5, 1872–discontinued during 1960s; Pop. 16.

Globe *(Lamar)*

The first name sent by T. H. Wheeler to the postal authorities had been claimed by another station. When he asked his family for new suggestions, one of his sons spied a kerosene lamp, noticed the globe, and offered that name, which was accepted.

Glory *(Lamar)*

In the 1880s, Nick Ratliff, a general storekeeper, wrote the postal department that he wanted to call the town

Richland for its fertile earth. A wit in Washington, reading Ratliff's glorious description of the surrounding farmlands replied, "Only *Glory* would do your town justice."
PO Aug. 29, 1881–June 15, 1915; Pop. 30.

Golden Acres *(Harris)*

"A golden opportunity" for prospective home owners was advertised when real estate men started a development of 160 acres, dividing them into one-acre blocks. The area was subsequently known as *Golden Acres* because of the sales slogan. When the post office was established, it was given that name.
PO 1946–discontinued Mar. 31, 1959.

Goliad *(Goliad)* ['go lɪ æd]

In his notes for an unpublished revision of *Texas Towns*, Fred I. Massengill wrote that the Congress of Coahuila-Texas issued a decree on February 4, 1829, that the fortress of La Bahía del Espíritu Santo in the Department of Texas might be called *Goliad*. Prior to that date, it was sometimes referred to as *Goliat*, Spanish for "Goliath," because it was such a large fortress or prison. When spelled *Golhiad*, the word forms an anagram of the name of Hidalgo, father of Mexican independence.
PO Jan. 18, 1847–; Pop. 1,738; Inc.

Goober Hill *(Shelby)* ['gu bər]

Because peanuts (also known locally as goobers or ground peas) were a major crop, the name was a natural development.

Goodnight *(Armstrong)*

Charles Goodnight established the first ranch in the Texas Panhandle in 1876 after he homesteaded in the Palo Duro Canyon near the town of Canyon. He became a partner in the J. A. Ranch with John Adair and left his name on the Goodnight Trail.
PO Nov. 19, 1888–Dec. 30, 1965; Pop. 25.

Gooseneck *(Young)*

A loop on the Brazos River makes a gooseneck at this point. An earlier name for the town was *Honey Bend*, in reference to the numerous wild bees.

Government Creek *(Robertson)*

This canyon provided the timber for the government to use in building Fort Elliot.

Gozar *(Reeves)* ['go zar]

Because this place was an enjoyable stop on the long trip from Pecos to El Paso on early cattle drives, the Spanish word meaning "to enjoy" was chosen.

Grand Prairie *(Dallas)*

The name at the close of the Civil War when the town was first established was *Deckman*, in honor of Alexander Deckman, owner of the townsite. When the Texas and Pacific Railroad was built through here in 1876–1877, the name was changed to describe the location on the eastern edge of the grand prairie region. The story is told of a lady destined for Dallas who mistakenly

got off the train here. As she stepped off the train, she exclaimed, "My, what a grand prairie!" Her remark allegedly inspired the name.
PO Oct. 27, 1874 (Deckman)–Aug. 13, 1877 (Grand Prairie)–Pop. 70,500; Inc.

Grand Saline *(Van Zandt)* [græn sə 'lin]

The town was originally called *Jordan's Saline,* in honor of John Jordan, who discovered the saline prairie and marked a trail to it in 1844. The present name was given in 1872 when the railroad passed through and a depot was built. Grand Saline was the first county seat of Van Zandt County and housed its first post office. Underground mining operations of the Morton Salt Company, once a tourist attraction, are now closed to the public.
PO Feb. 19, 1874–; Pop. 2,276; Inc.

Grassland *(Lynn)*

Enos L. Seeds, the first settler, was a friend of Grover Cleveland. He chose the name for the Texas village from President Cleveland's country home near Washington, D.C.
PO Jan. 12, 1889–May 7, 1900; Pop. 31.

Grayback *(Wilbarger)*

Lowly lice of the grayback species gave their name first to Grayback Crossing of Beaver Creek, then to a line camp established on the W. T. Waggoner Ranch at the crossing, and finally to the post office created when an oil field was developed in the area.
PO May 24, 1930–Dec. 31, 1955; Pop. 25.

Grayburg *(Hardin)*

The Thompson-Fort Lumber Company that founded the town in 1905 used gray paint on all the company houses, making the town literally a "gray burg." The community served as a lumber shipping point for the surrounding area. One story accounts for the choice of paint as loyalty to the Confederate gray.
PO Mar. 2, 1909–; Pop. 116.

Greenfield *(Johnson)*

Two separate communities existed, with a Methodist church at Stubblefield and a Baptist church at Greenbriar, until an explosion in a whiskey still in Stubblefield brought economic ruin to the community. Then the two settlements joined forces as *Greenfield*.

Grit *(Mason)*

Both the gritty soil and the perseverance of the early settlers suggested the name. The name is also found in Medina County.
PO June 29, 1901–; Pop. 63.

Grow *(King)*

Jim Goodwin, who opened a cotton gin here in 1908, incorporated into the name he chose his wish that the town would prosper and grow. The population had grown to eighty-five in 1970. *Grow* was only one of the wishful names submitted on a list to the post office department.
PO Aug. 24, 1912–Aug. 31, 1954; Pop. 85.

Gruhlkey *(Oldham)*

W. H. Gruhlkey was roadmaster of the Rock Island Railroad and owner of land on both sides of the track when the small railroad station was built.

Gunsight *(Stephens)*

Amid the hills that adjoin the town is a ridge as straight as a gun barrel, with a projecting peak at one end that resembles a gunsight. A less reliable explanation is the tale about an enemy bullet that knocked the sight from a sharpshooter's gun as he prepared to shoot an Indian.
PO Mar. 31, 1880–late 1930s; Pop. 6; Mountain El. 1,550.

Happy *(Swisher)*

Cowboys named the area *Happy Draw* because they were so elated on cattle drives to find spring-fed water here. It has also been recorded that long before White settlers came to the region, the spring was known as the happy hunting ground by Indians who roamed the plains. Happy is proud to be known as "the town without a frown."
PO Mar. 14, 1891–; Pop. 678; Inc.

Hard Luck Creek *(Hardin)*

The creek is aptly named if the story told about it can be believed. It seems that a merchant from Woodville took the fortune he had assembled and came to this area to

buy land. Camping along the creek, he heard someone coming and took the precaution of hiding all of his money in the hollow of a holly tree before riding away on his horse. The next morning when he returned, he discovered that many of the holly trees along the creek had hollows in them. He never found his money, and the name he gave Hard Luck Creek was adopted by others who heard of his woe.

Hardshell Creek *(Anderson)*

The name refers not to sealife, but to Hardshell Baptists who were dominant in the early days of the county. Their staunch religion provided the name of the stream.

Harmony Hill *(Rusk)*

The harmonious relations of early settlers probably inspired the official name in 1856, but a more interesting name is the nickname of *Nip'n'Tuck*, for two fox hounds chasing a fox down the main street.
PO May 2, 1854–Jan. 23, 1867; July 14, 1868–June 30, 1905.

Hashknife *(Baylor)*

The community is located on the Hashknife Ranch established by Colonel Simpson and Colonel Hughes in the 1890s and named for the resemblance of its shape to a hashknife with the top as the chopper.
PO Apr. 28, 1879–Nov. 17, 1879.

Heckville *(Lubbock)*

Rather than a euphemistic expletive, the Heck family was the source of the town name.

Helotes *(Bexar)* [hɛl 'o tɪs]

Three circumstances surrounding corn are given as explanations for the name. All agree that the name is derived from an Indian word later borrowed by the Spanish, meaning "green roasting ear of corn." One tradition says that early white settlers had considerable trouble with Indians stealing their corn when it was in the roasting ear stage. Another reports that San Antonio vegetable peddlers could always rely on the town for corn, even in time of drought. A third states that a man named Chaca was the first to build his hut and cultivate his cornfield in the settlement of Mexicans, who intermarried with Apaches.
PO Sept. 12, 1873–; Pop. 226; Inc.

Henrietta *(Clay)*

The explanation that the name combines the two given names of Henry and Etta Parish does not satisfy the desire of many residents to connect it to Henry Clay, for whom the county was named. One county historian suggests that Mrs. Henry Clay, who was Lucretia Hart until her marriage to the Kentuckian in 1799, then took the name Henrietta Clay. However, although biographies of the Clays report a daughter named Henrietta, there is no mention that Lucretia took the name herself. Another supposition is that Henry Clay's first name was feminized in a pattern of naming towns for the first name of the person whose surname provided the county name.
PO July 7, 1874–; Pop. 2,986; Inc.

Hereford *(Deaf Smith)* ['hər fərd]

The Hereford breed of cattle has been popular in the area since Deaf Smith County, of which this town is county seat, was founded. The first herd was brought here by

L. R. Bradly and G. R. Jowell. Early names for the area were *La Plata* and *Blue Water.* Fluorine iodides in the soil have given Hereford the motto of "Town without a Toothache."
PO Nov. 22, 1898–; Pop. 14,160; Inc.

Hermleigh *(Scurry)* ['hɜr mə li]

Harry W. Harlin and R. C. Herm donated land for the original townsite in 1907, and citizens asked that the post office become *Hermilin.* Washington officials chose to name it *Hermleigh,* however. During World War I, it became *Foch,* since *Herm* is a German name and *Foch* was the name of a French general. In 1921 the town changed back to *Hermleigh.*
PO Sept. 19, 1890 (Wheat)–Mar. 29, 1907 (Hermleigh)–Dec. 31, 1918 (Foch)–Dec. 16, 1920 (Hermleigh)–; Pop. 724.

Herronn Creek *(Bowie)*

No explanation has been given for the spelling of the map name. It refers to a large number of herons inhabiting the swamp formed at the point where the creek joins the Sulphur River.

Hico *(Hamilton)* ['haɪ ko]

Dr. J. R. Alford founded the town and was given the privilege of naming it. He chose the name of his home town in Kentucky. Residents accept this origin rather than reports that he named the town for the Hico Indians, alternately spelled *Waco* or *Hueco* from the Spanish meaning "a notching" or "a hole," probably for a gap in the hills.
PO Oct. 4, 1860–Jan. 23, 1867; Oct. 12, 1871–; Pop. 1,043; Inc.

High Hill *(Fayette)*

High Hill, elevation under five hundred feet, was established by German settlers in 1848. It originally consisted of three villages: Blum Hill, named for Robert Blum, who was murdered in Vienna on November 9, 1848; Wursten, where good wurst (sausage) was sold; and Oldenburg, transplanted from Oldenburg, Germany. When the post office was established for the group of villages, the new name was *High Hill.*
PO Jan. 30, 1860–Jan. 31, 1907; Pop. 116.

High Island *(Chambers)*

In this part of Texas, an island need not be surrounded by water; it need only be a contrast to the adjoining terrain. In this case, High Island is the highest point between Point Bolivar and Sabine Pass, a salt dome where refuge is sought during floods and hurricanes—when water does sometimes surround the point.
PO Apr. 8, 1897–; Pop. 500.

Hi-Lonesome Oil Field *(Midland)*

The oil discovery was made on a ranch named *Hi-Lonesome* because of its distance from other settlements and the fact that the buildings on the ranch headquarters were the highest elevation of the ranch.

Hitchland *(Hansford)*

J. H. and Charles A. Hitch were early settlers and landowners in the area that became a town when the Chicago Rock Island and Gulf Railroad was built across the county.
PO July 1, 1930–Feb. 15, 1955; Pop. 27.

Hog Eye *(Bastrop; Gregg)*

When B. F. Chapman applied for a post office at his Gregg County store, he submitted the name *Sabine* because of the proximity of the river. One day soon after he was told that *Sabine* was already in use, he was talking with a group of men in front of his store. One suddenly exclaimed, "Look," and pointed down the hill to a man generally believed to be a hog thief. "Yes," said another, "yonder goes old Hog Eye." Thus the post office got its name. In Bastrop County, a community south of Elgin was named *Hog Eye* for a catchy tune that a strolling fiddler played at a dance given in the John Litton home. *(Gregg Co.) PO Jan. 27, 1902–June 15, 1903.*

Hogg *(Burleson)*

When a post office was established here in 1893, the name was chosen to honor Governor Jim Hogg of Texas. The governor's only daughter Ima became a prominent Texas benefactress, but despite recurring reports there was never a daughter named Ura Hogg. A post office operated under the name of *Hogg* in Fannin County from 1890 until 1893.
PO Mar. 26, 1893–Nov. 15, 1905.

Hogholler Creek *(Llano)*

Wild hogs once roamed the canyon or hollow, given the Southwestern pronunciation of *holler*.

Hog Wallow Creek *(Medina)*

Pigs like to roll or wallow in the cool mud of the stream.

Hollar Creek *(King)*

Before anyone guesses that Texans corrupted the name of Hollow Creek, it should be known that Pete Hollar lived near here in 1900.

Homer *(Angelina)*

Agreement has been reached that a Dr. Manning provided the name, but whether it came from his admiration for the Greek poet or for the fact that he had previously lived in Homer, Louisiana, has not be determined. Perhaps both influences were at work.
PO Aug. 4, 1858–Apr. 30, 1924; Pop. 360; Inc. since 1970.

Hondo *(Medina)* ['han do]

The Spanish meaning of the word is "deep," a name given not only to the town but earlier to the creek and a pass. The name was used by post offices in Gillespie County 1857–1859) and in Llano County (1877–1878).
PO Apr. 12, 1882 (Hondo City)–Nov. 22, 1895 (Hondo)–; Pop. 6,039; Inc.

Honest *(Delta)*

Saint Thompson, the postmaster, happened to notice a tin of Honest Snuff when citizens were seeking a name for their post office.
PO Feb. 23, 1900–Mar. 15, 1905.

Honey Grove *(Fannin)*

On his way to met William B. Travis in central Texas in 1835, Davy Crockett camped near the present site of the town. Crockett found honey in nearly every locust tree, in the grass, and even hanging on some of the bushes near his camp. He referred to the campsite as the honey grove. The words *honey grove* were found carved on one of the trees by W. B. Allen, who visited the area soon after Crockett.
PO May 22, 1846–; Pop. 2,010; Inc. 1875.

Hooker Creek *(Burleson)*

The name may cause a few contemporary eyebrows to raise, but it had completely innocent connotations when given to honor the Hooker family, early settlers in the region.

Hoot Index *(Bowie)*

The point at which the Kansas City Southern and the
Texas and Pacific railroads cross was named in honor of
"Hoot" White.

Hoover *(Gray)*

Although Roosevelt (for FDR) and Woodrow (for Wilson)
lie only a few miles away, there is no presidential honor
in this name. It came from H. E. Hoover, lawyer and
landowner from Canadian, Texas. The settlement started
as a switch on the Santa Fe Railroad in 1887. The name
Hoover was also used for communities in Burnet,
Guadalupe, and Lamar counties.
*PO Jan. 31, 1910–Feb. 14, 1914; Jan. 9, 1915–after 1958;
Pop. 35.*

Hranice *(Lee)* [hə 'ræn ɪs]

Czech and Moravian settlers in the area chose the name
for a town in Moravia. The word denoted "a dividing or
boundary place," "high place," or "watershed."

Hub *(Parmer)*

Like the hub of a wagon wheel, this town in the center
of the county claims that everyting goes outward from
here.

Humble *(Harris; Throckmorton)*

Humble in place names in the proud Lone Star State
rarely refers to the virtue of humility and almost always
to the Humble Oil Company, now Exxon. When a Mr.
Stribling in Throckmorton County allowed the company
to build a lake on ten acres of his land for research in
1921, the company name designated the body of water as
Humble Lake. The original Humble Oil Field in Harris
County was named for the town of Humble, whose name
honored P. S. Humble, the town founder.

Humline *(Bee)*

This community name refers to the Humble Oil Company, which boosted development of homesites by
running a pipe line through the area. The Humble Pipe
Line Company purchased land here in 1937 for a booster
station.

Hurlwood *(Lubbock)*

Claude Hurlbut and W. M. Wood were two landowners in the area when the community was established around a railroad switch in 1924. A combination of their last names designated the town. An aviation school was established here in 1941.
PO Jan. 23, 1926–.

Iago *(Wharton)* ['aɪ ə ˌgo]

M. D. Taylor, operator of a general store, is usually given credit for naming the post office for the Shakespearean villain in *Othello*. Some sources give the credit to Mrs. S. W. Cates.
PO July 21, 1891–June 2, 1895; Sept. 6, 1900–; Pop. 56.

Ibex *(Shackelford)* ['aɪ bɛks]

The name was taken from the Ibex Oil Company from Colorado.
Pop. 25.

Icarian *(Denton)*

This ghost settlement, now absorbed into the present town of Justin, was settled by immigrants from France in 1848. About 150 Frenchmen calling themselves socialists or "Icarians" landed in New Orleans, sailed up the Red River to Shreveport, and then came to Denton via wagons. After rains ruined the wheat crop in 1849 and many died of fever and malaria, the colony disappeared, with some members returning to France, others going to New Orleans, Dallas, or another Icarian colony in Illinois.

Illinois Bend *(Montague)* [ɪl ə nɔɪ 'bɪnd]

Located in the bend of the Red River, the settlement was first called *Waidville* for C. M. Waid, the first store operator. After the post office rejected that designation, *Maxville* was submitted, for Max McAmos, another early home builder. With *Maxville* also rejected, the third name, *Illinois Bend*, was chosen because the first four families had come from Illinois in 1862. The third name was accepted.
PO Sept. 17, 1877–.

Illusion Lake *(Lamb)*

The alkali surface of this area gives the illusion of being a large body of water when the site is actually dry.

Impact *(Taylor)*

Dallas Perkins, owner of the Impact Advertising Company, gave the name to the small trailer park area which was incorporated in 1960 for the purpose of voting legal liquor sales at the northern edge of then-dry Abilene. A decline in Impact was predicted after the city of Abilene voted to permit operation of liquor stores in 1978.

Imperial *(Pecos)*

The town location in a fertile valley of the Pecos River led early settlers to believe it would be as productive as the Imperial Valley of California. The name was also used for a post office in Fort Bend County in 1908.
PO May 11, 1910–; Pop. 720.

Inari *(Refugio)* [aɪ 'nɛr ɪ]

Names came from all parts of the world to designate Texas places, but India rarely made a contribution to the Lone Star State. The railroad community taking its name from Inari, India, is an exception.

Independence *(Washington)*

The area was first known as *Cole's Settlement*, for J. P. Cole, who arrived in 1824 and served as first alcalde of the precinct. On March 2, 1836, when Texas independence from Mexico was proclaimed at Old Washington, twelve miles east, Dr. Asa Hoxey suggested the name of the place be changed to *Independence*, commemorating the great event. Texas records other places named *Independence* in Cherokee and Hopkins counties and *Independent* in Leon County.

India *(Ellis)*

When the post office was established, the name of the community was changed from *Morgan* to *India*. The reason for the choice of both names was lost with the death of A. J. Moyers and other early settlers. The original settlement dates to 1853.
PO Jan. 12, 1892—May 25, 1899; Nov. 18, 1899—July 30, 1904; Pop. 12.

Indianola *(Calhoun)*

The extinct town, called the gateway to Texas, was known as *Carlschafer* or *Karlshaven* in 1844, when it was established by Prince Carl of Solms-Braunfels, who began a tent colony for thousands of Germans soon to arrive in Texas. Later the name changed to *Indian Point* because Indians had once established a village here. In 1849 Major John Henry Brown changed the name to *Indianola*. Hurricanes of September 17, 1875, and August 20, 1886, destroyed the town and led to its abandonment.
PO Sept. 7, 1847 (Indian Point)—May 12, 1849 (Indianola)—Sept. 29, 1881; Sept. 20, 1882—Apr. 13, 1887; May 21, 1887—Oct. 4, 1888 or 1889.

Indio Ranch *(Maverick)*

The community gets its name from the Spanish word for "Indian" or "Hindu," referring to the shape of the Rio Grande as it flows through the ranch land, resembling a turbaned head. Places named *Indio* in Presidio and Zavala counties refer to American Indians.
PO June 28, 1880—Apr. 3, 1884.

Industry *(Austin)* ['ɪn dəs trɪ]

The first German colony in Texas was named in 1831 for its industrious pioneer leaders. Inhabitants of nearby San Felipe were so pleased at cigars produced by Frederich Ernst that they called him an industrious man. Tradition has it that Indians taught Ernst to grow, cultivate, and cure tobacco. Men of prominence soon requested Indus-

try cigars, popularizing the name of the town. An earlier name was *Seiper*, for Ernst's son-in-law, who received the mail from Galveston.
PO May 22, 1846–; Pop. 475.

Innocent City *(Denton)*

In prohibition days, anyone brought to trial on bootlegging charges was regularly declared innocent, so much in fact that residents earned the name of Innocent City for their community.

Iola *(Grimes)* [aɪ ˈo lə]

Like the town of Ariola in Hardin County, Iola took its name from that of Edward Ariola, one of Stephen F. Austin's original colonists who settled here in 1836. Attempts have been made to link the name to the tribe of Iraola Indians who once inhabited the area.
PO Aug. 7, 1871–Apr. 24, 1872; July 23, 1877–; Pop. 331.

Iraan *(Pecos)* [aɪ rə ˈæn]

Some folk mistake the name for a misspelling of the oil-producing, headline-making country in the Middle East, but its origins are strictly local. It comes from the names of Ira and Ann Yates, owners of a large ranch. When oil was discovered in 1926, a townsite was laid out, and a choice lot was offered as prize for the best name submitted for the town. While V. T. Hamlin was working as a reporter in Iraan during the oil boom, he developed the idea for his "Alley Oop" comic strip. A park in Iraan now

offers an Alley Oop top hat slide, a replica of "Dinny" (an eighty-thousand-pound dinosaur), and a museum of prehistoric life in the area.
PO Jan. 6, 1929–; Pop. 1,500; Inc.

Ireland *(Coryell)*

Although Kildare, Dublin, and other Texas towns trace their name origins to Ireland, this community took its name from John Ireland, governor of Texas from 1883 to 1887. This name replaced its early designation of *Hamco*, for its location on the line between Hamilton and Coryell counties.
PO Mar. 30, 1911–; Pop. 60.

Irish Creek *(De Witt)*

Arthur Burns, an Irishman, settled on Irish Creek in 1826. Later the post office became *Burn's Station*, and then *Verhelle* for Eugene Verhelle of the Gulf West Texas and Pacific Railroad.
PO June 9, 1851 (Irish Creek)–Oct. 27, 1853; Nov. 7, 1853–Aug. 14, 1854; July 1, 1872 (Burn's Station)–June 18, 1877.

Ironton *(Cherokee)*

The nearby ruins of the Chapel Hill Iron Manufacturing Plant explain the name of the town promoted by C. H. Martin, immigration agent for the International and Great Northern Railroad.
PO Sept. 17, 1904–discontinued during 1960s; Pop. 110.

Israel *(Freestone; Polk)*

The name of the ghost town in Freestone county is traced both to Uncle Israel Twaweek, first postmaster, and to the mother of Tom Newman, who took the name directly from the Bible. In Polk County *Israel Community* was founded in 1895 by a sect called the Israelites, who settled a tract of 144 acres and built a church called the New House of Israel. They deeded the land to "Lord God of Israel and Creator of Heaven and Earth."
(Freestone Co.) PO Jan. 25, 1897–Apr. 30, 1909.

Italy *(Ellis)*

Gabriel J. Penn named the town in 1880, presumably because he had visited "sunny Italy" and found similar

climatic conditions in Ellis County. An earlier name was *Houston Creek*, given in the belief that Sam Houston camped here, but that name was rejected by the postal department.
PO Mar. 24, 1880–; Pop. 1,220; Inc.

Itasca *(Hill)* [aɪ ˈtæs kə]

A Katy Railroad worker from Minnesota took the name in honor of Lake Itasca of that state, headwaters of the Mississippi River. The Indian word means "head of the waters" or "where the waters rise." The town was founded in 1881.
PO Feb. 9, 1882–; Pop. 1,438; Inc.

Ivanhoe *(Fannin)* [ˈaɪ vɪn ho]

Joe E. Dupree had just finished reading *Ivanhoe* by Sir Walter Scott when the post office department asked that a name be submitted for a new station. Earlier names were *Greenberry* before 1850 and *Hawkins Prairie*, honoring the first settler, until it was learned it duplicated *Hawkins* in Wood County.
PO Sept. 20, 1877 (Hawkins Prairie)–June 8, 1885 (Ivanhoe)–; Pop. 110.

Izoro *(Lampasas)* [aɪ ˈzo rə]

At the time of the settlement in the early 1880s, a respected resident had a beautiful daughter named Izoro Gilliam. An earlier name was *Higgins Gap*.
PO Aug. 18, 1888–discontinued by 1966; Pop. 31.

Jaboncillos Creek *(Duval, Jim Wells, Kleberg)*
[ja bən ˈsil əs] [ha bon ˈsi yos]

A Spanish-English dictionary quickly clears up the mystery of the name. The word means "soapstones" and is also the name of the Spanish grant of Antonio Ramírez in nearby Jim Wells County. The course of the stream was a source of soapstone for area residents.

Jack Mountain *(Coryell)*

Burros or donkeys, according to legend, carried a priceless treasure from the San Saba silver mines to the mountain where Indians tried to rob a caravan. The treasure has never been seen or heard of since that day, although prospectors often try their luck at finding it.

The burros are remembered by the slang expression which gave the mountain its name.
El. 1,059.

Jacobs Creek *(Comal)*

Jacob de Cordova was surveying land in the area on his birthday when he came upon the stream. He gave himself a birthday present by naming it for himself.

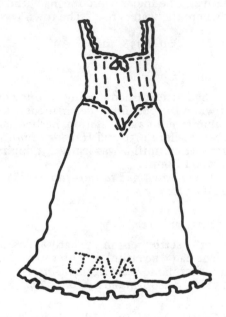

Java *(Cherokee)*

Java dates from the late 1880s, and by the 1890s J. L. Brown of Jacksonville was spinning a yarn on a fishing trip on the Neches River about the loss of a petticoat by a young lady at a community ball. Lettering still visible on the garment proclaimed it was made from a Java coffee sack. The post office was established while the town tongues were still wagging about the young lady's misfortune. Another version says the undergarment was lost in a creek.
PO Dec. 28, 1895–Apr. 2, 1906.

Jericho *(Donley)*

Judge John Altizer named the station on the Rock Island Railroad after Jericho in biblical Palestine.

Jiba *(Kaufman)* ['hi bə]

Multiple names and pronunciations caused so much confusion in the early days of the community that a song
was composed and entitled "Jiba (Heba), Jiba (Jeyeba),
Jessie Green." The name of the song title alludes to the
following transitions in the onomastic history of the
community: (1) In the late 1880s, the place was known as
Jessie when a post office was established. (2) In 1900, the
name was changed to *Green*, believed to have been a
tribute to E. H. R. Green, owner of the Midland Railroad.
Mail service was confused with another Texas postal station named *Green*. (3) The next designation was *Jiba*,
pronounced "Heba" in the Spanish fashion. The name
has been attributed to a Spanish-speaking railroad employee who labeled the community with a word said to
mean "the end" or "going away." (4) The Anglicized pronunciation of *Jiba* became "Jeyeba."
PO Feb. 1, 1901 (Green)–Aug. 30, 1905 (Jiba)–July 30, 1927.

Jim Ned Lookout *(Montague)*

Located between Montague and Forestburg, the mount or
high prairie ridge was used by a wary Caddo Indian spy,
Jim Ned, who would climb to the top and survey the
countryside to ascertain the movement of suspicious
White intruders.

Johnson Creek *(Kimble)*

The name of the creek was intended to honor General
Albert Sidney Johnston, but it was misspelled.

Jollyville *(Williamson)*

A family, rather than a jovial spirit, produced the town
name. John T. Jolly operated the first general store and
blacksmith shop here, beginning in 1866.
Pop. 150.

Jonah *(Williamson)*

When Dallie C. Davidson was assigned the task of finding a new name for Water Valley with the establishment
of the post office she was to manage, she went about her
work diligently. After several attempts to find names of
beauty and elegance acceptable to the postal department,
she became discouraged to learn that offices were already
using the names she submitted. "I feel just like Jonah,"
she remarked, alluding to someone believed to bring bad
luck. Hearing her comment, John Whitney jokingly suggested, "Why don't you call the place *Jonah*?" Davidson

then experienced some good luck in registering that name.
PO Aug. 21, 1876–; Pop. 60.

Jot 'Em Down *(Delta)*

When Dion McDonald built a new store in 1936, Lum and Abner, homespun comics who operated their fictional Jot 'Em Down store in Pine Ridge, Arkansas, were national favorites with radio listeners. Bob Roderick and others dubbed the new store a Jot 'Em Down, but McDonald rejected the name as undignified. Later a Jot 'Em Down Gin Corporation was organized, and the state highway department picked up the name as the official one for the community. Until 1936, the settlement was known as *Mohegan*, for the Mohegan Indian tribe, and some people called it *Bagley* for an old school here.
Pop. 30.

Joy *(Clay)*

When the area was settled about 1880, it was known as *Fanninton* or *Fannin Town* because so many of the home builders had come from Fannin County to the east. When a post office application was made, however, *Joy* was selected because everyone was so elated over abundant crops in the first year of planting. The selection of the name was also influenced by the desire of the post office department for short names. *Joy* is also the name of communities in Cass and Smith counties.
PO Jan. 26, 1895–; Pop. 150.

Jozye *(Madison)*

The name *Jo* was submitted to the postal department for Willie Jo Shannon, daughter of Joe H. Shannon, a major land holder. Postal authorities added the *-zye*.
PO Sept. 9, 1912–discontinued between June 15, 1943, and June 30, 1947.

Julia Pens *(Victoria)*

Julia Rose Anderson, once owner of the land, and the many cow pens which were once used by the railroad beginning in 1887 gave the name. The pens were torn down after 1945.

Juno *(Val Verde)* ['ju no]

Greek mythology had nothing to do with this name. The owner of a cantina served only two things—frijoles and

beer—but he always greeted his Spanish-speaking customers by asking, "What'll you have?" "Juno [You know]," they supposedly replied.
Pop. 10.

Justiceburg *(Garza)*

Jeff D. Justice was a landowner and rancher who gave the right-of-way to the Santa Fe Railroad when a station was established in 1910. He also gave a section of land for the townsite. Members of the Justice family have been involved in the operation of the post office from time to time since its opening. The earlier name of *LeForest* came from the two sons—Lee and Forest—of Mr. and Mrs. Arthur Tuffing, who opened the post office in their home in 1902.
PO Mar. 28, 1902 (LeForest)–July 31, 1905; July 25, 1906–June 3, 1910 (Justiceburg)–; Pop. 76.

Kaffir *(Schleicher)*

Kaffir is the grain sorghum grown in the vicinity of this rural community, where William M. Smith became the first and only postmaster in 1915.
PO Dec. 8, 1915–Mar. 31, 1921.

Karnack *(Harrison)*

The distance between this town and Caddo Lake was found to be the same as that between ancient Karnack in Egypt and the Nile River. Karnack is the hometown of Lady Bird Johnson.
PO Sept. 29, 1898–; Pop. 775.

Katemcy Creek *(McCullough)* [kə 'tɪm sɪ]

The name was taken from the Indian chief, Katumse, when John O. Meusebach negotiated a treaty. It was applied first to the stream and then to the community.
PO Nov. 17, 1884–; Pop. 162.

Katy *(Fort Bend, Harris, Waller)*

Although some people believe the town was named for the Missouri, Kansas, and Texas Railroad, known as the Katy, a former mayor and the postmaster disagree. Former mayor Arthur Miller claims he has good evidence that the town was named to honor Katy Mares, a saloon keeper who lived in her saloon with her husband and four children and who had people calling the town Katy

Mares long before the railroad came. D. Stanberry, postmaster, says his grandfather heard railroad workers say, "Let's go to Katy's."
PO Jan. 23, 1896–; Pop. 4,993; Inc.

Keechie *(Leon)* ['ki čaɪ]

The community was named for the Keechie Indians, whose name is spelled variously as *Kichai, Quichi,* and *Quihi.* The name of the tribe is translated as "peaceful" or as a reference to the white-necked Mexican eagle buzzard.
PO Mar. 1, 1852 (Milton)–Nov. 13, 1853 (Keechi)–Nov. 5, 1866; Jan. 1, 1872 (Keechie)–June 9, 1880; June 23, 1883–Nov. 15, 1889; May 15, 1890–Nov. 5, 1890; Nov. 9, 1895 (Fay)–Aug. 9, 1906 (Keechie)–Feb. 28, 1954; Pop. 67.

Kemah *(Galveston)* ['ki mə]

The town faces the winds of Galveston Bay and is appropriately given an Indian name meaning "facing the winds." An earlier name was *Evergreen.*
PO Nov. 12, 1907–; Pop. 1,229; Inc.

Kensing *(Delta)* ['kɪn sɪŋ]

This name is the composite of the last syllables in the names of two early settlers—Flenniken and Sansing. *Pop. 50.*

Kermit *(Winkler)*

In 1910, the year after he left office, President Theodore Roosevelt made a speaking tour of the West. His family was in the news frequently that year, and the name of his twenty-one-year-old son Kermit was chosen for the town. *PO July 18, 1910–; Pop. 7,506; Inc.*

Ketchum Mountains *(Irion)*

Two brothers, James and John Ketchum, were killed by Indians near the hill. *El. 2,730.*

Kickapoo Creek *(Tom Green)*

Settlers making an exploratory trip to El Paso in 1849 met a band of Kickapoo Indians just after they crossed the creek. At least eight other Texas streams also bear this name.

Killeen *(Bell)* [kə 'lin] [kɪ 'lin]

Named for Frank P. Killeen, civil engineer of the railroad, the depot town on the Gulf, Colorado and Santa Fe Railroad displaced the community of Palo Alto, about two and one half miles to the northeast. *PO Nov. 8, 1872 (Palo Alto)–Aug. 4, 1883 (Killeen)–; Pop. 49,307.*

Kiomatia *(Red River)* [ˌkaɪ əˈmi ši] [ˌkaɪ əˈmɪ ši]

One of the most complicated post office histories in Texas, involving at least four separate post offices, is to be found at Kiomatia. The bend of the Red River first called *Pecan Point* and currently known as *Kiomatia* bears an Indian name meaning "clear water." The name was transferred to the community south of the river. *PO July 5, 1850 (Kiomatia)–Nov. 5, 1866; Oct. 16, 1855 (Flintham's Tan Yard)–Oct. 9, 1866 (Milton)–June 26, 1868 (Kiomatia)–Oct. 27, 1868; July 12, 1871–Nov. 17, 1875 (Hooks Ferry)–Dec. 26, 1876 (Kiomatia)–July 10, 1886; May 17, 1898 (Kiomache)–Oct. 26, 1908 (Kiomatia)–June 29, 1918; Aug. 17, 1903 (Scrap)–Oct. 16, 1924 (Kiomatia)–; Pop. 61.*

Kittle *(Live Oak)*

Although George West, an important rancher, had the honor of lending his name to the county seat, his wife, Kittle, could claim that a community was also named for her. Settlement began here about 1915.

Knickerbocker *(Tom Green)*

Ollie Tweedy named the community for his home in New York. In turn, the New York town had been named by Morgan and Lawrence Grinnell, great-nephews of Washington Irving's famous Father Knickerbocker character.
PO Aug. 17, 1881–; Pop. 250.

Knox City *(Knox)*

The area was settled in 1907 and at first called *Orient* for the Kansas City, Mexico, and Orient Railroad. The new name came from Knox County, honoring Henry Knox, secretary of war in George Washington's cabinet.
PO Sept. 29, 1903 (Orient)–Sept. 16, 1904 (Knox City)–; Pop. 1,492; Inc.

Koon Kreek Klub *(Henderson)*

Established by Captain Gaston of Dallas, the private lake and club is a respelling of *Coon Creek*, named for the abundance of raccoons found in the area. Early members would go from Dallas to Athens by train, get in buggies, and travel fourteen miles south of Athens. Membership is now a social distinction.

Kosciusko *(Wilson)* [kə ˈšus ko]

In the early 1880s, a colony of Polish people bought the settlement, which dated from about 1850, and named it for the Polish patriot Thaddeus Kosciusko (1746–1817). *PO June 1, 1896–May 31, 1909; Oct. 9, 1909–Feb. 14, 1920; 1979–; Pop. 81.*

La Belle *(Jefferson)*

Because the postmaster's fiancée was Mary Bell Dordages, the new post office was requested in 1886 under the name of *Belle*, but postal authorities named it *La Belle* instead. An earlier name was *Lower Taylor's Bayou*.

LaCasa *(Stephens)*

This town was established when James C. Bargsley built
a log cabin near the site in 1880. In 1890, E. T. Bradford
operated the post office and general store in his white
house. Translated into Spanish, *The House* became *La
Casa*, spelled as one word in early postmarks.
PO Sept. 11, 1889–Aug. 14, 1926.

Lagarto *(Live Oak)* [lə ˈgar to]

The number of alligators reportedly in a nearby lake
when the town was established provided the name, from
the Spanish *lagarto*, meaning "alligator." A Mexican settlement here dates to 1858.
PO Aug. 17, 1874 (Lagarta, spelling later changed to
Lagarto)*–discontinued 1940; Pop. 80.*

Laguna Plata *(Kinney)*

In Spanish, *laguna* means "lake," and this one was called
plata or "silver" because the dry gypsum in its bed
flashed brilliant in the sunlight. The name gave rise to
stories of buried treasure, but no trace of silver has been
found.

Lake Raven *(Walker)*

The origin of the name of the lake is believed to be
derived from the nickname of Sam Houston, known as
"The Raven" and closely identified with the county.

Lake Surprise *(Chambers)*

The surprise of a stranger at finding a lake while walking
through high stretches of cane grass surrounding the
water is the supposed allusion of the name.

La Marque *(Galveston)* [lə ˈmark]

The original settlement of *Highland*, for its elevation
above the coastal plain, came to be known as *Buttermilk
Station* during the Civil War because soldiers stopped
here to buy buttermilk. During the late 1860s, Madam
St. Ambrose, French-born postmaster of an adjoining area
also known as Highland, was given the honor of renaming
Buttermilk Station. She thought *La Marque*, meaning
"the mark" in French, best designated the place she loved.
PO Jan. 25, 1887(LaMarque, later changed to La Marque)*–;
Pop. 14,588; Inc.*

Lambs Head Creek *(Throckmorton)*

The stream is believed to have received its name from the Lamb's Head Ranch, sometimes called Old Stone Ram. A doctor named Culver bought a large number of sheep and raised them on the ranch.

Lamesa *(Dawson)* lə 'mi sə]

A. L. Wasson, a member of the first board of the townsite company, suggested the name of *La Mesa*, Spanish for "tableland." M. C. Lindsey is given credit for influence in the selection of the name. An earlier name was *Chicago*.
PO July 13, 1904–; Pop. 11,204; Inc.

Langtry *(Val Verde)* ['læŋ trɪ]

Contrary to reports of movies, dictionaries, and other sources, the town was not named for Lily Langtry, the famous British beauty with whom Judge Roy Bean, "law west of the Pecos," became infatuated. The hanging judge was infamous for the justice he decreed from his Jersey Lily Saloon. But the town's name had been given in 1881 for a young English civil engineer who was in charge of a surveying crew for the railroad and who came to the area four years before Roy Bean.
PO Dec. 8, 1885–; Pop. 145.

LaParra Creek *(Live Oak)* [lə 'pær ə]

The name is usually written locally as *Lapara*. It came from Spanish *la parra*, "the grapevine," referring to the mustang or wild grapes found growing along creeks in the county.

Laredo *(Webb)* [lə 're do]

Established in 1755, with a mission founded in 1762 when the site was named *Villa de San Augustine de Laredo*, the name later was shortened to *Laredo*, probably for the town of Laredo in Santander, Spain. A far-fetched story is that monks tuned chimes in the church belfry to ring out "la, re, do."
PO Feb. 3, 1849–; Pop. 76,998; Inc.

La Reunion *(Dallas)* [ˌla rɪ 'yun yən]

When French settlers left their homeland for their utopian colony in Dallas County, they spoke of *la reunion* in Texas. Their reunion at their communal townsite in 1855 was followed by a severe blizzard which reduced their ranks and caused survivors to move across the Trinity to the town of Dallas. Historians attribute Dallas's cultural foundations to early leadership by artists and scholars among the French colonists. The name has now been popularized by the 1978 opening of the Reunion development around Union Station in downtown Dallas, including Reunion Tower and Reunion Sports Complex.

Lariat *(Parmer)* ['læ rɪ ət]

Only a few miles from Lasso is Lariat, where W. A. Simpson, official for the Santa Fe Railroad, was impressed by the lariats used by employees of the XIT Ranch.
PO Dec. 9, 1925–; Pop. 200.

Larissa *(Cherokee)*

The first settlement of 1837 was abandoned the following year because of a Cherokee uprising, but colonists returned in 1846. Two years later, the Reverend T. N. McKee, Cumberland Presbyterian minister from Tennessee, founded a village he called *Larissa*, for the ancient city of learning in Thessaly, Greece. A college begun in 1855 continued to the Civil War as Larissa College. A meningitis epidemic in 1872 left the site in ruins by 1885.
PO Dec. 23, 1847–Sept. 14, 1905.

La Salle *(Jackson)* [lə 'sæl]

The French explorer La Salle landed about five miles from this site in February 1685. The community was originally called *Benwest* for J. M. Bennett and Sol West, civic leaders in 1875. Then the name became *Bennview* until it was replaced by *La Salle*. Other post offices named La Salle operated in Calhoun, La Salle, and Limestone counties at different times without overlapping, the last one discontinued in 1908.
PO May 24, 1928 (Bennview)–Aug. 1, 1937 (La Salle)–; Pop. 75.

La Sal Viega *(Willacy)*

The name, from Spanish *la sal vieja,* "the old salt," refers to the salty water in the lake. At one time, a great salt lake existed here, supplying northern Mexico with salt.

Lasara *(Willacy)* [lə 'sɛ ɪə]

Residents wanted to honor both Laura Harding and Sara Gill, combining the *La* from *Laura* with *Sara*. The

townsite was laid out in 1924 with husbands of the two women, Will Harding and Lamar Gill, as land promoters.
PO Oct. 28, 1926–; Pop. 100.

Latexo *(Houston)* [lə 'tɛks o]

Stark's Switch was established in 1872 as a shipping point for cotton, lumber, and other products on the International and Great Northern Railroad. After the Louisiana and Texas Orchard Company was located in the town, the new name was created from *La* (Louisiana), *tex* (Texas), and *o* (Orchard).
PO Dec. 10, 1907–; Pop. 93.

La Vernia *(Wilson)* [lə 'vər nɪ ə]

About 1850 William P. Wiseman and his family from Mississippi organized a Presbyterian church in a location he called *Live Oak Grove*. In 1853, a post office was established here under the name of *Post Oak*, changed to *La Vernia* in 1859. One version attributes the name to a Spanish word said to mean "the tree," referring to the same grove of live oaks that had provided the name given in English by Wiseman.
PO Feb. 2, 1853 (Post Oak)–May 7, 1859 (La Vernia)–; Pop. 474; Inc. after 1970.

Lazbuddie *(Parmer)* ['læz bə dɪ]

Two ranchers in the early part of the century were D. L. "Laz" Green and A. "Buddie" Shirley. Their names form this compound.
PO May 2, 1926–; Pop. 248.

Leesburg *(Camp)*

While most citizens agree that the name honors members of the Otis H. Lee family who came from Alabama, some attribute the name to Robert E. Lee, Confederate general.
PO June 15, 1874 (Leesburgh, spelling changed in 1904 to Leesburg)–temporarily closed in 1979; Pop. 115.

Legion *(Kerr)*

The Texas Division of the American Legion established a hospital here in 1922. Llano County also had a Legion post office in 1859 and from 1894 to 1899.
PO Nov. 22, 1922–.

Leo *(Cooke)*

Because Dr. Stamper of Era thought the community settled in 1894 had such a rough and wild locale, he decided that the Latin word for "lion" would be an appropriate name. The spur on the Texas and New Orleans Railroad was originally called *Field's Spur*, for Dr. J. A. Field. *Pop. 80.*

Leona *(Leon)* [li 'o nə]

A party of travelers camped on a small prairie near the present town. During the night they were attacked by a Mexican lion (or yellow wolf, according to some reports), which they killed, and from that time the prairie has been known as *Leon Prairie*, suggesting the name for the county and then for nearby Leona.
PO Dec. 28, 1846–; Pop. 98; Inc.

Levita *(Coryell)* [lə 'vaɪ tə]

Originally *Simpsonville*, for M. Simpson, who operated a general store, gin, and mill, until it was discovered that another Texas post office had claimed the name, the community took its new designation from Levita Jay, mother of the first postmaster, Charles Jay. One source insists, however, that Simpson had two daughters named

Lee and Vita, who kept the town name in the family
when *Simpsonville* had to be relinquished.
*PO June 3, 1886—discontinued between July 1, 1965, and
June 30, 1967; Pop. 70.*

Liberty *(Liberty)*

The settlement begun on the Trinity River in 1756 by the
Spanish and called *Atascosito* was one of the earliest
outposts of the Spanish regime in Texas. In 1831 J. Francisco Madero named the settlement *Villa de la
Santissima Trinidad de la Libertad* ("Town of the Most
Holy Trinity of Liberty"), shortened to *Liberty*. By 1840
Liberty was a port of some importance, with regular
transportation to and from Galveston. From 1838 to 1878,
more than 133 steamers ran the Trinity River, stopping at
Liberty. In December 1836 the Republic of Texas established the first post office here. The present postmaster
represents the third generation of the Calhoun family,
who have served the Liberty post office over sixty years
and under eleven presidents.
PO May 22, 1846—; Pop. 9,180; Inc.

Little Hope *(Wood)*

Founders of the First Baptist Church, around which the
community grew, felt it would not exist long, and therefore they had little hope for the town.

Lively *(Kaufman)*

The frequency of dances held in the community caused
folk to call it a "lively little place" and then to shorten
the phrase to create the official name.

Liverpool *(Brazoria)*

The seaport city in England provided the name for this
Texas coastal town.
*PO May 22, 1846—Apr. 24, 1867; Aug. 5, 1879—; Pop.
422; Inc.*

Lockhart *(Caldwell)*

The original name of *Plum Creek* was changed when the
site was chosen as county seat for the new county in
1848. The person honored by the name change is Byrd
Lockhart, an official surveyor of De Witt's colony, who
received the land for the townsite from the Mexican government in recognition of his services. Later he

commanded a company at the capture of Bexar in 1835, became a messenger from the Alamo, and served as an officer in the Texas Army.
PO June 14, 1847 (Plum Creek)—July 27, 1848 (Lockhart)—; Pop. 6,489; Inc.

Loco *(Childress)*

The loco weed caused livestock that ate it to go crazy (Spanish *loco*) and become ill. The name of the weed that grew in the region was submitted to the post office department and accepted. A previous name for the post office serving the area was *Arlie*, for Arlie Griffith Weddington, an early resident.
PO June 18, 1887 (Arlie)—Aug. 1, 1930 (Loco)—Dec. 11, 1964.

Lodi *(Marion; Wilson)* ['lo daɪ]

The town in Marion County was first known as *Monterey*, but its name was confused with that of Monterey, Louisiana. The new name was given the community by an Italian railroad worker named J. Lopresto, remembering his former home in Lodi, Italy. In Wilson County, Francisco Flores de Abreyo chose the name, also for Lodi, Italy. Another story contends that the name is a corruption of the Latin word *lutum*, "mud," referring to the adobe homes in the early days of the town. The ghost town, which traces its origins to 1832, has been absorbed by Floresville.
(Marion Co.) PO Nov. 23, 1876—; Pop. 164.

Loire *(Wilson)* [lor]

J. M. Swindler, the first postmaster, came to the area
with a group from the Loire region of France, for which
the town was named.
PO July 17, 1895–Nov. 15, 1912.

Lolita *(Jackson)*

The town was named for Lolita Reese, great granddaughter of C. K. Reese, who fought at San Jacinto, and
granddaughter of C. K. Reese, Jr., a member of the Mier
Expedition who dug his way to freedom after the "black
bean lottery" in which every tenth man was shot. During
the 1950s when Nabokov's novel *Lolita* scandalized the
nation with the antics of a preteen nymphet, the town
grew so self-conscious about the new connotations of the
town name that a meeting was called to consider a
change, but *Lolita* was retained with the hope that the
novel and film would soon be forgotten.
PO Mar. 3, 1910–; Pop. 1,200.

London *(Kimble)*

Whether the name refers to London, England, or London,
Kentucky, remains in dispute. Several settlers had come
from England, and John Pearl's family, which lived
nearby, had come from London, Kentucky. London, Old
London, and New London are to be found in Rusk County.
PO Dec. 18, 1882–; Pop. 180.

Lonesome Dove *(Tarrant)*

After Josiah Hodges preached the first sermon in a new
Baptist church, some members of the congregation
wanted to name the surrounding settlement *Platte* because most of them had come from Platte, Missouri.
When a dove began to coo in a big oak tree, they were
impressed by the lonesome dove. They decided to let the
bird rather than their former home be their new town
namesake. The community was founded on February 21,
1846.

Lone Star *(Morris)*

One of the newer towns in the county provided a home
for employees of the Lone Star Steel Company, which
had taken its name from the Texas nickname. An earlier
settlement on this site was *Iron Bluff*, for the iron ore
deposits and the terrain.
PO May 1, 1948–; Pop. 1,924; Inc.

Lone Wolf Mountain *(Mitchell)*

Lone Wolf was a chief of the Kiowas who used the mountain as a lookout point. He was one of the nine signers of the Treaty of Medicine Lodge, Kansas, in 1867 when the Kiowa tribe first agreed to be placed on a reservation.

Long Mott *(Calhoun)* [lɔŋ 'mat]

German immigrants arriving in 1853 settled in the vicinity of two large motts (clumps or groves of trees): Upper Mott and Lower Mott. Because Upper Mott was the larger and the longer of the two, it was also called *Long Mott*, and that name was assigned when the post office was established.
PO May 24, 1887–Dec. 31, 1909; Jan. 10, 1910–; Pop. 76.

Long Taw *(Delta)* [lɔŋ 'tɔ]

Early freighters with horse-, mule-, or ox-drawn wagons referred to a haul as a taw. The trek from the water supply at De Spain Bridge across the South Sulphur River to the community was considered a long taw.

Long Tom Creek *(Polk)*

Long Tom was a chief of the Creek Indians.

Longview *(Gregg)*

A notarized statement by William Wyatt Pierce has been accepted by the Gregg County Historical Society as the official explanation of the naming of the community that was to become the county seat. Pierce, who was then eighty-four, stated in 1942 that he often heard his guardian, O. H. Methvin, Sr., say the name of Longview was applied to the new platted townsite from the fact that a person standing on Rock Hill, sometimes called Methvin Hill, could see a long-distance view. Rock Hill, situated on the north boundary of the townsite, is considerably higher than the surrounding land. Three other accounts, given no credence by city historians, supply slightly different details: (1) A group of men were standing on the porch of Dr. Stansbury's house when one of them looked over the land that was to be the new town and exclaimed, "What a long view there is from here!" "Sure," agreed another, "and what a good name for our new town." (2) R. M. Kelly, who came to Longview in 1882, attributed the name to a Mrs. Long, wife of a railroad engineer. One day as she ascended a hill with her husband to see the newly surveyed town, she commented,

"What a long view there is from here!" Her husband replied, "You have just named the new town." (3) According to an Indian legend, the Great Spirit spoke to Chief White Feather, saying, "Ahead lies the land of abundance that thou dost gaze upon from a long, long view." The Indians had been traveling toward the present site of Longview from the north to escape a drought.
PO Jan. 27, 1871–; Pop. 52,034; Inc.

Looneyville *(Nacogdoches)*

Coincidence places Looneyville near a creek called *Loco* or *Crazy Creek* because of the wild patterns of its flow, but Looneyville was named in honor of the Looneys, a very stable pioneer family.
PO July 10, 1874–Apr. 15, 1878; July 15, 1889–Jan. 14, 1905 (Mt. Cushing).

Loop *(Gaines)*

As Edgar Belcher, who was to be the first postmaster, considered a name to be submitted, he began to twirl a

lasso in his hand, making a loop and then jumping through the whirling loop. The old cowboy trick gave him the idea of the name which gained acceptance with the postal department.
PO March 7, 1905–Oct. 31, 1905; Jan. 13, 1906–; Pop. 315.

Loraine *(Mitchell)* [lo 'ren]

The shipping point for cattle on the Texas and Pacific Railroad was established in 1898. The name comes from Loraine Crandall, wife of a landowner in the area. A persistent story reports that the railroad threw off the wrong sign, and *Loraine* was intended for another station.
PO Aug. 19, 1890–June 20, 1896; Aug. 5, 1896–Sept. 15, 1903; Oct. 24, 1903–; Pop. 677; Inc.

Lord *(Ochiltree)*

No religious significance is found in the name of this railroad switch, only an honor for an official of the Santa Fe Railroad. The same name was used for a Harris County post office operating from 1883 to 1886.

Los Angeles *(La Salle)* [lɔs 'æn jə ləs]

In 1923 when the town was developed by the F. Z. Bishop Land Company of San Antonio, a promoter familiar with Los Angeles, California, saw similarities in the soil, climate, and topography.
PO Oct. 22, 1923–; Pop. 140.

Lost Creek *(De Witt)*

The name was given prior to 1850 to the spring-fed creek which bubbles to the surface and then disappears underground, literally becoming a lost creek. At least nine other Texas creeks also carry this name.

Lost Draw *(Dawson, Lynn, Terry, Yoakum)*

The behavioral pattern of the intermittent water course which runs through the town of Brownfield suggested the name. It appears, then disappears, scatters out, and "gets lost."

Lost Pines of Texas *(Bastrop, Fayette)*

The pine forest, an island of loblolly pine, is considered "lost" because it is about eighty miles west of the state's principal pine forests.

Lover's Retreat *(Palo Pinto)*

Most Lovers' Retreats or Lovers' Leaps involve romantic love, but this spot north of Gordon recalls a man named Lover, who leaped from a steep boulder, slid down a tree and landed on the rocks beneath as he escaped Indians in hot pursuit.

Loving *(Jack)* ['lə vɪŋ]

Between 1855 and his death in 1867, the fame of Oliver Loving, early trail driver, led to naming of Texas villages for him, as well as Loving County in West Texas, Loving Bend of the Pecos River, and Loving and Lovington in New Mexico. The Jack County settlement was founded in 1903 on the route of the Goodnight-Loving Trail. A Loving post office still operates in Young County; a post office with that name was listed for Cooke County, 1889–1891.

Lowake *(Concho)* [lo 'we kɪ]

The two oldest residents at the time the railroad came were J. L. Lowe and C. G. Schlake. The *Low-* was taken from *Lowe* and the *-ake* from *Schlake*.
PO Oct. 28, 1909—; Pop. 40.

Luckenbach *(Gillespie)* ['lu kɪn bak]

The town famous through country and western songs and the charm of its leading resident, the late Hondo Crouch, was founded in 1850 by Jacob and August Luckenbach and named for Mrs. Albert Luckenbach, who established the post office.
PO Apr. 30, 1886—discontinued 1975; Pop. 25.

Mabank *(Kaufman)*

Names of two pioneer families are combined here. Citizens took *Ma-* from Dodge Mason's name and *-bank* from Tom Eubank's name to create *Mabank*.
*PO Nov. 10, 1887 (Lawndale)—Jan. 2, 1900 (Mabank) ;
Pop. 1,652; Inc.*

Macedonia *(Liberty)*

Slavic settlers remembered the name from the old country when suggestions were asked for naming a railroad station on the Texas and New Orleans line.

Magic City *(Wheeler)*

A large number of oil derricks sprang up in this location overnight, as if by magic, in 1926. Nine years later, they disappeared in the same manner because the wells were shallow and of short duration. The once living town was abandoned, and nothing remains today.

Magnet *(Wharton)*

Early planters believed the fertility of the soil would attract other settlers, drawing them like a magnet. A post office in Smith County was also given this name, in 1901–1902.
PO Nov. 20, 1911—July 31, 1954; Pop. 42.

Mahomet *(Burnet)* [mə 'ha mɪt] [mə 'ha mɛt]

Every Texas school child learns of the Arab camel drivers brought to Texas in the late 1850s in the U.S. Army

experiment for western wilderness transportation. That era survives in the town name, believed to refer to a person of the Moslem faith who came on the dromedary adventure.
PO Dec. 14, 1857–July 31, 1916.

Marathon *(Brewster)* [ˈmær ə ˌθən]

When Albion E. Shepherd, a sea captain who was an engineer for the Southern Pacific Railroad in 1882, saw this plain between jagged mountains and a thorny wilderness called *Hell's Half Acre*, it reminded him very much of Marathon, Greece.
PO Feb. 13, 1882–; Pop. 800; El. 3,043.

Marfa *(Presidio)* [ˈmar fə]

The wife of the chief engineer of the Southern Pacific was given the privilege of choosing the name of a watering place and freight headquarters in 1882. She happened to be reading Dostoevski's *The Brothers Karamazov* (published in 1880) at the time, and she named the town *Marfa*, for the servant in the Karamazov household.
PO Apr. 30, 1883–; Pop. 2,497; Inc.

Margaret *(Foard)*

First known as *Peace*, the town was renamed in honor of Margaret Wesley, the daughter of Mr. and Mrs. John Wesley and the first Anglo-American child born in the county.

Marion *(Angelina)*

The first county seat of Angelina County was named for General Francis Marion, American Revolutionary War hero. One hundred miles to the north, Marion County also honors the same general. As early as 1828, the area in Angelina County was known as *McNeill's Landing*.
PO Mar. 8, 1847 (Marion)–Aug. 9, 1869; Oct. 4, 1869–Oct. 10, 1976.

Maryneal *(Nolan)*

Neal S. Doran was an auditor of the Kansas City, Mexico, and Orient Railroad. His wife Mary was also a stockholder in the company. Their combined first names were given when the town plat was filed in 1907.
PO Oct. 9, 1907–;

Matate Creek *(Atascosa)*

The term is a variant of *metate*, a carved stone, in the shape of an inclined plane, resting on three feet and used for grinding maize for tortillas. The creek yielded such hard stones that the Indians could use them as metates.

Matthew, Mark, Luke, and John *(Williamson)*

When the Gospel Railroad was active in the county, four of its switches were named for the New Testament gospels. The railroad was chartered in 1909, and Tim Cronin, a deeply religious man, was its chairman of the board, president, engineer, and owner. He framed a copy of each gospel and hung them on the walls of his depot.

Maydelle *(Cherokee)*

Maydelle was established in 1910 and named for Maydelle Campbell, daughter of Governor Thomas M.

Campbell, whose term was 1907–1911. She had grown up in three older villages—*Pine Town*, named for the pine forests surrounding it; *Java*, named when a girl lost her petticoat made from a Java coffee sack; and *Ghent*, derived from the salutation "Howdy, gent." Maydelle sang on the occasion of the opening of the new townsite.
PO May 27, 1910–; Pop. 250.

Mayflower *(Newton)*

The sight of blooming flowers in the spring caused John Wells to submit this name for a post office. The area was first known as *Surveyville* or *The Survey* because the first known surveying in the county began here on the William Williams league.
PO Sept. 19, 1890 (Surveyville)–Feb. 10, 1892; June 11, 1895–Nov. 2, 1898; Oct. 26, 1912 (Mayflower)– discontinued 1953; Pop. 100.

Maypearl *(Ellis)*

A post office was granted under the name of *Eyrie*, named by pioneers who found the hills and hollows a sanctuary for birds and wildlife, but the name was changed to honor May Pearl Trammel, wife of J. H. Trammel, chief engineer of the International–Great Northern Railroad when it reached the town on June 25, 1903. Railroad officials had considered naming the town *Trammel*, but decided instead to submit the name *Pearl City* and then offered *Maypearl* when the earlier name was rejected as duplication.
PO Aug. 24, 1894 (Eyrie)–June 25, 1903 (Maypearl)–; Pop. 598; Inc. 1914.

May West Oil Field *(Brown)*

Although GIs in World War II named their inflatable life jackets for Mae West, the buxom blonde screen star, there is no such influence here. The oil field is located west of *May*, named for Nathan L. May, one of the first settlers who operated a store and a post office. Instead of taking the usual locational name that would have yielded *West May*, this oil field was designated as *May West*.

Medicine Mound *(Hardeman)*

The town is *Medicine Mound*, even though there are four mounds in the area. Comanche and Kiowa Indians frequented the area to gather herbs that restored their health and happiness. They also held religious cere-

monies and medicine dances on the mesas. According to the old Comanche legend, this area provided the only source of certain medicinal herbs.
PO Nov. 3, 1908–; Pop. 50.

Melon Creek *(Goliad)*

Although melons grow in this region, it is believed that the Spanish pronunciation of the name of John Malone produced the stream name. Malone was one of the original settlers on a land grant at the head of the creek.

Mentone *(Loving)* [mɪn 'ton]

The original town was west of the present site, about one mile closer to the Pecos River. The present town was laid out in 1933, but it was not developed until the Wheat Oil Pool became active later in the 1930s. Named by an early settler for Menton, France, it is the only town in the West Texas county that has the distinction of being the least populated county in the United States, with 114 in residence in 1975.
PO Sept. 29, 1893 (Mentone)–May 18, 1896; Nov. 19, 1909 (Juanita)–Feb. 21, 1910 (Porterville)–May 1, 1931 (Mentone)–; Pop. 50.

Mentz *(Colorado)*

The former home town of many of the German settlers was Mentz, Germany.
PO June 17, 1889–Dec. 29, 1896; Dec. 4, 1897–Jan. 15, 1913.

Mercedes *(Hidalgo)* [mər 'se diz]

Mexican ranchers settled the area in the late 1770s, and in 1904 a townsite was called *Lonsboro,* nor Lon C. Hill, agent and promoter. A new site was chosen two miles west on the Capisallo Ranch, and a new name was picked to honor Mercedes Díaz, wife of the president of Mexico, Porifio Díaz (1877–1880, 1884–1911). Her name was offered in an attempt to persuade Porifio Díaz to exert his influence to prevent the growing number of Mexican raids in the area.
PO Dec. 26, 1906–; Pop. 306; Inc.

Mercury *(McCulloch)* ['mər kyə rɪ]

The large deposits of minerals in the area led to the name when the town was founded by J. A. Austin in

1904. The town is located one mile from the spot often considered the center of Texas.
PO Mar. 16, 1904–; Pop. 166.

Meridian *(Bosque)* [mə 'rɪ dɪ ən]

The source of Meridian Creek lies at the ninety-eighth meridian. The nearby town and state park took their names from the waterway. Major George B. Erath laid out the town in 1854 on land donated by Dr. J. M. Steiner, and he also named the stream.
PO June 12, 1856–; Pop. 1,209; Inc. 1874.

Mesmeriser Creek *(Navarro)* ['mɛz me ˌraɪ zer]

The stream was named for a pioneer who had some skill as a hypnotist. He tried to hypnotize some wild buffalo bulls, but failed. The bulls stampeded over the hypnotist, and the creek took its name from the buffaloed mesmerizer.

Miami *(Roberts)* [maɪ ˈæm ɪ]

Miami was an Indian of the Algonquin tribe who once occupied the area between the Wabash and Maumee rivers in Ohio. The word *Miami* is said to mean "sweetheart," and the name is interpreted here as "sweetheart of the plains."
PO Nov. 1, 1887–; Pop. 725; Inc.

Mico *(Medina)* [ˈmi ko]

The name is an abbreviation of the Medina Irrigation Company, taking water from Medina Lake and the Medina River.
PO Aug. 21, 1911–Dec. 12, 1912; Feb. 16, 1919–June 19, 1916 (Medina Lake)–Apr. 28, 1923 (Mico)–; Pop. 98.

Midland *(Midland)* [ˈmɪd lənd]

Both the city and the county of Midland are named for their location halfway between Fort Worth and El Paso. The original name of the town was *Midway*, marking a post on the Texas and Pacific Railroad which was 307 miles equidistant from Fort Worth and El Paso, but the name was changed when Midland County was organized. Known as "Tall City" because of the large number of office buildings, Midland ranks fourth in Texas for office space.
PO June 4, 1884–; Pop. 82,000; Inc.

Midway *(Dickens; Madison)*

The town in Dickens County was located halfway between Dickens and Afton. The same name was given for a halfway location in the following counties: Bell, Bowie, Dawson, Henderson, Lavaca, Midland, Polk, and Tom Green. In Madison County, the name refers to Midway, Kentucky.

Milvid *(Liberty)* [ˈmɪl vɪd]

Because the lumbering center depended for its livelihood upon the Miller-Vidor Lumber Company, the name for the town was created by combining the first three letters of the surnames of the company's owners. Settled in the early 1900s, the town declined when the timber supply was depleted.
PO Apr. 26, 1907–Oct. 7, 1925.

Mineral Wells *(Palo Pinto, Parker)*

After Judge J. W. Lynch built a cabin on the site of the present town and dug a well in which water was abundant, but apparently unfit to drink, the water from the well gained a reputation for curing hysterical manias and other maladies. As people began to come to Mineral Wells for health reasons, a resort city developed quickly, and Crazy Water Crystals were marketed in reference to the alleged curative powers for mental disturbances.
PO Apr. 4, 1881 (Ednaville)—Sept. 20, 1882—; Pop. 13,005; Inc. 1882.

Missouri City *(Fort Bend, Harris)* [mə ˈzʊr ə ˈsɪ tɪ]

The realty firm of Cash and Luckle promoted the town in 1890, primarily in Missouri newspapers, bringing in a number of settlers from that state.
PO Aug. 21, 1897—; Pop. 8,873; Inc.

Mitchell Bend *(Somervell)*

Although there is nothing unusual in the name, it is a novelty in that it was given for "Cooney" Mitchell, the only man ever legally hanged in adjoining Hood County. The hanging tree still stands.

Mohat *(Colorado)*

The name carefully disguises the honor it bestows upon Mose and Harold Thomas, taking the *Mo-* from *Mose*, the *-ha-* from *Harold*, and the *-t* from *Thomas*.

Montalba *(Anderson)* [man 'tæl bə]

The first postmaster's wife, Lizzie Hamlett, produced the descriptive name on a rare day when snow covered the hill near the community. Some sources state that the whiteness referred to in the Latin phrase meaning "white mountain" was white sugar sand. An earlier name was *Beaver Valley*, encompassing the communities of Black Rock and Pace's Chapel.
PO Mar. 20, 1882–; Pop. 110.

Montcola *(Bee)* [man tɪ 'o lə]

When a traveling salesman discovered that Mase Lynch's general store served a community with no name, he volunteered his name, Monty, and that of his wife, Ola, to create *Monteola* for the nameless landscape. The area had been called *Butler's Neighborhood* in 1883 because a ranch was operated here by L. G. and A. B. Butler.
PO Mar. 9, 1907–Mar. 15, 1929.

Monticello *(Titus)* [man tə 'sɛl o]

In 1886 John Brantley named the community in honor of President Thomas Jefferson's Virginia home, after he had seen a picture of the mansion on a visit to Jefferson, Texas.

Moon Chapel *(Sterling)*

The building of the church which the community surrounds was instigated by an early Methodist pastor named R. D. Moon.

Moonshine Hill *(Harris)*

The story is told that the town had so many bootleggers at the time of its founding that the famous product they sold was a natural choice for a name. A more profitable product was discovered in 1904 when an oil field opened here.

Moravia *(Lavaca)* [mo 're vɪ ə]

Moravia in Europe was the former home of Ignac
Jakufak, a Czech-Moravian settler, who named the com-
munity in 1880.
PO Sept. 20, 1882−Sept. 1, 1906; Pop. 165.

Moscow *(Polk)* ['mas ko]

The original choice in 1844 was *Green's,* for the founder,
David G. Green. Later there was a petition to change the
name to *Greenville,* but another Texas post office, in
Hunt County, had claimed the name. "Send in *Moscow,"*
said one citizen; "that town is far enough away; there
will be no objections." *Moscow* was also significant as
David G. Green's hometown in Tennessee.
*PO May 19, 1847 (Green's)−Jan. 20, 1853 (Moscow)−Apr.
24, 1867−; Pop. 716.*

Mount Nebo *(Gillespie)* [maunt 'ni bo]

In 1875 a group of Anglo-American settlers constructed a
little log church on one of the hills near Willow City,
taking the name of the biblical *Mount Zion* for the
church and for the hill. The name of the hill was later
changed to *Mount Nebo,* also referring to a biblical
mountain, and around 1890 the old church was blown
away in a storm. The name of the mountain where
Moses stood when he took his first and last view of the
Promised Land is found in several Texas counties where
churches were established.
El. 1,825.

Mount Vernon *(Franklin)*

The area was settled in 1830 by Joshua T. Johnson and
named *Keith's* for Stephen Keith, who donated twenty-
four acres for a townsite when the post office was established. Two years later the name changed to *Lone Star* in
reference to the nickname of Texas, but some confusion
developed with a community of the same name. At the
first commissioners' court meeting, held in J. E. Brooks's
barn after the county was established in 1875, saloons,
gambling, and race tracks were outlawed and a new
name was chosen for the county seat, honoring George
Washington's home near Alexandria, Virginia. The name
was used in Lamar, Limestone, and Montgomery counties as well.
*PO June 20, 1848 (Keith's)−Nov. 19, 1850 (Lone Star)−
Sept. 21, 1875 (Mount Vernon)−; Pop. 1,977; Inc.*

Mucorrera Creek *(Goliad)*

In early days, a woman blacksmith lived on the creek, called by the Spanish name of *Arroyo de Mujer Herrera* or "Creek of the Woman Blacksmith." German-speaking residents hearing the name pronounced in Spanish interpreted it as *Mucorrera*.

Mudville *(Brazos)*

At one time in the history of this community, sweeping rains left the streets memorably muddy and impassable. The mud of the Texas blackland prairie is also noted in *Mud Creek* (Smith), *Mud Spring* (Bell and Denton), *Mud Town* (Hill), and *Mud Dig* (Fannin).

Muenster *(Cooke)* ['mən stər] ['myun stər]

In 1889, led by Emil and Carl Flusche, a group of Roman Catholics of German descent came to Texas from Westphalia, Iowa. Others came directly from the province of Westphalia in Germany. Their first choice for a name was *Westphalia,* but upon hearing there was another Texas settlement with that name, the group chose *Muenster* instead, for the capital of Westphalia.
PO Dec. 19, 1889–; Pop. 1,376; Inc.

141

Mukewater *(Coleman)*

An unsuccessful attempt to pronounce the name of the Comanche named Mukewarrah, Mukewaka, or Mugua-ra produced this version. Because the name referred to a creek, at least the *-water* part of the name made sense. Some say that the Indian word means "muddy water."

Muldoon *(Fayette)* [məl 'dun]

The namesake of Muldoon was only partially Irish. He was Miguel Muldoon, son of an Irish father and Spanish mother, who served as resident priest of Stephen F. Austin's colony. The area was settled in the 1830s, and the town began in 1886.
PO Jan. 18, 1888–; Pop. 98.

Muleshoe *(Bailey)*

The Muleshoe Ranch of this vicinity used an inverted *U* over a bar for its brand, and the resemblance to a mule shoe soon gained the brand a new name, later transferred to the city.
PO Jan. 7, 1913 (Janes)–May 2, 1914 (Muleshoe)–; Pop. 4,668; Inc.

Mushaway Mountain *(Borden)*

Frank X. Tolbert, *Dallas Morning News* columnist, believes *Mucha-Koogato* is Comanche for "buzzard excretion." Charlie Miller, cowman and a native of Borden County for more than sixty-five years, maintained that *Mushaway* in Comanche could only be translated as the slang derivative of the act of sexual intercourse. Neither translation has been tied directly to the mountain. Another translation is "planting stick." To the Spanish explorers, it was *Cordova Peak*.
El. 2,862.

Mustang Lake *(Aransas)*

Horse dealers drove the mustangs out into the lake until they bogged down, making their capture much easier than on high, dry ground.

Mutt and Jeff *(Wood)*

Contrasting physical dimensions of the town's two leading merchants suggested the tall and short characters in the comic strip of the same name.

Naclina *(Angelina, Nacogdoches)* [næk 'li nə]

A blending of the first syllable of Nacogdoches County and the last two of Angelina County created the name for this community on the boundary line between the two counties.

Nacogdoches *(Nacogdoches)* [næ kə 'do čəs]

A legend has been composed for those who expected an explanation more romantic than the one that this oldest town in Texas was named for the Nacogdoche Indians, a Caddoan tribe and one of the nine major members of the Hasinai Confederacy. The tale also accounts for the similarity of the names of Nacogdoches, Texas, and of Natchitoches, Louisiana. Once upon a time, the story begins, an old Indian chief had two sons: Natchitoches and Nacogdoches. When they grew to manhood, their father sent them out to make homes and establish tribes of their own. Natchitoches was to travel three days and three nights in the direction of the rising sun, and Nacogdoches was to travel three days and three nights into the setting sun. Thus, the Louisiana and Texas towns were established, linked by a route later followed by the Spaniards and named El Camino Real.
PO 1843 (Republic of Texas)—May 22, 1846 (U.S.)—; Pop. 27,351; Inc. 1939.

Nada *(Colorado)* ['ne də]

Founding fathers and mothers from Czechoslovakia adapted the name from that of the city of Nadja in their home country.
PO Apr. 17, 1894—Apr. 7, 1914; May 24, 1915—; Pop. 165.

Nameless *(Travis)*

The site, first surveyed in the 1850s, attracted numerous settlers by 1852. In 1880 the town applied for a post office, and after authorities rejected six names, the citizens replied, "Let the post office be nameless and be d____d." The implied name was accepted, and a post office operated with the post mark of *Nameless* from 1880 until 1890.
PO Jan. 10, 1880—Jan. 13, 1890.

Nanhattie *(Sterling)*

W. F. Kellie combined the names of his wife, Nan, and her sister, Hattie.
PO Feb. 28, 1898—May 14, 1904.

Narcisso *(Cottle)* ['nar 'sɪs] [ˌnar 'sɪs o]

The community was supposedly named for a Mexican horse who must have been very fond of himself. Several ranches moved cattle to this shipping point on the railroad.

Naruna *(Burnet)* [nə 'ru nə]

The name is traced to a ship on which pioneers in the area had traveled on the Mississippi on their way to Texas. William Spitler, who had been a passenger aboard the *Naruna*, chose the name.
PO June 19, 1878–Oct. 15, 1906; Pop. 45.

Navasota *(Grimes)* [næv ə 'so tə]

When the town was first founded about 1855 at the intersection of La Bahia–San Antonio and Nacogdoches Road and the Indian trail from Waco, its name was *Nolansville*, for James Nolan, who arrived from Mississippi in 1846 and later operated a stage stop here. Three years later, the name was changed to *Navasota* because it is located near the junction of the Navasota and Brazos rivers. Two translations are given the name: the Spanish *Navasota* was derived from the Indian *Nabototo*, whose name means "Muddy Waters," or the word was derived from Spanish "nativity of De Soto." A statue of the French explorer La Salle was erected on the main business street, commemorating his death at the

hands of his own followers in 1637, probably in the vicinity of Navasota. For seven years during the mid-nineteenth century, the post office serving the adjoining area was named *Hollandale*, for Colonel J. K. Holland, who came from Louisiana in 1822 and established a community near Navasota.
PO June 24, 1854 (Navasota)–July 22, 185⅓; Jan. 5, 1859–Oct. 8, 1865; Sept. 15, 1858 (Hollandale)–Oct. 18, 1865 (Navasota)–; Pop. 4,993; Inc.

Nazareth *(Castro)*

With the advent of a new colony under the leadership of Father Reisdorff, a Roman Catholic priest, the little settlement in Castro County, which had previously been designated by the names of *Wynne, Shamrock,* or *Dimmitt,* received the name it now bears. It was Father Reisdorff's intention to place the parish under the invocation and protection of the Holy Family of Nazareth. As a consequence, the locality developed under that name, and in subsequent advertising Father Reisdorff wrote of "this new colony, Nazareth."
PO Mar. 6, 1903–; Pop. 240.

Necessity *(Stephens)*

The town was named through necessity in the 1880s when citizens were informed by postal authorities that a post office was absolutely essential to their community. The area was formerly called *Cottonplant.* A drought in 1886 also gave the citizens a sense of necessity.
PO July 19, 1893–Sept. 30, 1912; Nov. 4, 1919–Oct. 15, 1925; Pop. 10.

Nechanitz *(Fayette)* ['nɛk e nɪts]

Wenzel Matejowsky, who was postmaster as well as a leading musician and merchant, remembered his birthplace in Bohemia with this name. A national record was established in 1946 when the post office had been operated for seventy-three years by members of the same family: first Wenzel and later Charlie Matejowsky.
PO Jan. 27, 1874–Apr. 15, 1954; Pop. 21.

Neches River *(Anderson, Angelina, Cherokee, Hardin, Henderson, Houston, Jasper, Jefferson, Orange, Polk, Smith, Trinity, Van Zandt)* ['ne čɪs]

The Hasinai Indians had given the waterway a name meaning "Snow River" when the Spaniards found them living in villages along its banks. The present name is traced to Alonso de León, who named it for the Indian tribe he encountered nearby in 1869.

Needlepoint Road *(Chambers)*

The road ends at a "needlepoint," a sharp bend in Cedar Bayou.

Needmore *(Hemphill; Terry)*

When a school building was being completed in Terry County, it was discovered that the residents were always needing more of everything; thus the name of *Needmore*. In Hemphill County, the trading post was always needing more supplies to sell in the days when the stagecoach ran only once a week, and the name of *Needmore* was suggested. Other communities named *Needmore* are found in Bailey, Delta, and Nacogdoches counties.

Needville *(Fort Bend)*

Just before the state of Texas offered to sell twenty sections of school land in Fort Bend County in 1887, August Schendel had built his residence and a small store on the high prairie at a place known as *Schendelville*. Soon Schendel decided to change the name to *Needmore* as a joke because the people were poor and always in need of something else. When he petitioned for a post office, both *Needville* and *Needmore* were suggested, and the postal authorities chose *Needville* since *Needmore* was a duplicate of an existing office.
PO Apr. 14, 1894–; Pop. 1,662; Inc.

Nemo *(Somervell)* ['ni mo]

At the time the community was named, local residents proposed the name *Cleburne, Johnson Stop*. The postal department rejected it as being too long. Thus the village was left with "no name." Uncle Jimmie Johnson, to whom the Johnson Stop referred, was so angered by the post office response that he declared that if the name Johnson wasn't good enough, the town couldn't be named for any man. A school teacher suggested that it be called *Nemo*, for the Latin word for "no one" or "no name." And so it was.
PO Dec. 20, 1893–; Pop. 56.

New Baden *(Robertson)* [nyu 'bed n̩]

J. G. Meyer, German-born colonizer, founded this Robertson County community in 1880. He decided to name it in honor of Baden in his native land.
PO Apr. 12, 1882—; Pop. 105.

New Berlin *(Guadalupe)*

Early settlers of German origin thought they were establishing a new city that might match the achievements of Berlin, Germany.
PO Apr. 1, 1878—June 30, 1906.

New Braunfels *(Comal)* [nyu 'braun fɛlz] ['bran fəlz]

Prince Carl de Solms-Braunfels of Wassau, Germany, brought a colony of German immigrants to the area for settlement on March 21, 1845. He named the new townsite for his estate, Braunfels on the Lahn River in Germany.
PO May 22, 1846—; Pop. 20,308; Inc.

Newcastle *(Young)* ['nyu kæs əl]

The town was founded in 1908 for the purpose of developing the extensive deposits of coal in the region. Because Newcastle, England, was noted for its coal mining industry, it was decided that Newcastle, Texas, would be its American counterpart. Such success did not materialize, however. Before the founding of Newcastle, the area was served by post offices named for the fort established by General William G. Belknap in 1851.
PO Aug. 14, 1856 (Fort Belknap)—Nov. 5, 1866; Jan. 20, 1874 (Belknap)—Feb. 24, 1875; May 4, 1876—Nov. 3, 1908; Nov. 13, 1908 (Newcastle)—; Pop. 659; Inc.

New Deal *(Lubbock)*

It is easy to guess that the town was established after the election of President Franklin D. Roosevelt in 1932, since the name alludes to his New Deal administration. Originally named *Monroe*, the community discovered that it duplicated another name when a post office was sought. The new name came from a consolidated school built during the Roosevelt era. Texans named schools, towns, and other institutions for this president. Some families even referred to their outhouses as *FDR Memorials* because his administration provided subsidies for families that would build their outdoor conveniences according to government specifications.
PO June 1, 1949—; Pop. 537; Inc. since 1970.

New Fulp (Fannin)

The original name was *Fulp,* honoring Russell Fulp, an early resident. When the Fulp and Longbranch schools consolidated at Fulp, the town and school took the name of *New Fulp.*

Newport (Clay)

This town holds the Texas record for the number of persons whose names were incorporated into one word. The name was formed from the surname initials of seven prominent men: *N*ewton, *E*zell, *W*elch, *P*ortwood, *O*wsley, *R*eigis, and *T*urner. Naturally, someone not familiar with this origin had to spin a tale about an early homesteader being a sailor on the high seas. Upon his arrival here, he called his latest stop *Newport.* The name used during the 1870s was *Bear Hill,* in reference to a bear killed on the hill near J. H. Hardy's home. The town of Newport in Walker County was a port on the Trinity River with a post office between 1855 and 1875.
PO July 11, 1878–; Pop. 70.

New Salem (Rusk)

Colonel John Ruitt settled the area which was named *Salem* by Oscar Wilson in honor of his previous home in Victoria County. After malaria diminished the population of Salem, *New Salem* appeared.
PO Sept. 19, 1849–discontinued between 1931 and 1964; Pop. 31.

New Waverly (Walker)

New Waverly originated when the Houston and Great Northern Railroad was forced to lay tracks ten miles west of Waverly because they were unable to obtain land there. Waverly, named for Sir Walter Scott's Waverly novels, became a ghost town by 1884.
PO Aug. 7, 1854 (Carmel)–Nov. 30, 1885 (Waverly)–Mar. 12, 1872 (Phelps)–Jan. 21, 1873 (New Waverly)–; Pop. 573; Inc.

New York (Clay; Henderson)

Realizing there would never be a city here, Henderson County citizens named the community, cemetery, and church for New York City as a joke in 1860. Population declined drastically when the community was missed by the railroads. The name is also found in Clay County, where Happy Willis, a store owner, thought of the na-

tion's largest city when she chose the name for the small settlement.
(Henderson Co.) PO Sept. 11, 1876–Feb. 28, 1907.

Nickle Berry *(Cass)*

The name was given for the son of one of the first settlers, whose last name was Berry. The actual first name of the son is no longer remembered, and only his nickname survives.

Niederwald *(Hays)* ['ni dər wɔld]

In German, the name means "lower wood" or "underbrush," referring to a low forest of mesquite. The area was settled about 1900 by German colonists.
PO April 5, 1902–Sept. 15, 1904; Pop. 79

Nigger Arroyo *(Randall)* ['nɪ gər ə 'ro yo]

A leader of the Comanches in the Panhandle was known as Nigger Horse and associated with the area of the draw that bears his name.

Nigton *(Trinity)*

The progressive farm community was settled in 1873 by former slaves. The name was suggested by one of the former slaves, Jeff Carter, who served as the first postmaster.
PO June 14, 1894–; Pop. 34.

Nineveh *(Leon)* ['nɪn ə və]

When the town was given permission to establish a post office, a Miss McCreary suggested the name of *Nineveh* because a great deal of squabbling in this town brought to mind the biblical Nineveh, the Assyrian capital known as a seat of wickedness.
PO June 18, 1900–; Pop. 101.

Nipple Mountain or Nipple Peaks *(Coke)*

The mountain was so named because of its shape.
El. 2,350.

Nogalus *(Trinity)* [no 'gæl əs]

Two horse thieves were put to death by being hanged from a limb. Soon the surrounding community was known as *Nogallows*, but when the post office was granted, the spelling was changed to *Nogallis*, and it later became *Nogalus*.

PO Sept. 17, 1858 (Nogallis Prairie)—Nov. 20, 1858; July 20, 1860 (Nogallis Prairie)—Jan. 23, 1867; Feb. 11, 1867 (Nogallis Prairie)—May 14, 1868; Nov. 27, 1894 (Nogalus)—Dec. 3, 1920.

Nome *(Jefferson)* [nom]

Three stories compete as explanations for the naming of this town which started as Sour Lake Junction in 1860. By 1901 the Sour Lake oil boom north of the community caused problems with the similarity of names, and a new name was sought. One account of the new name is that a train stopped here one morning, and a lady passenger asked a young man standing on the platform if she had arrived in Liberty. "No'm," he replied in Southern fashion. The second version reports that no name had been given when maps were being made for the region. One cartographer wrote on his map "Name?" and the printers later interpreted it as *Nome*. Finally, because the Sour Lake oil boom occurred at the same time as the Alaskan gold rush, passengers would tell the train conductors they were going to Nome in Texas for "liquid gold."

PO Apr. 19, 1894 (Buttfield)—May 18, 1903 (Nome)—; Pop. 567; Inc. since 1970.

Noonday *(Smith)*

Captain Edward W. Smith, a leading planter, took the name from the Noonday Baptist Church he knew back home in Georgia.

Pop. 56.

Nopal *(McMullen)* ['no pæl]

Nopal, is the Spanish name for the prickly pear cactus, which grows throughout the southwestern part of the state. This community shares its name with settlements in De Witt, Dimmit, Gonzales, and La Salle counties, where the cactus is found.

PO Dec. 4, 1860—Nov. 5, 1866; June 16, 1871—May 4, 1891; Pop. 75.

Normangee *(Leon, Madison)* ['nɔr mən ji]

Earlier names of *Roger's Store* and *Roger's Prairie* for this station on the Texas and Brazos Valley Railroad were

changed in 1906 to honor Norman G. Kittrell. The attorney served as judge and member of the Texas legislature. He also wrote editorials for the *Houston Chronicle*.
PO July 10, 1874 (Roger's Prairie)—Oct. 20, 1906 (Normangee)—; Pop. 670; Inc.

Normanna *(Bee)* [nɔr ˈmæn ə]

The area had been called *San Domingo* for a nearby creek until Norwegians arrived between 1894 and 1898 from Norway, Iowa, Minnesota, Wisconsin, and Illinois. They settled four miles east of the present site at a spot called Norwegian Colony, Menonite Colony, or Colbay Settlement. In 1886 the railroad extended its line to the area and proposed the name of *Walton* for Sheriff D. A. T. Walton, a settler since 1884, but *Normanna* was selected to designate "home of the Norsemen."
Pop. 210.

North Pole *(Nueces)*

The area was named during the winter of 1937, an especially cold one. The name was suggested when A. Garner entered Bill Griffin's one-chair barbershop and said it was "as cold as the North Pole outside." Others say it was first applied at the Traumbley service station, which was a very cold sheet-metal building. Another tale argues that a railroad surveyor came through and said it was the highest point on the railroad between Brownsville and Houston.

North Zulch *(Madison)* [nɔrθ ˈzulč]

After the community was founded and named for Dr. Julius Zulch, the town's respected physician, its citizens moved one mile northward to the Trinity and Brazos Valley Railroad. The name soon changed to *North Zulch*.

Notla *(Ochiltree)* [ˈnat lɪ]

First called *Halfway* because of its location on the freight route between Canadian and the ranching area of the county, the town changed to *Notla* in the early 1900s. The name reverses the name of the Alton Grocery Company of Enid, Oklahoma, which owned a store in the area.
PO Dec. 21, 1920—Oct. 4, 1944; Pop. 20.

Notrees *(Ector)* ['no triz]

The first postmaster, Charles J. Brown, Jr., thought the name described the barren landscape. Discouraged by rejection of a number of names he had submitted that duplicated existing post office names, Brown was asked what was distinctive about his area. "No trees," he replied, and it was accepted. "We had one native tree when we moved here on February 2, 1946, and they moved it to put in the Shell Gasoline Plant," Mrs. C. J. Brown, postmaster, reports.
PO Dec. 3, 1946–; Pop. 338.

Novohrad *(Lavaca)* ['no vǝ rad]

Early Bohemian settlers named the community for Novohrad in Bohemia.
PO Oct. 31, 1894–May 31, 1905; Pop. 35.

Nubbin *(Hood)* ['nǝ b ɪn]

The official name of the school located here was *Bald Knob*, but everyone referred to it as *Nubbin Ridge* since the soil was so poor that only nubbins (small ears of corn) could be raised. The church was also known as *Nubbin Ridge Baptist Church*, but it now goes by the more dignified name of *Cedar Grove Baptist Church.*

Oakalla *(Burnet)* [o 'kæl ǝ]

In 1879 petitioners for the post office wrote that they had selected *Oak Valley* for their community located in a valley of oak trees. But due to incompetent penmanship or reading ability, the postal department read the name on the form as *Oakalla*, and it went into the books as just that.
PO May 19, 1879–May 26, 1882; Dec. 12, 1883–; Pop. 45.

Oatmeal *(Burnet)*

Wheaties has no ground on which to request equal space on Texas road signs if the explanation is accepted that the name is a corruption of the name of a Mr. Othneil, owner of the first grist mill in the community. On the other hand, it could have been a translation of a name of a Mr. Habermille, a German settler who lived in the area between 1849 and 1852. The name *Oatmeal* was given to a creek and later the town.
PO Dec. 13, 1853–Oct. 11, 1866; Jan. 5, 1867–Dec. 30, 1867; June 26, 1868–Sept. 5, 1874; May 24, 1875–Jan. 26, 1876.

Ocaw *(McLennan)* [o 'kaʊ]

By spelling the name of the Waco Indian tribe backward, the name of *Ocaw* was created for a community in the county where Waco is county seat.

Odds *(Limestone)*

To comply with a post office request that the name be changed, the citizens of the town of Buffalo Mott chose the word *Odds*, perhaps from Odds, Kentucky. Their earlier name referred to the buffalo and to a mott or grove of trees.

Odessa *(Ector)*

The first settlers believed the rolling prairies resembled the steppes of Russia, and they expected a plentiful harvest of wheat. They hoped the new town would be a shipping center of a vast area, so they named it for the wheat distribution center of the Old World at that time—Odessa, Russia. Various stories are told to link the name to women of that name—a little girl who survived a massacre, a railroad man's Indian sweetheart, and a rancher's daughter. A post office operated in Cooke County under this name, 1855–1856.
PO Aug. 19, 1885–; Pop. 84,476; Inc.

Offatt Bayou *(Galveston)* ['ɔ fət]

If the legend can be taken seriously, the name comes from Galveston-bound train passengers who asked to be let off at the bayou in such a manner that it sounded like "Offatt Bayou."

Old Egypt *(Collin)*

William Sherley was reminded of biblical descriptions of Egypt as he walked to and from school, constantly on the lookout for snakes, tarantulas, and white cattle.

Old Glory *(Stonewall)*

Farmers of German descent, who first called the place *New Brandenberg* in 1903, demonstrated their loyalty to the United States on July 14, 1918, by changing the name to *Old Glory*. The selection of a new name constituted highly visible American flag-waving.
PO July 13, 1908 (Brandenburg)–Oct. 3, 1908; Sept. 23, 1909–Aug. 9, 1918 (Old Glory)–; Pop. 125.

Old Granny's Neck *(Delta)*

An elderly widow raised goats on a peninsula or neck of the South Sulphur River. Travelers from the north crossed Granny's neck of land on their way to Andy's Saloon across the river.

Omen *(Smith)* ['o mɪn]

After a series of name changes, Omen got its new name because W. W. Orr thought it might bring good luck.
PO Dec. 18, 1849 (Round Rock)–Jan. 30, 1851; Feb. 17, 1852 (Clopton)–April 29, 1879 (Old Canton)–June 18, 1880 (Omen)–April 14, 1906; Pop. 150.

One-Eye Creek *(Cherokee)*

A one-eyed Indian lived on the bank of the creek until he was driven from the area by White men.

Orange *(Orange)*

The county and its county seat were named for the early orange groves near the mouth of the Sabine River. The area was known by several names—*Strong's Bluff, Green's Bluff, Town of Jefferson,* and *Madison,* for President James Madison. Confusion with *Madisonville* caused the name change to *Orange* in 1858.
PO Sept. 7, 1848 (Grand Bluff)–Nov. 30, 1848 (Green's Bluff)–Apr. 29, 1852 (Madison)–Aug. 18, 1858 (Orange)–; Pop. 25,782; Inc. 1858.

Orangeville *(Fannin)*

Visitors from New York admired the large "oranges" growing around the store owned by Mr. Parmelee, the

founder of Valley Creek a few miles away. Because the large balls were not oranges but bois d'arc apples, the people in the area found the incident so amusing they named the town *Orangeville.*

Oslo *(Hansford)*

Norwegian settlers hoped that the city would prosper in Texas in the same manner that its namesake had done in Norway.

Oxford *(Llano)*

In 1880, A. J. Johnson moved here and laid out the present community, naming it for his former home in Oxford, Mississippi. The nickname of *Cat Town* developed because drunk young men at a dance threw a cat into a large pot of coffee. Another Oxford post office operated in Milam County for a short time in 1877.
PO Aug. 3, 1880–Dec. 31, 1924; Pop. 33.

Oyster Creek *(Hunt)*

The large number of mollusk shells in the area suggested oysters to the early settlers.

Ozona *(Crockett)* [o 'zo nə]

The great quantity of free air or ozone in the area is advertised by the town name, which had a slight alteration in form.
PO Sept. 3, 1891–; Pop. 3,500.

Ozro *(Ellis)*

One source traces the name to Ozro High, son of an early leader; another source attributes the name to Ozro Cheatham, son of T. O. Cheatham.

Padre Island *(Cameron, Kenedy, Kleberg, Nueces, Willacy)* ['pa dre]

The island stretching along the southern Texas coast was named for Padre Nicolas Balli, to whom the government of Spain granted the island. The first Spanish name was *Islas Blancas* ("White Islands"). Later the northern end was called *Isla de Corpus Christi*, for its proximity to Corpus Christi, and the southern end was *San Carlos de las Malaguitas*. The present name was given when Padre Balli established residence here in 1811.

Paducah *(Cottle)* [pə 'du kə] [pə 'dyu kə]

The former home of some of the town's first residents was Paducah, Kentucky. Both A. F. Neff, county surveyor, and R. E. Avant, county attorney, had come from that city.
PO Sept. 19, 1891–; Pop. 2,185; Inc. 1910.

Painted Bluff *(Edwards)*

Picture writing of the Indians can still be seen on the walls under this bluff located on the Cedar Creek Fork of the Nueces River.

Paint Mare Ranch *(Terrell)*

The name came from a band of wild horses, most of which were paint mares, once running free here.

Paint Rock *(Concho)*

Indian paintings were found on rocks and on a bluff along the Concho River near the town. More than 1,500 paintings made by various tribes at widely differing dates were scattered along the bluff for half a mile.
PO July 1, 1879–; Pop. 224.

Palestine *(Anderson)* ['pæl ə ,stin]

The county seat was founded on March 24, 1846, and named by the Reverend Mr. Daniel Parker, who had moved to the area from his hometown of Palestine, Illinois. In turn, the Illinois town had been named for biblical Palestine in Syria.
PO Mar. 8, 1847–; Pop. 15,510; Inc.

Palito Blanco *(Jim Wells)* [pə 'li to 'blaŋ ko]

In Spanish the name means "little white stick," a reference to the hackberry trees along the Palito Blanco Creek, for which the town was named.
PO Oct. 25, 1904 (Eva)–Nov. 16, 1916 (Palito Blanco)–discontinued by 1968; Pop. 35.

Palo Duro Canyon *(Armstrong, Briscoe, Randall, Swisher)* [pæ lə 'du rə]

The Spanish name means "hard wood," referring to the canyon's supply of strong cedar brush from which Indians made arrows. The canyon, created by water erosion ninety million years ago, is on the Prairie Dog Town

Fork of the Red River. The gorge is 120 miles long, with an altitude of 3,500 feet at the rim and 2,380 on the floor.

Pampa *(Gray)* ['pæm pə]

George Tyng, manager of the White Deer Land Company, had seen the pampas of South America before he bestowed the Spanish name for "flat rolling plains" on this town. Earlier the railroad had designated the town as *Ontario*, then *Sutton*, and then *Glasgow*.
PO Oct. 29, 1892–; Pop. 20,312, Inc.

Pancake *(Coryell)*

A man, not a flapjack, provided the name. Joseph Russell Pancake, who was born in Virginia, came to the county to establish a ranch and to serve as first postmaster.
PO June 19, 1885 (Pancake)–July 9, 1886; Mar. 29, 1894 (Bush)–June 7, 1901 (Pancake)–Jan. 31, 1908.

Panhandle *(Carson)*

Located in the central part of the Texas Panhandle, the town was first called *Carson City* for the county and then *Panhandle City* for its location when the Southern Kansas (Santa Fe) Railroad built into Texas in 1886. In the 1920s, when the discovery oil well for the Texas Panhandle was drilled, the population rose to 25,000 almost overnight.
PO Aug. 13, 1887–; Pop. 2,237; Inc.

Panna Maria *(Karnes)* ['pæn ə mə 'ri ə]

Early Polish immigrants named the town for the Virgin Mary in fulfillment of a vow. The first Polish church in the United States was established here on December 24, 1854.
PO Aug. 30, 1856 (Pana Maria)–Jan. 3, 1870; June 15, 1871–April 1872; Feb. 13, 1874–Dec. 4, 1883 (Panna Maria)–; Pop. 2,500.

Pansy *(Crosby)*

The original name was *Pansy Mills*, because the first postmaster, H. S. Shives, was partial to pansies and because two windmills stood nearby. The community developed on the Kentucky Land and Cattle Company ranch. Another post office named *Pansy* served a community in Navarro County from 1900 to 1910.
PO June 15, 1894–Apr. 3, 1896.

Panter *(Hood)* ['pæn tər]

The local pronunciation of *panther* gave the name to the creek and to a post office that existed at the turn of the century. The name is a reference to wild cats that roamed the area.
PO Sept. 11, 1889–Nov. 15, 1907.

Pantex *(Carson)* ['pæn tɛks]

The location of the town in the Panhandle of Texas suggested the abbreviated compound. The post office was established to provide service for employees of the Pantex ordnance plant, which loaded bombs with TNT for the army from 1942 to 1945, but the town vanished after World War II.
PO Nov. 15, 1944–now a rural branch of the Amarillo post office; Pop. 115.

Panthers Chapel *(Titus)*

George Panther was the wagon master of a small wagon train that settled in Titus County about 1835.

Papalote Creek *(San Patricio)* [pa pə 'lo tɪ]

The Spanish word meaning "kite" was suggested by the kite-shaped rocks in the bed of the stream.

Paradise *(Foard; Wise)*

In 1862 a Confederate post office was established in Wise County and called *Eldorado*. In 1872, when Bill Ander-

son built the first store in the same community, its name was *Paradise Prairie*. W. L. Burress had declared the surroundings made the place "a paradise on earth," and cowboys seeking a place of rest and relaxation while driving cattle to Kansas were attracted to the green prairie. Communities with this name are also found in Hunt and Winkler counties, indicating that Paradise exists in more than one spot in Texas. In Foard County, a Church of Christ minister once visited a community near a stream, where lived a Jobe family and a Pigg family. The minister jokingly wrote a progress report to his wife in which he stated, "I preached to Jobe, and baptized a Pigg in Paradise." Paradise Creek has ever since held that name.

PO Mar. 10, 1876—; Pop. 275.

The Pass of the Camels *(Culberson)*

The canyon was named when a U.S. Army expedition, including two dozen camels, paraded through the Big Bend in July 1859. One of the camels died, and this event caused the gorge to be named The Pass of the Camels.

Patella *(Walker)*

The community is a switch on the railroad tap line between Phelps and Huntsville. When it was established, a couple lived there. He was Pat; she was Ella.

Pattowatomie Creek *(Henderson)* [pa tə 'wa tə mɪ]

The creek was named for the Pottawatomi Indians, an Algonquin tribe whose name means "people of the place of fire." The first historical records that mention them locate them in Wisconsin. About 1852 a group associated with the Kickapoos migrated to Texas and settled along headwaters of the Sabine and Trinity rivers. Appropriately, there is a Kickapoo Creek nearby.

Peach Creek *(Colorado; Gonzales; Matagorda; Montgomery; Wharton)*

The creek in Montgomery County was originally called *Pete's Creek* because a wild steer named Peter was frequently found along its banks. People unfamiliar with Peter turned the name into *Peach*. In Colorado, Gonzales, Matagorda, and Wharton counties, peach trees probably provided the name.

Pearl City *(De Witt)*

The pearls alluded to by the community came not from oysters but from the bubbles of Pearl beer, a San Antonio brew sold in such large quantities in a store built here in 1935 that the product gave the town its name.

Peatown *(Gregg)*

The community was known as *Edwardsville* until one year when the only crop produced was peas. Such an abundance of peas was harvested that a new name was given.

Pedernales River *(Blanco, Gillespie, Hays, Kimble, Travis)* [ˌpər də 'næl ɪz] ['pərd n̩ˌnæl ɪz]

The river gained international fame during the years President Lyndon B. Johnson turned his ranch house into the Texas White House. The name, which means "flint rocks" in Spanish, was spelled *Pierdernalis* at one time.

Peerless *(Hopkins)*

The community has been known by four names. First, in the 1850s, it was called *Gays Mill* for a water-powered flour mill operated by John D. Gay. Second, for a time, it was referred to as *Hilldale* because of its location near a hill. Third, in the 1880s, the residents charged with selecting a new name chose *Fairyland*, taking pride in their dances attended by young ladies who looked like fairies. Fourth, by 1891, a family named Cotton planted some Peerless type potatoes. Near havest time, a series of hard rains prevented digging the potatoes and the overripened crop began to rot, releasing a strong odor in the community.
PO Jan. 29, 1880 (Fairyland)–Mar. 20, 1891 (Peerless)– Dec. 10, 1919; Apr. 30, 1920–July 31, 1934.

Pegasus Oil Field *(Upton)*

The trademark of the Magnolia Petroleum Company is the flying red horse, a representation of the Greek winged Pegasus. The company symbol is still seen atop the Magnolia Building in Dallas. Originally a single horse was placed on the downtown skyscraper, but when visitors accused Dallas of being a one-horse town, two red-winged horses were given visibility. The Upton County oil field was a producer for the Magnolia Company.

Pelican Island *(Galveston)*

The island or land spit just north of Galveston Island suggested its name by its pelican shape. Visitors who see pelicans on the island assume that the birds themselves were responsible for the name.

Pen Branch *(King)* [pɪn]

The stream was named for an early settler named Pin, but since honest-to-goodness Texans don't pronounce a difference between *Pin* and *Pen*, Pen got written down on the map.

Pep *(Hockley)*

The energy of the citizens supplied the name for the post office. Sale of forty-two thousand acres of land to the Yellowhouse Land Company in 1924 brought settlers of German descent to cultivate a site for a Catholic colony. They did their work with great zest, causing a visitor to remark, "By golly, you people are sure full of pep to get this thing going that fast!" What had been a ranch only a few months before had become a block of farm homes, with windmills, fencing, and cultivation.
PO Apr. 13, 1936–; Pop. 50.

Pert *(Anderson)*

The person who bestowed the name had faith that the community was going to be a "right peart" (spirited) town.

Petrolia *(Clay)* [pə ˈtrol yə]

After being called *Oil City* following the first oil discovery in 1901, the community was bypassed by the railroad, and residents moved to the tracks, naming their new town *Petrolia*, like a town in Pennsylvania.
PO June 25, 1904 (Oil City)–Nov. 14, 1904 (Petrolia)–; Pop. 695; Inc.

Picketville *(Stephens)*

The county seat from 1858 to 1864 was probably named for Bill Picket, an early settler, but some insist that the name was derived from the number of "picket houses" (constructed from tree limbs placed on end and chinked with mud) here.

Pickton *(Hopkins)*

Several versions compete in explaining the origin of the name. According to one, when the town was founded in 1879, J. P. King and Cable Richardson were appointed to pick a name. The oddity of their assignment resulted in their decision to call it *Pick Town*, a name shortened by the postal department to *Pickton*. M. D. Jackson had suggested the name of *Jacksonville*, but a town in deep East Texas had a prior claim on that name. Another explanation links the name to the picks of workers building the Louisiana, Arkansas, and Texas Railroad, causing the town to be known as *Pick Town*, and then as *Pickton*.
PO Aug. 29, 1881–; Pop. 90.

Pigeon Roost Prairie *(Hardin)*

Amid thick growths of pine and palmetto is a mile and a half of open country, said to have been a roosting place for wild pigeons at one time. The prairie was created when settlers cut down the trees to discourage the birds, and the area has been barren of trees ever since.

Pike's Peak or Pike Peak *(Edwards)*

Colorado is not the only state with a peak named for Zebulon Pike, whose exploring party passed near the spot on the return trip from the Rockies in 1807. The Texas peak offers no dangers from altitude sickness, however.
El. 1,905.

Pilgrim Rest *(Rains)*

Marshall, Jefferson, and Shreveport were the leading markets for early settlers in Northeast Texas. A spot near the present Pilgrim Rest Church became a favorite camping place for tired travelers en route to the trade centers.
Pop. 72.

Pilon or Pelon Creek *(Dimmit)* [pi 'lon]

Opinion is divided in tracing the name to the Spanish word *pilón*, meaning "watering trough" or "basin" or "loaf" (of sugar), also used in several regions of Texas to mean a "a gift" or "something extra," or to the Pelone Indians. *Pelone* means "bald" or "hairless" and was a name given by the Spaniards to various Indian groups that removed their hair.

Pilot Knob *(Denton)*

Three sandstone knobs nine miles southwest of Denton rise above the surrounding area some 180 feet. Because the knobs can be seen for many miles, they became a feature by which travelers were piloted through the area. The name of the surrounding community was changed to *Argyle* by settlers from Argyle, Georgia.
PO July 24, 1878 (Argyle)–Nov. 28, 1881; El. of knobs, 900 feet.

Pilot Point *(Denton)*

Named for its location on a high ridge which can be seen for some distance, the townsite was platted by George W. Newcomb on Christmas Day, 1853. A large grove of post oak timber on the ridge extends into the surrounding prairie.
PO June 12, 1885–; Pop. 1,782; Inc.

Pine Island *(Chambers)*

No water is involved in this island, which refers to an area of land where a clump of pine trees grows in the midst of an open prairie.

Pipe Creek *(Bandera)*

Three men made a lunch stop on the creek while traveling to Boerne. One later discovered he had lost his pipe, and as the trio returned from Boerne they stopped to look for the lost pipe. Upon finding it, they decided that the stream should be called *Pipe Creek*. Oral historians report that O.B. Miles is the one who lost the pipe while riding with P. D. Saner and John Odem. County residents are skeptical about the adventurous stories that developed later that the pipe was lost while the men were being pursued by Indians. A post office at this location later assumed the name of the creek.
PO Oct. 3, 1873 (Pipe Creek)–Dec. 4, 1895 (Pipecreek)– between July 1, 1964, and July 30, 1966 (Pipe Creek)–.

Pisgah *(Nacogdoches)*

The Biblical name refers to one of the ancient high places of Moab east of the north shore of the Dead Sea, where sacrifices were offered. The mountain is also known as *Nebo*. The name *Pisgah* was also used by post offices in Eastland County, 1900–1903, and in Navarro County, 1891–1892.

Plaska *(Hall)* ['plæs kə]

The name was suggested by N. M. Orr for his old home in Pulaski, Tennessee. Through error, the name came back from Washington spelled *Plaska,* and so it has remained. An earlier name was *Lodge.*
PO Mar. 7, 1905 (Lodge)–Apr. 30, 1909; Apr. 30, 1920 (Plaska)–Jan. 31, 1954; Pop. 21.

Pleasant Valley *(Hunt)*

Settlers expressed both their liking for the site of their rural community and their desire that its name have pleasant connotations when they changed its nickname of *Sodom,* in reference to the city of wickedness in the Bible.

Pluck *(Polk)*

In the opinion of George H. Deason, a resident when the name was chosen in 1918, it required pluck to locate here. An earlier name was *Stryker,* for Henry Stryker, who, with his cousin D. W. Angle, established a sawmill in 1885.
PO Feb. 17, 1885 (Stryker)–July 29, 1897; Nov. 5, 1899–Nov. 30, 1913; Oct. 25, 1918 (Pluck)–discontinued, 1953.

Poetry *(Kaufman)* ['po ɪ trɪ]

Agreement has been reached that the community was originally named *Turners Point* for the Turner family. Why the name was changed to *Poetry* has been disputed. Some say a young man who wrote for the local newspaper loved poetry and filled the columns with various selections. Others believe the name was derived from the many amateur poets who met under the brush arbor at the town campground to recite verse. The most commonly accepted version tells of a drummer passing a home in the area and seeing a small, ragged boy and a scrawny dog. He explained, "Now there's a poor Tray if I ever saw one." At the time *Tray* was a common name for a dog. Citizens trying to select a name for the community heard the expression "poor Tray" and altered it to *Poetry.*
PO Jan. 29, 1880–Jan. 31, 1905.

Pointblank *(San Jacinto)*

The present name is a misinterpretation of the name of *Blanc Point* ("White Point") given by Florence Dissiway,

a French woman who came from Alabama to be governess for the R. T. and Henry Robinson families. Later the name was placed in reversed order, and *Point Blanc* soon became *Pointblank*.
PO May 13, 1884–; Pop. 183.

Point Enterprise *(Limestone)*

The name was suggested at a quilting party by a visitor who knew that four points of a survey met here and who thought the community was an enterprising one. Whether Lizzie Robertson Herring or William Pearson was the giver of the name is a point of contention.

Pole Cat Branch *(Walker)*

An "impossible" branch delayed roadbuilding efforts for so long that people showed their dislike for the stream by saying it "stunk." Over the years their statement came to be associated with the stink of a polecat, and the new name remained even after the branch no longer presented obstacles to roadbuilders. *Polecat* is a variant of *skunk*, and the term is found primarily in the South. At least six other Texas streams have this name.

Pole Cave Creek *(Real)*

Early settlers built pole ladders to reach the bee caves on this creek.

Polly's Peak *(Bandera)*

Few associate the name today with its namesake, José Policarpo Rodrigues, a scout, hunter, preacher, and Indian fighter. The first two syllables of his middle name provided the name of the peak.

Ponta *(Cherokee)* [pan 'te]

This town has one of the few Texas names taken directly from Latin. Ponta started as the village of *Donoho*, named for the location on the Donoho Survey. When the railroad bypassed the community, residents moved toward the tracks in an area called *Hubb*, for Hubbard Guin, surveyor. Because there were two railroad bridges crossing Mud Creek, the ablative form of the Latin word for "bridge"—*ponte*—was suggested as the new name, and the first postmaster, Robert Montgomery, altered the word to its present spelling, contending that no one would pronounce the Latin *e* correctly.
PO Apr. 1, 1903–?; Pop. 50.

Pontotoc *(Mason)* ['pant ə tak]

R. Kidd moved to Mason County from Pontotoc, Mississippi, and Benjamin J. Willis decided the name of Kidd's hometown would be suitable for the settlement which grew up at road junction in 1854. In Chickasaw, *Pontotoc* means "cattails growing on the prairie," perhaps an accurate description for the Mississippi town but not for the Texas namesake. A post office operated under this name in Bastrop County, 1871–1872.
PO Jan. 5, 1880–Dec. 12, 1883; Feb. 18, 1884–; Pop. 106.

Popher Creek *(Angelina)* ['po fər]

An Indian chief named Popher lent his name to this stream and to some of the legends of Angelina County. After his son was sentenced to be shot for killing two peddlers, Chief Popher persuaded White settlers to let him take his son's place when they carried out the death sentence. Allowed to select the time and place of his execution, he chose the banks of a creek where he had killed many deer and which came to bear his name.

Possum Kingdom Lake *(Jack, Palo Pinto, Stephens, Young)*

Water in the reservoir was impounded by the Morris Sheppard Dam, so named by an act of Congress for Congressman Morris Sheppard. Because the area was a paradise terrain of hills and valleys, post oaks, and cedars for opossums, the local name could not be supplanted even by congressional designation.

Post *(Garza)*

C. W. Post, the cereal king who created Post Toasties, owned 400,000 acres of land in the county. Between 1911 and 1914, he spent more than $50,000 on rain-making experiments using dynamite.
PO July 18, 1907–; Pop. 3,876; Inc.

Potato Hill *(Comanche)*

The soil here is hardly suitable for growing potatoes, but the large hill standing by itself resembled a potato in form and structure.

Pot Rack Creek *(Collin)*

Pot racks, wooden racks built around trees to hold clay or metal pots, were used by passing settlers who stopped to refresh themselves with water from the stream.

Potters Point *(Marion)*

For his efforts in the war for Texas independence, Robert Potter was awarded a land grant near Caddo Lake. At the end of his tenure as Secretary of the Navy for the Republic of Texas, he retired to his land. On the scenic point which bears his name, political enemies shot and killed him as he ran from his home and dived into Caddo Lake. His exploits as recorded in the memoirs of his widow, Harriet Potter, are reported in the novel *Love Is a Wild Assault* by Elithe Hamilton Kirkland.

Praha *(Fayette)* ['pra ha]

The original name was *Mulberry,* but Czech pioneers went round and round in their efforts to change it until the decision was made in 1856 that the new name should be *Praha* (Prague) for the city in Czechoslovakia. It was here that the first Bohemian Catholic parochial school in the United States was established.
PO Mar. 25, 1884–Nov. 31, 1906; Pop. 25.

Prairie Lea *(Caldwell)* [ˌprer ɪ 'li]

Like *Rio Grande River, River Thames,* and *River Avon,* this repetitive name draws frowns from language purists. *Prairie,* meaning "a grassy plain," is coupled with *lea,* also meaning "a grassy spot."
PO Aug. 23, 1851–; Pop. 100.

Prospect *(Clay)*

William Richard thought the place had fine prospects for becoming a sizable town. The name was used for communities in Burleson, Collin, McLennan, and Milam counties also.
PO Apr. 15, 1893–.

Providence *(Jefferson)*

A thankful family arriving in 1829 named their new community in the Big Thicket region *Providence.* Communities sharing this name are to be found in Angelina, Polk, and Van Zandt counties.

Pullman *(Potter)*

A Pullman car housed part of the construction crew for the Fort Worth and Denver City Railroad in 1887 when the line reached this area.
Pop. 12.

Pumpkin Center *(Wichita)*

Here a man established a blacksmith shop, and his helper erected a sign showing a picture of a pumpkin and the name *Pumpkin Center Blacksmith Shop.* When asked why he named the blacksmith shop that, the helper replied that he needed a name; he had only yellow paint; he couldn't draw a horse; and he had seen this name in a cartoon strip applied to a crossroads town. *Pop. 70.*

Pyote *(Ward)* [ˈpaɪ ot]

Pyote is a misspelling of the hallucinatory cactus button peyote. Another, less likely version of the name states that Chinese laborers on the Texas and Pacific Railroad, unable to pronounce *coyote*, said *pyote* instead. The town was developed in the 1880s.
PO Mar. 20, 1907–; Pop. 162; Inc.

Quanah *(Hardeman)* [ˈkwa nə]

A favorite Texas frontier story involves the capture of the fair-haired Cynthia Ann Parker by Comanches. She became the wife of Nocona, for whom the town in Montague County was named, and the mother of Quanah, chief of the Comanches, for whom the county seat of Hardeman County was named. *Quanah* is a Comanche word translated as "bed of flowers" or "sweet odor." Quanah was so pleased that the town had been named in his honor that he visited it many times between 1895 and 1911, the year of his death. His mother's family is the same Parker clan for whom Parker County was named.
PO Jan. 11, 1886–; Pop. 3,669; Inc.

Quemado *(Maverick)* [ke 'ma do]

The Spanish name refers to the "burnt" valley near the town. Some say it received its name during the Spanish exploration when the heat was terrific; others say the naming occurred because it was thought the valley had been burned by a volcanic eruption.
PO Dec. 22, 1903–June 15, 1918; May 23, 1934–; Pop. 426.

Quicksand *(Newton)*

Early homesteaders found quicksand in a creek. After the creek was named, the nearby community assumed the designation.
PO June 19, 1871–July 18, 1871.

Quihi *(Medina)* ['kwi hi]

The name was given by Henri Castro in 1845 when he laid out the town on Quihi Lake. The name refers to the white-neck Mexican eagle buzzard, whose name is spelled *Quichie, Quichi, Quihi,* or *Keechie.*
PO June 24, 1854 (Quihi)–May 21, 1857 (New Fountain)–Nov. 22, 1871 (Quichi)–Apr. 24, 1872 (New Fountain)–Jan. 15, 1914; Pop. 96.

Quitaque *(Briscoe)* ['kɪt ə kwe]

A legend about the name is derived from the presence of wild horses and two buttes in the area. Because the two buttes looked like a pile of horse manure, that meaning was assigned to the Indian word *quitaque.* Another explanation is that the name was taken from the Quitaca Indians who supposedly dealt in stolen livestock; their name was translated by the Whites as "whatever one steals." The name was first assigned to a creek, then a ranch, and finally the town.
PO Sept. 6, 1882–; Pop. 522.

Rabbit Creek *(Gregg)*

The creek, which flows near an old Cherokee campsite, was named for the Indian Chief Rabbit.

Race Track *(Delta)*

The community grew up around a prairie race track where horses attracted Sunday afternoon crowds during the 1880s.
PO May 24, 1888–June 15, 1904.

Rainbow *(Somervell)*

William L. Stewart, a leader in the community, chose a committee to name the settlement, but nothing could be agreed upon. Seeing a rainbow after a Texas thundershower, one of the committee members suggested the name *Rainbow*. The same name was given to a Newton County post office, 1880–1883 and 1884–1888.
PO Dec. 6, 1895–; Pop. 76.

Raisin *(Victoria)*

Vineyards which once grew in the area provided the name of this station on the Southern Pacific Railroad.
PO Sept. 22, 1892–June 30, 1914; Pop. 50 (including Colletoville).

Ramirito *(Jim Hogg)* [ra mə 'ri to]

The original name of the post office was *Ramirez*, for A. Ramírez, who had established ranch headquarters here before organization of the county in 1913. However, the name was altered to *Ramirito* to avoid repetition of the name of a Duval County post office operating at that time.
PO July 21, 1922–Oct. 31, 1957.

Randado *(Jim Hogg)* [ræn 'da do] [ræn 'da ðo]

The Spanish meaning of the word is "fringed with lace," possibly referring to itinerant salesmen of Spanish lace. The name may have come from the lace made by the Indians, which they called *randa*. Frank X. Tolbert of the *Dallas Morning News* reports the fringe of lace could have been the adobe walls surrounding the town and offering protection from Comanches, Apaches, and others who might have brought harm.
PO June 5, 1882–Dec. 4, 1883; Feb. 19, 1891–May 31, 1959; Pop. 15.

Ranger *(Eastland)*

The town developed around a ranger camp, where oil was discovered in 1917. The population grew to twenty thousand by 1920. Rangers camped here to give protection to builders of the Texas and Pacific Railroad.
PO Dec. 27, 1880–; Pop. 3,055; Inc.

Rangerville *(Cameron)*

The Texas Rangers, who supposedly sent only one man to a riot because there was only one riot, are honored in

the names of *Rangerville* in Cameron County and *Ranger* in Eastland County. Border disturbances in southern Cameron County made Rangers active here until about 1917.
PO Nov. 13, 1924–; Pop. 80; Inc. since 1970.

Razor *(Lamar)*

The name refers to a popular brand of tobacco sold in the A. K. Haynes general store.
PO Sept. 26, 1904–Apr. 30, 1935; Pop. 15.

Red Light *(Hudspeth)*

Hopes for a bawdy origin of the community name are extinguished when the local explanation is given. The settlement was so small that at night when a train passed through the area, the passengers could see nothing but one red signal light at the depot.

Red Paint Creek *(Haskell)*

The color of the soil bordering the creek makes the water red when it rises to that point.

Redwater *(Bowie)*

The number of unbelievers in the community earned it the name of *Ingersoll*, for the renowned agnostic orator and critic of the Bible, Robert Ingersoll. In 1889, E. T. Page of London, England, settled here at about the same time the community was experiencing a religious revival. By petition, he had the name changed to describe sulphurous springs in the vicinity which spout red-tinted waters.
PO June 27, 1881 (Ingersoll)–Dec. 13, 1894 (Redwater)–; Pop. 460.

Reklaw *(Cherokee, Rusk)* ['rɛk lɔ]

After the decision was made to honor the owner of the townsite, Margaret L. Walker, it was discovered that another post office had been registered as *Walker*, Texas. Determined citizens insisted upon honoring Walker, even if they had to spell the family name backward.
PO Oct. 5, 1903–; Pop. 152; Inc.

Relampago *(Hidalgo)* [re 'lam pa go]

In Spanish, the name means "lightning." Literally, the source could be an electrical storm in the 1880s which destroyed homes and killed several people. Figuratively,

the name is traced to a pioneer who was unusually dynamic. He soon earned the nickname that was transferred to the town.
PO Apr. 30, 1910–July 15, 1918.

Reliance *(Brazos)*

The reliability of the area in supporting a settlement rested on its fertile soil and plentiful water supply. An earlier name was *Little George,* referring to the colony of settlers from Georgia.
PO Oct. 13, 1899–Nov. 30, 1907.

Remlig *(Jasper)* ['rɪm lɪg]

The backward spelling of *Gilmer,* taken from the Alexander Gilmer Lumber Company, provided the name. The site was established in 1904 and abandoned when the sawmill closed in 1925. Reason for the reverse spelling was the existence of the Gilmer post office in Upshur County.
PO Dec. 26, 1905–June 30, 1926.

Resaca del Rancho Viejo *(Cameron)* [rə 'sa kə dɛl 'ran čo vi 'e ho]

A distinctive term in the Brownsville area is *resaca,* a Spanish derivative meaning "day stream channel," alluding to the old tributaries of the Rio Grande now cut off from the main course. This resaca takes its name from its location on an old ranch, now being developed as a country club of luxury homes and condominiums.

Reynard *(Houston)*

Instead of naming the community for the local Fox family, citizens chose *Reynard,* meaning "fox." Coincidently, the fox is among the animals inhabiting the region.
PO Jan. 14, 1901–Sept. 30, 1907.

Rhineland *(Knox)*

German settlers came from the Rhineland section of Germany to settle in a colony directed by Joseph R. Reisdorff in 1895.
PO June 15, 1898–Aug. 1917; Pop. 196.

Rising Star *(Eastland)*

When T. W. Anderson applied for a post office, he first suggested the name of *Rising Sun,* but that petition was

denied because another office was using that name at the time. He then submitted the name of *Star*, but that also was in use, and the postal department replied by assigning *Rising Star*. It is also reported that the name came from the belief of D. D. McConnell, postmaster at Eastland, that the locality was a "rising star country" because of its excellent crops.
PO Apr. 19, 1880–; Pop. 1,061; Inc.

Rita Santa *(Reagan)*

The community was originally called *Santa Rita* for the discovery well on University of Texas lands in West Texas where oil was found on May 28, 1923. The railroad changed the name to *Rita Santa* to avoid confusion with a similarly named station in New Mexico.

Riviera *(Kleberg)* [rɪ ˈvir ə]

The location of the town along the Texas coast reminded T. F. Koch, a land promoter, of the French Riviera. Nearby Loyola Beach was named for Ignatius Loyola Unterbrink, one of Mr. Koch's associates.
PO May 27, 1907–; Pop. 550.

Robstown *(Nueces)* [ˈrabz taʊn]

The person honored by the town name is Robert (Rob) Driscoll, Jr., son of a rancher and financier, and owner of the land on which the railroad station was built in 1903. His father lent his name to Driscoll in the same county.
PO Aug. 3, 1905–; Pop. 10,912; Inc.

Rockne *(Bastrop)* [ˈrak nɪ]

Notre Dame was finally victorious in the naming of this town for its famous coach, Knute Rockne. First the community was *Lehmanville* for a local family, and next *Hilbigville* in honor of William Hilbig and his family, who came in 1871 and started a store. Soon after the death of Rockne, on March 31, 1931, school children and other residents, especially those who were of Norwegian abstraction as was Rockne, began to petition for a new name. Father Strobel suggested the name change at a town meeting in the parochial school.
Pop. 400.

Rockwall *(Rockwall)*

In 1851 T. U. Wade was digging a well for his farm when he discovered a dike or wall of rock which surrounds the

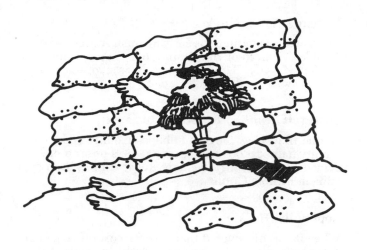

present city and appears occasionally at ground level. Wade was assisted in his excavations by B. F. Boydstun and a Mr. Stevenson. Each wanted to lend his name to the new settlement, but *Rockwall* was selected as a compromise for the town that was to become county seat when the smallest county in Texas was organized in 1886. Although scientific analyses indicate the wall is a natural geological formation, stories persist that it was built by prehistoric residents.
PO Aug. 31, 1854–; Pop. 4,192; Inc.

Rockwood *(Coleman)*

The first postmaster of the town was A. J. Wood, whose name was combined with the location of the town near a rock hill. An earlier name was *Discord*, Uncle Jim Foreman's reference to the disagreements when almost everyone proposed a different name. Civic pride and the insistence of Flossie Thompson led to the change to *Rockwood*.
PO May 24, 1889 (Discord)–Jan. 30, 1890 (Rockwood)–; Pop. 80.

Roma *(Starr)* ['ro mə]

Roma was chosen in 1821 by early Spanish-speaking settlers because the community was built on a hill and surrounded by hills very much like the Italian capital Rome.
PO Apr. 15, 1850–July 20, 1852; Sept. 27, 1852–Oct. 23, 1868; Jan. 6, 1869–; Pop. 2,696 (including Los Saenz).

Romero *(Hartley)* [ro 'mɛ ro]

The town was named for early Spanish settlers—either Trinidad Romero or the Casimero Romero family.
PO Mar. 6, 1903–May 4, 1903; July 23, 1907–Jan. 11, 1908; Aug. 7, 1908–Aug. 31, 1964.

Roosevelt *(Kimble; Lubbock)* ['ru zə vəlt]

Not far from New Deal in Lubbock County is the community named *Roosevelt*. Since 1898, a post office named *Roosevelt* for Theodore Roosevelt has been operating in Kimble County.

Ropesville *(Hockley)*

When it was discovered that a Texas post office had already been named *Lariat*, the town had to settle for *Ropes* as the closest name the cowboys could find to their first choice. Then the postal department reported that the name was too similar to *Ropers* to be used. Although the post office was designated as *Ropesville*, the railroad station retained the name of *Ropes*.
PO May 3, 1920–; Pop. 547; Inc.

Rosenberg *(Fort Bend)* ['roz ṇ bərg]

Admiration for Henry Rosenberg, a Swiss banker and philanthropist of Galveston, is reflected in the name of the mainland city. Rosenberg served as president of the Gulf, Colorado, and Sante Fe Railroad at the time the post office was established.
PO Nov. 1, 1881–Dec. 11, 1882; Mar. 2, 1883–July 18, 1883; Dec. 1, 1884–; Pop. 14,995; Inc.

Rosharon *(Brazoria)* [ro 'šɛ rən]

Because there were so many wild roses which reminded him of his native Rose of Sharon in England, George W. Collins named his new tract of land in Texas "The Rose of Sharon Garden Ranch," later shortened to *Rosharon*. An earlier name was *Masterson Switch*.
PO Feb. 9, 1912–June 15, 1920–; Pop. 435.

Round Lake *(Chambers)*

The near-perfect round shape of the lake provided its official name. But it is also known as *Murder Pond*,

where General Thomas Jefferson Chambers is said to
have killed John O'Brien while arguing over land titles.

Round Rock *(Williamson)*

Named *Brushy* when the area was settled in 1850, the
community changed its name when it moved across
Brushy Creek to the north bank in 1854. The new name
acknowledged a massive, toadstool-shaped rock in the
middle of Brushy Creek. In 1876, another move was
made about two miles northward to the present location.
*PO May 27, 1851 (Brushy Creek)—Aug. 24, 1854 (Round
Rock)—; Pop. 6,067; Inc. 1913.*

Rowena *(Runnels)* [ro 'i nə]

After the town was laid out by P. J. Barron, it was first
called *Barronville* and later named *Bolf*, a name supplanted by *Rowena*. Some believe *Rowena* is derived
from the Bohemian word *rovina*, meaning "level," an apt
name for this flat region. Others report that Jonathan
Miles was permitted to name Miles and one other station between San Angelo and Ballinger. His son, John S.
Miles, persuaded his father to let him name Rowena for
the girl he was courting at the University of Missouri.
*PO Jan. 10, 1900 (Bolf)—Mar. 26, 1901 (Rowena)—; Pop.
466; Inc.*

Royalty *(Ward)*

Until a post office was applied for after the discovery of
oil in 1927, the town was known as *Allentown*, for an
early land owner. Then the money or royalty the residents received from petroleum producers inspired the
new name.
PO Aug. 26, 1929—; Pop. 196.

Rule *(Haskell)*

W. A. Rule was an official of the Kansas City, Mexico,
and Orient Railroad when the route was surveyed in 1905.
PO 1903—; Pop. 907; Inc.

Rumley *(Lampasas)*

A threshing machine gave the town its name. The settlement was established in the late 1870s, and two men,
Smart and Clay, owned an unusually large machine
called a *Rumley*, for the equipment brand.

Sacred Heart *(Lamb)*

Early settlers were Roman Catholics, who hoped the name would draw others of their faith to the area.

Sacul *(Nacogdoches)* [sæ 'kəl]

When *Lucas* proved to be an unacceptable name for the post office, settlers were so determined to honor John Lucas that they reversed the spelling of the surname to gain approval. The town of *Reklaw* (*Walker* spelled backward) is only five miles away.
PO June 29, 1903–; Pop. 170.

St. Helena *(Cass)*

A former teacher and World War I veteran, Walter Mitchell, was instrumental in building a new school in the community in 1933 and naming it *St. Helena* because it was surrounded by pine trees similar to those on the island of St. Helena, where Napoleon spent his final days.

St. Lawrence *(Glasscock)*

A bishop named Lawrence came from Amarillo to dedicate the Catholic church in the community, which was later named *St. Lawrence.*

St. Paul *(San Patricio)*

No saint is involved here, only the nickname of George H. Paul, a land agent, lumber dealer, and operator of a gin and store. The name is also found in Collin and Falls counties.
PO Dec. 3, 1910–; Pop. 180.

Samnorwood *(Collingsworth)* [sæm 'nɔr wʊd]

The name takes on obvious meaning when it is discovered that S. (Sam) W. Norwood was a county pioneer.
PO Oct. 12, 1932–; Pop. 110.

San Augustine *(Shelby)* [sæn 'ɔ gəs ˌtin]

The town was built on a tract of 640 acres of land bought by Thomas S. McFarland from Chichester Chaplin for $200. The name chosen was the Spanish spelling of *Saint Augustine,* apostle to the English nation and first Archbishop of Canterbury. The town was first in Texas to be laid out according to a purely American plan, with two lots near the center kept for a public square.
PO May 22, 1846–; Pop. 2,599; Inc.

Sanctuary *(Parker)*

The inspiration for the community name was economic, not religious. Several families in the Ash Creek addition, fearing annexation by nearby Azle, held a meeting to discuss incorporation and voted to adopt the name *Sanctuary*, designating their new town as a sanctuary from high taxes. When the votes in the election were canvassed on May 12, 1969, twenty-nine of the thirty ballots cast favored incorporation. R. R. Baker and T. O. Brown were among the leaders attending the first meeting of neighborhood families when the name was chosen and the election petitioned.
Pop. 175; Inc.

Sand *(Dawson)*

Anyone who has visited the town during a high wind would agree that it is aptly named. It is located in sandy post oak land once called *The Sands of Texas*, where homesteaders began to arrive in 1860. A post office with this name operated in Bastrop County, 1898–1929.

San Gabriel River *(Milam, Williamson)* [sæn 'ge brɪ əl]

Fray Isidro Felix de Espinosa and Domingo Romón named the stream *San Francisco Xavier*. In 1828 Stephen F. Austin on his map spelled the name *San Javriel*, and field notes as late as 1833 continued to use that spelling, but the corruption to San Gabriel soon thereafter became set.

San Miguel Creek *(Atascosa, Frio, McMullen)*

The stream was first seen by the Spanish on San Miguel's Day, September 21.

San Saba *(San Saba)* [sæn 'sæ bə]

An early Christian saint provided the name for the San Saba Mission, then for the nearby river, and later for the county and county seat. The area was settled in 1854.
PO May 5, 1857–; Pop. 2,555.

Santa Monica *(Willacy)*

Clarence Ayres, President of the American Life Insurance Company, which furnished capital in 1925 for clearing and developing for the Missouri Pacific Railroad, named the town for Santa Monica, California.

Sarita *(Kenedy)* [sə 'ri tə]

This cattle shipping station was named for Sarita Kenedy, granddaughter of Captain Mifflin Kenedy, original partner of Richard King, founder of the King Ranch. Captain Kenedy lent his own name to Kenedy County and to Mifflin, a town in the county.

Saspamco *(Wilson)* [sæ 'spæm ko]

This community may very well be unique in explaining that its name was derived from a sewer pipe company, the only business in the area. The San Antonio Sewer Pipe and Manufacturing Company established the town when a sewer pipe factory was built nearby. The company acronym was transferred to the town and to a nearby oil field.
PO Aug. 22, 1901–; Pop. 475.

Satin *(Falls)* ['sæt ṇ]

The name of *Laguna* had to be forfeited after application was made for a post office and another Laguna, Texas, was discovered. It was decided that twenty-one names would be submitted, including that of *Westbrook* for T. C. Westbrook. Twenty names came easily, and while a group of citizens were sitting in a local dry goods store struggling to produce number twenty-one, a clerk handling a bolt of satin remarked that it was "as fine as split silk." *Satin* became the twenty-first name and the one chosen by postal authorities. Some sources say the name was derived from the surname of a railroad employee.
PO Dec. 20, 1917–; Pop. 138.

Saxet Oil and Gas Field *(Nueces)* ['sæk sɪt]

The name reverses the spelling of *Texas.*

Scalp Creek *(Menard)*

Scalps were associated with the creek following an Indian attack.

Scatter Branch *(Hunt)*

The rural community lies along Highway 24 near a stream called *Scatter Branch*, which runs out of its banks and scatters water over the countryside during rainy seasons.

Science Hill *(Henderson)*

The first school in the county was Science Hill Academy, established in 1859 by the Reverend Mr. Hezekiah Mitcham, a Methodist minister, and his six sons. The community was later absorbed along with Wildcat and Willow Springs into the Cross Roads area, named for its location on two intersecting roads.
PO Jan. 18, 1859–Nov. 5, 1866.

Scotland *(Archer)*

The name does not refer to bonnie Scotland, but rather to Henry J. Scott of Toronto, Canada, who represented English capitalists in the sale of land here in 1905. The name of *Scotland* was selected in 1907 at a picnic marking the arrival of the Southwestern Railroad. Not far away in the same county is *Dundee*, named by Morgan Jones in 1881 for his native town in Scotland. A post office in Harrison County also used the name *Scotland*.
PO June 3, 1908–; Pop. 345; Inc. since 1970.

Scrapping Valley *(Newton)*

The scrapping resulted from the thrashing a young lady gave her boyfriend after singing school when she discovered he had torn up her picture. The episode supposedly took place around 1900.

Scratch Eye *(Harrison)*

The Presbyterian church and cemetery were located in an area where low-hanging tree limbs caused visitors to stoop for fear that the sharp branches would scratch their eyes out. The original name was *Wilsons Chapel*, chosen for a Presbyterian preacher from Tennessee.

Scrougeout *(Anderson)* [ˈskraʊj aʊt]

It is said that the congregation of the church grew to such great proportions that they were scrouging out the sides of the building. The humorous name is also found in Fannin and other Texas counties.

Scrub Creek *(Angelina, Trinity)*

Saturday night bathers would scrub themselves in the stream before the days of bathtubs and indoor running water.

Scyene *(Dallas)* [saɪ 'in]

The name was given in 1854 by Sam Fisher, who bought land in the John Leonard survey for development which was never realized. Dallas County histories state that *scyene* means "key" or "opening" and was the name of a town in central Egypt built ca. 250–150 B.C. The location of the Dallas County community was considered the opening or the eastern entrance to the county.

Sebastopol *(Trinity)* [sə 'bæs tə pul]

The naval station of Russia was chosen as the name of the Trinity River community, a port on the Trinity as early as 1850.
Pop. 31.

Seclusion *(Lavaca)*

The secluded location of the town on the Lavaca River suggested its name. The area was settled in 1840, taking *Boxville* as its first name.
PO Apr. 28, 1879–May 31, 1914.

Segno *(Polk)* ['sɛg no]

A segno is a musical sign, marking the beginning and end of a repeat. A musical background led H. S. Knight, an early resident, to this name choice.
PO July 28, 1911–; Pop. 90.

Segovia *(Kimble)* [sɪ 'go vi ə]

George Van Buren, nephew of President Martin Van Buren, chose the name in reference to early settlers from Segovia in Spain. The terrain was said to resemble that of the Spanish region.
PO June 29, 1900–Nov. 30, 1959; Pop. 101.

Sejita *(Duval)* [sə 'hi tə]

A dam shaped like a *cejita*, Spanish for "little eyebrow," provided a water place for early range cattle. The half-moon-shaped, grass-covered bank of earth created a waterhole known as *La Sejita*, shortened to *Sejita* when the town was founded.
PO Sept. 25, 1914–July 15, 1954.

Seminole *(Gaines)* ['sɪm ə nol]

Before the county was organized, a post office named *Caput* served the region. When a new town was founded a mile to the northeast, it absorbed the Caput post office under the name of *Seminole,* named for the presence of the Seminole scouts here during the R. S. Mackenzie campaigns against the Indians in the 1870s. The scouts found some water wells on the site of the town, and they were called *Seminole Wells.* The common school district covers eight hundred sqaure miles, making it one of the largest in the country.

PO Dec. 19, 1904 (Caput)—Jan. 22, 1906 (Seminole)—; Pop. 7,002; Inc.

Seven Sisters *(Duval)*

Fred Massengill, the master of Texas town names in the 1930s, said that the surveyors named the seven small mounds that looked alike the *Seven Sisters* and that it was for the mounds that the post office was named. In the 1960s, Frank X. Tolbert reported in a column for the *Dallas Morning News* that the name paid homage to the seven attractive daughters of an important landowner named Don Refusio Serna.

PO established after 1930—discontinued between July 1, 1966, and June 30, 1968; Pop. 60.

Shadowland *(Red River)*

The name was suggested to J. C. Wright by clouds forming shadows on the prairie.

Shake Rag *(Rusk)*

Before the community came to be known as *Pleasant Grove* and now *Sardis,* it was called *Shake Rag* because of a poor boy who would come to school in rags, then rush home after school to do his chores in order to have time to study. Other school children would say, "Run, run, run, and shake your rags!" The boy later became a high-ranking government employee. The woman who tells this story is sure of her facts, but others contend that *Shake Rag* refers to the custom of farm wives of shaking a white rag to signal husbands in from the field or to the words of a school teacher who threatened, "I'll whip you students so hard you won't have anything left but rags to shake."

Shaky Springs *(Somervell)*

At times the ground provides a natural trampoline for anyone who jumps up and down at the edge of the springs. The earth will rise and fall like a shaky mattress.

Shamrock *(Wheeler)*

The first postmaster was an Irish immigrant named George Nickel, who offered the name for good luck and courage. A nearby post office operating under the name of *Exum*, for Frank Exum, manager of the general store and postmaster, was absorbed by the Wheeler County post office. Another post office was assigned under the name of *Shamrock* in Castro County, 1893–1894. *(Wheeler Co.) PO Oct. 6, 1890 (Shamrock)–June 2, 1893; May 14, 1900–May 30, 1903; Apr. 30, 1902 (Exum)–June 10, 1903 (Shamrock)–; Pop. 2,476; Inc.*

Sherlock *(Lipscomb)*

The town was named by the railroad for an official, employee, or friend of the Panhandle and Santa Fe Railroad. Such a naming pattern is found for most of the communities in the county. No written record remains to identify the namesake.

Shoe String *(Harrison)*

The first oil developers in the community operated on a shoe-string budget during the early days of their oil exploration.

Shorters Defeat *(Cherokee)*

This marsh located near Boxes Creek took its name from a man named Shorters who narrowly escaped some Indians by riding his horse into the marsh to avoid his pursuers. Why the marsh is called *Shorters Defeat* rather than *Shorters Escape* remains unexplained.

Shovel Mountain *(Blanco)*

The U.S. Geological Survey mapmaking crew considered the mountain to be shaped like a shovel.

Shumla *(Val Verde)* [ˈšum lə]

The community was named for a Turkish fort with a similar geographical surrounding. *Shumla* is a corruption of *Shulmen*, a town built in 1387 within a cluster of hills on the northern side of the Balkans.
PO June 27, 1906–Sept. 30, 1909.

Silver City *(Navarro)*

A small general store was run by a German family just before the Civil War. When Confederate money was offered for groceries, the merchant would refuse, demanding silver or gold. Because of his unusual demand for silver coins, people referred to his store as *Silver City.* Communities without post offices share this name in Fannin, Milam, and Red River counties.

Silver Creek *(Kerr)*

A silver bridle bit was found in the stream crossing. At least three other Texas creeks share this name.

Silver Lake *(Edwards)*

Treasure seekers will be disappointed at this large water-hole on the West Nueces River. Its name refers to the gypsum deposits nearby which shine brilliantly in the sunlight, giving the gypsum crystals the illusion of silver. Lakes with this name are also found in Harris, Kinney, and Van Zandt counties.

Sipe Springs *(Comanche)* [ˈsip sprɪŋz]

The springs were named for John C. Flott in 1870, and the town developing nearby assumed the name. The water source is a group of seep—or "sipe"—springs which oozed from the ground. The name is also applied to a community near natural springs in Milam County.
PO Feb. 4, 1873 (Siep Springs)–July 9, 1883 (Sipe Springs)–Sept. 1957; Pop. 110.

Sisterdale *(Kendall)*

A water source for the town is a pair of branches called the *Sisters.* The community lies between two mountains overlooking the valley. This parent German colony for Kendall County was founded by Nicolas Zink in 1847.
PO Oct. 23, 1851–1966; Pop. 63.

Skeeterville *(San Saba)*

In 1920 Roy Wilson opened a general store and named the village for the giant mosquitos in the area near the confluence of Wilbarger and Brush creeks.

Skellytown *(Carson)*

One of the first oil companies to operate here was the Skelly Oil Company, which brought in an oil field in the early 1930s and provided the name.
PO Jan. 31, 1927–; Pop. 658; Inc.

Slide *(Lubbock)*

When W. R. Standefer resurveyed the site in 1903, he discovered that nearly two hundred sections of land were located almost two miles farther west than people thought when they first settled there. After the mistake was discovered, the residents had no alternative but to slide over, moving all the schools, churches, and businesses with them to the west. An earlier name was *Block Twenty.*
PO July 12, 1904–Oct. 15, 1915; June 6, 1917–Jan. 15, 1929; Pop. 44.

Smackover Creek *(Titus)*

The creek took its name from a term used for classifying subterranean formations in nearby oil fields.

Smetana *(Brazos)* ['smɛt nə]

Czech settlers recalled their homeland in this name, which in Czech means "sweet cream."
PO Apr. 25, 1896–Nov. 15, 1906; Pop. 80.

Smoothing Iron Mountain or **Iron Mountain** *(Llano)*

From a distance, the mountain resembles a smoothing iron to those familiar with the domestic implement used before the days of wash-and-wear clothing.
El. 1,350.

Snap *(Panola)*

Dr. Snap Cariker was an early physician in the community.
PO Oct. 11, 1899–Jan. 31, 1906.

Snook *(Burleson)* [snuk]

J. S. Snook, a postmaster at Caldwell, was influential in getting a post office approved for this community.
PO Feb. 20, 1895–; Pop. 372; Inc. since 1970.

Snow Hill *(Morris)*

The school community was established in 1870 when J. J. Cason deeded the land for the school site with the stipulation that only Whites should be allowed to attend. An earlier post office here had been named *Buchanan.*

Soda Lake *(Crane)*

The name of the West Texas body of water announced its mineral content to thirsty travelers.

Soldier Lake *(Dimmit)*

Several soldiers were either lost to alligators or drowned while they camped on the banks of this lake. The mystery of their disappearance was never solved.

Solms *(Comal)* [salmz]

Most settlers consider themselves lucky if one town is named for them, but Prince Carl of Solms-Braunfels received a double honor in the names of *Solms* and *New*

Braunfels. Until 1886 the community was known as *Four Mile Creek.*
PO Aug. 27, 1894–Oct. 31, 1903; Pop. 40.

Sour Creek *(Comal)*

Many a thirsty person has avoided the cool, sweet water of this stream, not realizing that it was named for early settlers who were members of the Sauer family.

Sour Dough Creek *(Roberts)*

"Sour Dough" Charles Dietrich lived near this creek and cut cedar posts in the area, selling them to ranchers for fence posts. He got his name for letting his sour dough biscuits run over, and the creek was named for him in turn.

Sourlake *(Hardin)*

A spring of sour water formed a small lake which gave its name to the town. Indians looked upon the waters with awe for their healing powers. The founder of the settlement was Stephen Jackson, a loyal supporter of Stephen F. Austin, who came in 1835. When he took ponies to pasture in the Sour Lake area, the horses made for the lake, sniffed cautiously, but did not drink. Jackson tasted the sour water, felt sick, and then refreshed. "Don't take horses to Sour Lake," was the word he passed to others. From that warning, the town name developed.
PO Nov. 7, 1866 (Sour Lake)–Feb. 1, 1869; Sept. 29, 1871–Mar. 6, 1876; Apr. 28, 1879 (Sour Lake Spring)–Aug. 11, 1880 (Sour Lake)–Feb. 26, 1895 (Sourlake)–;Pop. 1,695;Inc.

Spindle Top *(Jefferson)*

The first oil field in Texas, located south of Beaumont, took its name from the geological formation shaped like a spindle. The famous Spindletop oil gusher dating to January 10, 1901, provided a name for a station established on the Southern Pacific Railway.
PO June 1, 1905–Aug. 31, 1906.

Splendora *(Montgomery)* [splɪn 'do rə]

M. Z. King, teacher and first postmaster, named the town for the splendor of its floral environments. No stock is placed in printed reports that the name came from the ship *Splendora,* about which the song "The Good Ship That Never Returned" was written.
PO May 1, 1896–; Pop. 318; Inc.

Sprayberry Oil Field *(Midland)*

One level of the oil-producing strata, called *Sprayberry*, is the sand from which oil is obtained.

Spunkie Ridge *(Rockwall)*

Mischievous children at the school here were so adept at getting into trouble that the school and community took a name to reflect the juvenile spunk.

Spur *(Dickens)*

The brand of the Espuela Land and Cattle Company was a spur, quite appropriately, since *espuela* means "spur" in Spanish. At first the post office department rejected the name, but through the influence of friends of the community the decision was reversed.
PO Sept. 15, 1909–; Pop. 1,559; Inc.

Spurger *(Tyler)* ['spər gər]

Whether the town was named for William Spurger or for the pronunciation a local drunk gave the Spurgeon brand of whiskey has not been settled.
PO 1881–; Pop. 472.

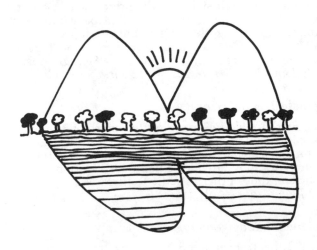

Squaw Tit Peak *(Pecos)*

Wyoming has its Grand Tetons, California its Nellie's Nipples, and Texas this boldly named peak in Pecos County, lying between Sheffield and Fort Stockton.

Staggers Point *(Robertson)*

The earliest large community in Robertson's colony was settled by Irish immigrants who came to America in 1821 and lived in South Carolina and then in Alabama before finding a permanent location here in 1833. In 1836, when relatives joined early arrivals to strengthen the settlement, the community name meaning "Strivers' Point" in dialect was given probably for the rugged zeal of settlers in the face of hardships. A community remained here until 1868, when the Houston and Texas Central Railway bypassed the community and business waned.

Stampede Creek *(Bell; McLennan)*

Usually nosies caused horses to stampede, but in McLennan County it was the stench of decaying buffalo and Indian bodies that sent them at a gallop. The victims had been killed after the Texas Rangers, under George Erath, surprised a hunting party in 1839; the creek was soon named for the event. In Bell County, a post office operated in the Stampede community between 1893 and 1901, taking its name after some cattle got out of hand on the old Chisholm Trail. A creek was first named for the event before the name was transferred to a nearby settlement.

Stanton *(Martin)* ['stant n̩]

When the town was established in 1881 as a section on the Texas and Pacific Railroad, it was called *Grelton*. Catholic settlers petitioned that the railroad change the name to *Marienfeld*, meaning "field of Mary," and their request was granted. By 1890, Protestants outnumbered the Catholics, and they changed the name to *Stanton*, honoring Edwin McMasters Stanton, Abraham Lincoln's secretary of war.
PO Dec. 28, 1882 (Marienfeld)—Sept. 26, 1890 (Stanton)—; Pop. 2,205; Inc.

Star *(Mills)*

The town was first known as *Star Mountain*, taking its name from a nearby hill shaped like a five-pointed star. The name had been shortened by the time the post office was established.
PO Aug. 5, 1884—; Pop. 90.

Star Creek *(Hood)*

The stream is usually called *Star Hollow Creek*, probably for the outlaw Belle Starr, who spent some time in the

area. The source of the name has also been traced to an employee of the Star Shoe Company, who owned a ranch here. He erected a large star in his pasture as the trademark of his company.

Starvation Creek *(Hutchinson)*

In the late 1870s, a cattle outfit camping on the creek lost all its food and horses to outlaws said to be associates of Billy the Kid. The cowboys avoided starvation by sending one of their number on a two-day hike sixty miles to Fort Elliott to seek help, while the others lived off beef from their herd and water from the creek.

Steal Easy Mountain *(Stephens)*

The story heard by Frank X. Tolbert, *Dallas Morning News* columnist, is that the Comanches and Kiowas had such an easy time sneaking over the rise and raiding the ranchers' horse and cow herds that the name developed naturally.
El. 1,500.

Stonewall *(Gillespie)*

In 1870, Major Israel Moses Núñez laid out a town site along the Pedernales River and called it *Millville.* When

he applied for a post office, Major Núñez requested that it be named *Stonewall Jackson* for the general under whom he had served in the Civil War. Because that name was in use, it was shortened to *Stonewall.*
PO Mar. 5, 1875–Oct. 31, 1900; Apr. 30, 1902–July 31, 1905; reestablished before 1930–; Pop. 245.

Stranger *(Falls)*

While the citizenry were having a hard time choosing a title for the new town, the task was assigned to the postmaster, who said, "I'm a stranger here myself." Someone latched on to *Stranger* as the post office name.
PO Nov. 24, 1879–Nov. 30, 1901; May 10, 1902–Apr. 15, 1907; Pop. 27.

Stratford *(Sherman)*

If it can be believed that Colonel Walter Colton, an early settler, paid homage to Stratford-on-Avon, birthplace of Shakespeare, then this Texas community is Stratford-on-Coldwater-Creek. A more likely influence, however, is Colonel Colton's admiration for General Robert E. Lee and his decision to honor Lee's birthplace at Stratford, Virginia. The colonel owned the townsite when the railroad came.
PO May 27, 1901–; Pop. 2,500; Inc.; El. 3,695.

Study Butte *(Brewster)* [ˌstyu dɪ ˈbyut]

Will Study managed the Big Bend Cinnabar Mining Company, established after Frederico Villalva discovered mercury in the area about 1900. The community in the Big Bend National Park lies in the Chisos Mountains of southern Brewster County and was first called *Big Bend,* for the loop of the Rio Grande nearby.
PO May 13, 1904 (Big Bend)–May 31, 1910; Sept. 14, 1917 (Study Butte)–Jan. 15, 1921; Pop. 120.

Styx *(Kaufman)* [staɪks]

The community was named by a Dr. Gordon for the principal river in the underworld of Greek mythology.
PO Jan. 18, 1899–Feb. 15, 1908.

Sublime *(Lavaca)*

Some sources trace the name to the inspiration of Robert Miller, who donated the townsite to the San Antonio and Aransas Railroad when he moved to the site from

Smoothing Iron, one mile east, and built a store and hotel in 1887. Others insist that settlers chose the name for their former home in Sublime, Germany.
PO June 14, 1875–; Pop. 75.

Sudan Lake *(Walker)*

When Raymond David, chairman of the board of directors of the Huntsville National Bank, was given the chance to name the lake in 1949, he took a syllable from the name of his daughter, *Suzanne,* and combined it with the name of his son, *Dan.*

Sugar Bottom *(Fannin)*

The rich soil of this "bottom," or lowland area along a stream, once produced a type of cane from which syrup was made.

Sugar Hill *(Titus)*

Large amounts of sugar were transported to the community's stills that made its moonshiners famous throughout East Texas. The same name was used for a post office in Panola County operated intermittently between 1850 and 1904 and as an early name for the community that became Farmersville (Collin County) in 1857.

Sugarland *(Fort Bend)*

The name evolved from the fact that the population earned its livelihood through the activities of Sugarland Industries and the Imperial Sugar Company. Sugarland claimed the largest sugar plantation and refinery combination in the world, developing at the turn of the century when Colonel E. H. Cunningham combined five plantations of 12,500 acres. A group from Venice, Italy, settled in the area and began to refine sugar, naming their development *Sugar Land.* Another post office in the county used the name of *Sugarland* from 1858 to 1886. It developed into *Imperial,* a shipping point on the Texas and New Orleans Railroad.
PO Feb. 28, 1890–; Pop. 4,173; Inc.

Sundown *(Hockley)*

R. L. Slaughter, a landowner, declined the honor of having the community named for his family and suggested that it be called *Sundown,* for the title of a movie he had seen photographed on family property in Mexico. Those

not familiar with Slaughter's inspiration devised the story that on the day the villagers were to choose a name, they debated all afternoon until almost sundown, when someone suggested that they call the place *Sundown* and go home. The town was laid off in 1928 on part of the old C. C. Slaughter ranch, where oil was discovered in 1938.
PO Mar. 29, 1938–; Pop. 1,195; Inc.

Sunnyside *(Waller)*

Jeff Rainwater, an early resident, chose the name because the community was located on the sunny side of a knoll. No one seems to know whether the name was based on morning or afternoon observations. *Sunnyside* is found also in Castro County.
PO Nov. 6, 1977–; Pop. 120.

Sunnyslope *(Swisher)*

"The place is real pretty when the sun hits it" was the explanation given by one resident.

Sunray *(Moore)*

The post office was named for the Sunray Oil Company of Tulsa, Oklahoma.
PO July 11, 1930 (Altaman)–Mar. 15, 1931 (Sunray)–; Pop. 1,743; Inc.

Sunset *(Montague)*

When the postal department decided that *Jacksonville*, for an early settler named *Jackson*, was a duplicate name that could not be used, the new appellation assigned in 1881 was *Sunset*, given according to some for Sunset Boone, an early resident, and according to others for the comment, "You are so far towards the setting sun, why not name it *Sunset?*"
PO Jan. 26, 1880–; Pop. 200.

Swamppoodle Creek *(Bowie)* ['swamp ,pu dəl]

The name originally referred to a puddle—not a dog—in a swampy area. Joseph Deucherman dreamed of building a canal along the route of the creek to connect Red River and Sulphur River. The idea was abandoned with the coming of the railroad.

Swartout *(Polk)*

Tradition traces the name to Samuel Swartout of New York, a speculator and politician, who advanced money to the Texas government in 1836 and organized an association for founding a trading post at the edge of the Alabama-Coushatta Indian village.
PO 1843–Jan. 7, 1875.

Sweet Home *(Lavaca)*

Early residents felt they had found ideal conditions for home life in this area, where George West stimulated community growth when he established the first hotel, store, and stable in 1860.
PO July 14, 1852–; Pop. 360.

Sweetie-Peck Oil Field *(Upton)*

The wife of the owner was known by a saccharin nickname—Sweetie-Peck.

Sweetwater *(Nolan)*

Texas Rangers provided the name in 1874 while they were scouting for Indians along a creek given the same name. The sweetness of the water in a land of bitter streams was much appreciated, and it made a strong impression. The sweetness has been traced to elm trees and to gypsum. The post office was registered as *Sweet Water* in 1879 and changed in 1918 to *Sweetwater* to conform to the spelling used in the town. Prior to the coming of the Texas and Pacific Railroad, a settlement in the area was known as *Blue Goose,* for the blue crane seen in a nearby creek. Residents moved to the railroad later and became a part of Sweetwater.

PO Mar. 27, 1879 (Sweet Water)–Jan. 24, 1918 (Sweetwater)–; Pop. 11,574; Inc.

Swiftex *(Bastrop)*

The now-extinct community, also known as Swiftex Village, faded swiftly once its function had been served—that of providing on privately owned property a residence for military personnel of the Camp Swift Military Reservation. The World War II army camp received the first German prisoners of war sent to the United States. The name is a contraction of *Swift, Texas.*

Swindler Creek *(Newton)*

Four men who lived by the creek refused to tell their names. Their secrecy led their neighbors to think they were up to no good, and soon they were referred to as swindlers.

Tahoka *(Lynn)* [tə ˈho kə]

The name is taken from nearby Lake Tahoka, an Indian name translated as "clear water" or "deep water." The Indians knew it as the hardest, strongest-smelling water around. The lake itself is a phenomenon found only on

the Llano Estacado. A great sink hole, one hundred feet deep and covering an area of four miles, the lake bed is dry most of the time, but fresh water springs along the west side have never been known to go dry.
PO Apr. 8, 1903–; Pop. 2,965; Inc.

Talco *(Titus)* ['tæl ko]

The oil town was named impulsively for a candy company. During a discussion of possible names, J. H. Brown, a merchant, noticed the name *Talco* on the end of a candy box produced by the Texas, Arkansas, and Louisiana Candy Company.
PO June 12, 1856 (Gouldsborough, for Nehemiah C. Gould, first postmaster)–Nov. 5, 1866; May 13, 1878–Dec. 5, 1882; May 1, 1883–Aug. 4, 1910 (Talco)–; Pop. 718; Inc.

Talking John Creek *(Foard)*

The following story was told by Mrs. Virginia Johnson of Crowell, member of the county historical survey committee: "An old cowboy once lived on this creek, and when he looked out and saw someone riding up, he always rode out to meet him. As the fellow left, he rode away with him for a short distance. Because his name was John, and because he loved so much to chat with these strangers, the name of the creek was established as *Talking John Creek*."

Talpacata Creek *(Bee)* ['tæl pə kæt]

The mysterious Karankawa name means nothing more than "tadpole."

Taminia *(Montgomery)*

Captain James H. Berry named this town for Tammany Hall, New York. It is presumed the writer of the letter submitting the name to the postal department had his own idea as to its spelling.

Tan Tought Creek *(Llano)*

In the early days of the county, an old settler who sold shoes tanned the leather in this stream.

Tarpley *(Bandera)*

The son of John T. Prichett, an early postmaster in Bandera County, was Clarence Tarpley Prichett. His middle

name, which was the maiden name of his mother, who had come from Tennessee, was taken for a new post office established near Bandera. An earlier name was *Hondo Cañón*, meaning "deep canyon" in Spanish.
PO Jan. 30, 1887 (Hondo Cañón)–Jan. 31, 1899 (Tarpley)–; Pop. 30.

Tarzan *(Martin)* ['tar zən]

In 1937, Tant Lindsey, who read widely, submitted fourteen book titles as suggested names for the post office. Postal authorities decided on *Tarzan of the Apes*, the novel by Edgar Rice Burroughs. Four years earlier, Lindsey had named the area around his small grocery store *South Plains*, but another name was required when he applied for a post office.
PO Mar. 31, 1927–; Pop. 500.

Tascosa *(Oldham)* [tæs 'ko sə]

Cassie Romero originally named the place *Atascosa*, meaning "boggy creek," but cowboys from the LIT and other ranches called it *Tascosa* because it was easier to say. As the settlement grew and needed a name, *Tascosa*

was chosen over *Atascosa*, which was the name of a town near San Antonio.
PO May 23, 1878–discontinued during 1960s; Pop. 85.

Teacup *(Kimble)*

The town lies near a mountain shaped like an inverted teacup.

Teepee Creek *(Motley)*

The source of the name could have been Indian teepees along the waterway or the first houses built with sharp roofs like tents. At least two other Texas streams have this name.

Teepee Draw *(Reagan)*

Although the name of the draw may call to mind pointed Indian tents, the source of the name is the T & P (Texas and Pacific) Land and Trust Company.

Tehuacana *(Freestone, Limestone)* [tə ˈwɔ kə nə]

The Tehuacanas were a tribe of Indians of the Wichita group whose name translates as "the three canes." They lived in the area between the Brazos and Trinity rivers. Variant spellings of their name are *Tawakoni* and *Tewockony*.
PO Mar. 8, 1847 (Tewockony Springs)–Nov. 27, 1860; Dec. 19, 1860–Nov. 5, 1866; Oct. 8, 1869 (Tehuacana)–; Pop. 283; Inc.

Telegraph *(Kimble)*

The first telegraph and telephone poles used in the county were cut from a canyon of the South Llano River opposite the community. The settlement claims onomastic kinship to Telephone in Fannin County.
PO Feb. 17, 1900–; Pop. 11.

Telephone *(Fannin)*

When the community applied for a post office, a store operator named Hinderman submitted several names which were rejected. Eventually he offered the name *Telephone* because he owned the only telephone in the community. The fact that the community is located between Bells and Dial is coincidental.
PO Feb. 26, 1886–; Pop. 210.

Tell *(Childress)*

For a time, the community was called *Lee*, but it became *Tattle Tale Flats* because some residents were exceedingly eager to go before the grand jury to report

unsolicited information about their neighbors. When the post office was established, the nickname was shortened to *Tell*.
PO Sept. 26, 1888 (Lee)—Sept. 30, 1893; May 4, 1905 (Tell)—; Pop. 51.

Teneha *(Shelby)* ['tɪn ə hɔ]

Teneha is an Indian word meaning "muddy water." The town was established in 1885 and named by the Hicks family for the municipality of Tenehaw (also spelled *Teneja*), a division of the Nacogdoches Municipality dating to 1833. On January 11, 1836, the name of the municipality changed to *Shelby*, which became the county name, and the name of *Teneha* was not revived until almost fifty years later.
PO Apr. 7, 1886—; Pop. 1,239.

Tennessee Valley *(Cottle)*

The area was called *Pleasant Hill* until so many new settlers started arriving from Tennessee. Bell County also has a Tennessee Valley, and Anderson a Tennessee Colony.

Tennyson *(Coke)*

After Samuel and J. W. Sayner, Englishmen, settled near the present site of the town in 1882, they suggested the name as a tribute to the poet Alfred Tennyson. The town lies at the base of Mount Margaret, named for a girl killed by Indians. Her father buried her on the highest peak nearby, marking her grave with a cross which still stands and attracts climbers.
PO June 26, 1894–; Pop. 35.

Tenth Cavalry Creek *(Wichita)*

A legend says that a party of soldiers from the Tenth Cavalry, a Black regiment stationed at old Fort Augur on Augur Creek, in Tillman County, Oklahoma, came across the Red River to clean up a band of Indians in 1872 or 1873. The Indians, however, ambushed the soldiers, killed them, and buried horses and officers alike in a common grave on the banks of the creek. Another story is that a detachment of the Tenth Cavalry was stationed at the mouth of the creek to chase Indians when the Red River was up and could not be forded.

Tequesquite Creek *(Kinney, Maverick)* [te ke 'ski te]

Two ranching families living along the creek had given it separate names. One called it *Texas Creek,* and the other *Mesquite Creek.* In a compromise name, they agreed upon *Tequesquite Creek.*

Terlingua *(Brewster)* [tər 'lɪŋ gwə]

The word providing the name of the creek which flows into the Rio Grande has been interpreted as "three languages," referring to the Spanish, English, and Indian spoken in the area, and as "three tongues," describing the three forks of the stream. Other interpretations of the name claim that the intended designation was *Los Linguas,* meaning "the tongues" or "the languages" (Comanche, Seminole, etc.) or that the name based on *tres lenguas* refers to the three tribes of Indians living on the upper branches of the creek—the Apache, Comanche,

and Shawnee. In recent years the picturesque town has gained recognition as the site of a chili-cooking contest. *PO Aug. 15, 1899–; Pop. 100; El. 2,720.*

Terrapin *(Nacogdoches, Wood)* ['tær ə pɪn]

In 1876, a picnic was held in the new Wood County community bordering Upshur County and extending north from the Sabine River to Big Sandy Creek. Instead of catching fish to fry, the picnickers caught only terrapins, providing the name *Terrapin Neck*. In Nacogdoches County, *Terrapin Creek* impressed its namers as being as slow-moving as a turtle. In Texas *terrapin* usually refers to the box land turtle, rather than to the flat-backed water turtle.

Tesnus *(Brewster)* ['tɛs nəs]

People wanted to name their town *Sunset*, but the postal authorities would not let them because of Sunset in Montague County. So they spelled *Sunset* backward. Some say the famous Southern Pacific Railroad symbol, as well as the spectacular western sunset, inspired the

sunset name. The sunset symbol was originated and designed by a bookkeeper named Allen who worked in the San Antonio division of the railroad. An earlier name for the area was *Tabor* in the 1870s.
PO Feb. 2, 1912–discontinued 1955.

Texana *(Jackson)*

The settlement was originally called *Santa Anna* when it was founded in 1832 as the first town in the county. Dr. F. F. Wells and Pamela Porter changed the name to *Texana* in 1835 to replace the name associated with an enemy of Texas independence. The town declined after it was bypassed by the New York, Texas, and Mexican Railroad in 1883.
PO Feb. 17, 1837–Nov. 27, 1885.

Texarkana *(Bowie)*

The name combines the first syllable of *Texas,* the first syllable of *Arkansas,* and the last two syllables of *Louisiana.* The Texas-Arkansas boundary divides the post office and the railroad terminal, and Louisiana lies some twenty miles south of the city. Promoters of Texarkana as hub of the four-state area suggest that the last letter in the name was taken from the last syllable in *Oklahoma,* since Texarkana is located some thirty miles southeast of Oklahoma.
PO Feb. 2, 1886–Dec. 13, 1892 (mail to Texarkana, Ark.)–Oct. 28, 1893–; Pop. 33,813; Inc.

Texhoma *(Sherman)* ['tɛks 'o mə]

The location of the Texas-Oklahoma state line suggested the blending of the name. In other locales along the state boundary, the blending produced *Texoma.*
PO Dec. 11, 1909–Apr. 30, 1910–; Pop. 336, combined population of community in Texas and Oklahoma is about 1,500; post office and banks are in Oklahoma.

Texla *(Orange)*

The first post office here was named *Bruce,* with Charles G. Bruce as first postmaster for the mill site operated by the Harrell-Votaw Lumber Company. In 1906, the R. W. Wier Lumber Company bought the mill and changed the name to *Texla,* coined from *Texas* and *Louisiana* because of the Texas mill's proximity to the bordering state.
PO Sept. 21, 1905 (Bruce)–July 10, 1906 (Texla)–July 31, 1929.

Texline *(Dallam)*

The town is on the line between Texas and New Mexico.
PO Oct. 24, 1888–; Pop. 411; Inc.

Tex-Mex Oil Field *(Gaines)*

The field was named for the border line of Texas and
New Mexico.

Texon *(Reagan)* [tɛks 'an]

The community was named by Levi Smith for Frank
Pickrell's and Hayman Drupp's Texon Oil and Land
Company.
PO Apr. 28, 1926–; Pop. 35.

Thalia *(Foard)* ['θel yə]

The name of *Paradise* was submitted because a nearby
stream bore that name, but the postal department rejected it as duplicative and suggested *Thalia*, a Latin
word meaning "blooming or luxuriant" and referring to
one of the nine muses, the one inspiring comedy and
pastoral poetry.
PO Mar. 3, 1890–Nov. 1, 1957; Pop. 104.

Thermo *(Hopkins)*

The Thermo Brick Plant located here was given its name
for the type of sand used in making brick. The community is also known as *Crush*, referring to the method of
crushing clay in the process of making brick.

Thicket *(Hardin)*

The community is located deep in the Big Thicket, a
name applied to the area between the old San Antonio
Road and the coastal prairie of South Texas. Early immigrants from Louisiana found their way effectually
blocked by impenetrable thickets rooted in the sandy
soils of hills bordering almost innumerable streams. The
nearest open land was ten miles away when the town
was founded.
*PO Jan. 22, 1906 (Williams)–June 25, 1906 (Thicket)–;
Pop. 350.*

Three Aces Oil Field *(Callahan)*

The crew of the oil company was playing poker in the
"doghouse," the small room at the entrance to the oil rig,

when the first well came in. Everyone threw in his cards and ran to bring the well in. One of the players tried to get the men to finish the game because, after losing all night, he had just gotten a hand of three aces when they quit. Hence, the oil company named the field *Three Aces.*

Threemile Creek *(Waller)*

At flood stage, the creek spread out for a width of three miles.

Three P *(Fannin)*

When the Prairie Hill, Portland, and Philadelphia schools were consolidated, the new school was called *Three P,* and the surrounding community assumed the name.

Three Rivers *(Live Oak)*

The proximity of the Atascosa, Frio, and Nueces rivers provided the name for this town, founded in 1914. Originally, the site was called *Hamiltonburg,* but the similarity of that name to the names of two other towns led to a change.
PO *Oct. 30, 1913 (Hamiltonburg)–May 1, 1914 (Three Rivers)–; Pop. 3,500; Inc. 1926.*

Three States *(Cass)*

The area at which Texas, Arkansas, and Louisiana join is known as Three States.

Tierra Blanca Creek *(Deaf Smith, Randall)*

The Spanish phrase for "white earth" aptly describes the film which develops on the land after a rain. The high acid content of the soil creates the phenomenon.

Tiffin *(Eastland)*

An Irishman working on a railroad crew remarked one noon that he was about ready for *tiffin*, meaning "lunch, a drink of liquor or small beer." The word was new to other citizens, who submitted it for their post office. *PO May 20, 1919 (Bull Creek)—July 8, 1920 (Tiffin)—1930s.*

Tigertown *(Lamar)*

Three stories account for the name: (1) A huge picture of a tiger was obtained from a circus playing in Paris, Texas, and hung over the bar of the town saloon. Soon a common expression was coined: "Let's go over and take a shot at the tiger." (2) Some drunks rode into town when all the store buildings were plastered with pictures of circus tigers. They went galloping down Main Street, yelling "Tigertown! Tigertown!" (3) Visitors from Bonham were bested by local boys at a community dance. The defeated Bonham lads returned to paint a tiger on a wall in the community to symbolize the fierceness of the fight. The name was also used for a town in Washington County.

Tilden *(McMullen)*

Tilden was originally called *Colfax* and later *Dog Town* because there were so many dogs in the community. M. F. Lowe, elected county judge when the county was organized in 1887, is credited with naming the county seat for Samuel J. Tilden, Democratic candidate for president in 1876. Although Tilden received a majority of more than 200,000 votes, the election was contested, and Rutherford B. Hayes, the Republican candidate, became the nineteenth president. *PO June 12, 1871 (Dog Town)—Sept. 14, 1877 (Tilden)—Pop. 500.*

Tinrag *(Hopkins)*

Indirect honor was paid the Garnit family when their name was spelled backward to produce the designation of this community.

Tin Top *(Parker)*

The community took its name from a gin established here. The galvanized iron roof could be seen for many miles. The settlement started in 1850 when a man named Cary Disk erected a cabin along the river. The same name is used in Polk County for a community that also never had a post office of its own.

Tioga *(Grayson)* [taɪ 'o gə]

In 1896, after the coming of the Texas and Pacific Railroad, the community which flourished near medicinal springs took its name from a tribe of Indians once inhabiting New York State. The tribe's name is translated as "fair and beautiful." Tioga's most famous son, Gene Autry, left home at eighteen to work as a telegraph operator in Oklahoma. After achieving fame as a movie cowboy, Autry offered to buy the townsite on the condition that the name be changed to *Autry Spring.* The citizens declined his offer. In the early 1970s, fourteen of the sixteen business buildings in Tioga were purchased by Mr. and Mrs. James Wendover, who attempted to turn Tioga into "Antique Town, USA," while reviving the mineral water sales and operating a flea market on the town square one weekend a month.
PO Aug. 29, 1881–; Pop. 381; Inc.

Tira *(Hopkins)* ['taɪ rə]

The original name of *Chapman Arms,* traced to the Chapman family, was changed with the establishment of a post office. One of the leading citizens jestingly remarked that it should be named for Tyre because it was just as wicked as the biblical city.
PO Dec. 24, 1898–Oct. 31, 1906; July 16, 1910–Apr. 30, 1919.

Tivoli *(Refugio)* [taɪ 'vo lə]

N. C. Gullet, a former riverboat gambler, gave the land for the post office and named it for Tivoli, Louisiana. The Tivoli resort near Rome, Italy, had inspired the Louisiana town name.
PO July 31, 1893–; Pop. 540.

Tobacco Creek *(Borden)*

The water of this creek had a bitter and brackish taste, reminding the namegivers of tobacco. The name was probably given by men serving General Randal S. Mackenzie and camping along the stream.

Toenail Oil Field *(Schleicher)*

The oil field takes its name from the small ranching community of Toenail, named because families would send their children on horseback to get the mail, and a ranch hand, seeing all the barefoot children, thought that *Toenail* would be a good designation for the area.

Tokio *(Terry)* ['to kɪ o]

Credit is sometimes given to Mrs. H. L. Ware, wife of the first postmaster, who had no particular reason for the name other than that she liked it. Present-day residents, pointing to newspaper coverage of the war between Russia and Japan about the time their town was named, believe the school and post office were named for Tokyo, Japan. *Tokio* was also used in 1882 as the name of a station on the Texas Central Railroad in McLennan County.
PO Sept. 21, 1912–; Pop. 60.

Toledo *(Newton)* [tə 'li də]

Settlers arrived from Toledo, Ohio, in the 1840s and brought the name with them.
PO July 7, 1873–Sept. 11, 1877.

Tomball *(Harris)*

The name of the town blends the first and last names of Thomas Henry Ball, 1859–1944, a congressman from Houston who earned the name of "Father of the Port of Houston." The town was first named *Tom Ball* and later became *Tomball.* The adjacent town of *Peck,* platted in 1906, was absorbed by Tomball in 1907. The community developed as a railroad stop on the Trinity and Brazos Valley Railroad. An earlier town given the name of *Tom Ball* became *North Houston* in 1909.
PO Mar. 5, 1908–; Pop. 4,651; Inc.

Tom Bean *(Grayson)*

The community came into existence in 1887 when the Cotton Belt Railroad was completed. A picturesque surveyor named Tom Bean gave fifty acres for the townsite to lure the railroad to the area.
PO Jan. 24, 1888–; Pop. 629; Inc.

Tonk Creek *(Throckmorton)*

The stream was named by abbreviating the name of the Tonkawa Indians. At least four other Texas counties claim creeks named for the same Indian tribe.

The Trap *(Tom Green)*

The "trap," or panhandle of the county stretches over a two-mile width for some thirty miles westward. When the county, which once spread over West Texas to New Mexico over an area of 12,500 square miles, was divided, residents of the county still wanted access to the outer reaches of their own land; hence the "trap" provided a westward access route.

Tres Marias Island *(Kenedy)*

The name is Spanish, "Island of the Three Marys," and probably refers to the three Marys in the Bible—Mary, mother of Jesus; Mary Magdalene; and Mary of Bethany.

Trickham *(Coleman)*

The present name evolved from *Trick 'em*, alluding to a store owner who enjoyed playing practical jokes—per-

haps putting mousetraps in the cracker barrel or pepper in the snuff. The most famous prank of Tom Peters was to fill liquor bottles with water for his cowboy customers. *Trick 'em* was submitted to the postal department, which dignified it a bit as *Trickham*.
PO Apr. 10, 1879–July 31, 1958; Pop. 40.

Troup *(Cherokee, Smith)* [trup]

This community was named for Governor George M. Troup of Georgia. In 1877, the nearby Zavala post office was merged with that of Troup.
PO June 7, 1854 (Troup, first of this name)–Dec. 19, 1877; Jan. 8, 1873 (Zavala)–Dec. 19, 1877 (Troup, second of this name)–; Pop. 1,771; Inc.

True *(Young)*

After *Liberty* was disqualified as a name since there was a southeast Texas post office by that name, Mrs. George Terrell, wife of the man who gave land for the settlement, offered *True* as a virtuous name. In 1877 George Terrell had wanted to start the town so badly he offered to deed an acre of land to every man who would build a home here.
PO Nov. 22, 1894–Feb. 29, 1912.

Tulia *(Swisher)* ['tul yə]

The town is near the Tule Canyon, Tule Creek, and Tule Draw, all deriving their names from the Spanish word *tule*, a kind of bulrush. An error in recording the name of the post office produced *Tulia* rather than *Tule*.
PO Aug. 22, 1887–; Pop. 5,328; Inc. 1909.

Turkey *(Hall)*

Wild turkeys which were plentiful along *Turkey Creek* also gave the town its name of *Turkey Roost*, later shortened to *Turkey*. Texas has at least twenty-three Turkey creeks.
PO Mar. 3, 1893–July 15, 1895; Mar. 5, 1900–; Pop. 684; Inc.

Tuxedo *(Jones)* [təks 'ı do]

The original name of the town was *Bonita*, which means "pretty" in Spanish. When the Texas Central Railroad opened the townsite in 1907, application for a post office required that the name be changed because of duplica-

tion. In discussing several possibilities for a name, Warren Foster suggested *Tuxedo,* and it was accepted immediately.
PO Aug. 29, 1907–; Pop. 42.

Twin Sisters *(Blanco)*

Two peaks in a chain of hills look so much alike that settlers decided they had to be sisters. The name of the peaks was transferred to the town that developed nearby.
PO Dec. 24, 1856–Jan. 23, 1867; July 10, 1867; Pop. 78; Mountain El. 1,767.

Umbrella Point Oil Field *(Chambers)*

The configuration of the point resembles an umbrella.

Uncertain *(Harrison)*

Several stories vie in explaining the name of the community. (1) Between 1832 and 1874, Caddo Lake was navigable for steamboats traveling from New Orleans to Jefferson, Texas. One of the ports in the area was called *Uncertain Landing* because boats had difficulty mooring here. (2) At the turn of the century a not-too-dependable fish buyer set up temporary headquarters in the area, but local anglers hoping to sell their catch knew they had an uncertain market, uncertain as to where the buyer would have his wagon and uncertain about his being there at all. (3) When the community was incorporated for the purpose of voting approval of liquor sales, the Texas attorney general stated he would see that such use of incorporation laws would not succeed. Hence, Uncertain was uncertain about its legal status. (4) Before incorporation, W. J. Sedberry and friends fished in the area and commented that they were uncertain about getting in and out if it rained.
Pop. 218; Inc.

Union *(Andrews; Falls; Lubbock)*

While most Texas communities with *Union* in the name refer to a sense of unity or a cluster of Union sympathizers, the settlement in Andrews County owes its name to the Union Oil Company of California. A church in the Falls County community was a union of all faiths during the 1870s, inviting all preachers to come and give sermons. A union Sunday school for five denominations provided the name for the community with this name in

Lubbock County. The name is also found in Eastland, Hopkins, Terry, Washington, and Wilson counties.

Utopia *(Uvalde)* [yu 'to pɪ ə]

The area was settled in 1852 by Captain William Ware, one of Sam Houston's fighting men at San Jacinto. His son-in-law, Robert Kincheloe, assigned the name of *Waresville*. In 1883, an attempt was made to change the name to *Montania*, in reference to the surrounding hill country, but it failed. George Barker, a school teacher impressed with the scenery, gave the settlement the name coined by Sir Thomas More for his famous book, *Utopia*, from the Greek roots meaning "not a place." Because Victor Prosper Considérant, a French socialist, owned land in Sabinal Canyon in the Utopia area, it has been suggested that the name came from his search for a Texan utopia. He left the state in 1869 to return to France after having failed to realize his utopias at La Reunion (Dallas County) and elsewhere in Texas. *PO Jan. 13, 1876 (Waresville)—Sept. 1, 1885 (Utopia)—; Pop. 360.*

Valentine *(Jeff Davis)* ['væl ən taɪn]

A construction crew for the Texas and New Orleans Railway chose the name of *Valentine* when they reached

the site on Valentine's Day, 1882. People from all over the United States and Canada send the postmaster their valentines for a Valentine postmark. Little credence is given to a competing story that a man named Valentine quit the railroad and built a café here.
PO Jan. 22, 1886–; Pop. 224; Inc.

Vanderbilt *(Jackson)*

The name refers not to the wealthy American tycoons but to the heroic captain of a cotton barge that was sunk in the mouth of the Navidad River near the end of the Civil War. The town was established with the coming of the railroad in 1904.
PO Apr. 8, 1907–; Pop. 667.

Vega *(Oldham)* ['ve gə]

A. M. Miller, who founded a store on the site in 1903, submitted the name of *Gusben* for his two sons—*Gus* and *Stephen*—as well as *Vega* and other names to be considered by postal officials. *Vega* was chosen as suitable because it described the level land. The Spanish word means "meadow."
PO Jan. 30, 1904–; Pop. 933; Inc.

Venus *(Johnson)*

Most sources report that Venus got its name from J. C. Smith, who wanted to honor Venus Housby, daughter of a local physician. Ruth Wilkerson insists, however, that her father always said the name came from the fondness of a Dr. Fontaine, one of the town founders, for a statue of Venus. He thought the site of the town was as pretty as the Greek goddess of love. It is understandable that the founders were looking for a name of beauty, since the settlement was first called *Gossip*.
PO Oct. 4, 1888 (Gossip)–Dec. 12, 1888 (Venus)–; Pop. 324; Inc.

Vercal *(Anderson)*

The switching stop on the railroad took its name as a shortened form of *Vern Calhoun*, who had a packing plant at a siding on the Texas South-Eastern Railroad.

Veribest *(Tom Green)*

The area had been known as *Mullin*, for Isaac Mullin, who settled in the area in 1873, but when a post office was sought in 1926 *Mullin* duplicated an office near Brownwood. In a contest to choose a new name, Mattie Bean submitted the winning entry of *Veribest*. She got the name from the Very Best brand of canned goods sold in her brother-in-law's store.

Viboras *(Starr)* [vi 'bo rəs]

Víboras, meaning "rattlesnake," was the name given this ranch town by Don Manuel Guerra when it was founded about 1890, because of the large number of rattlers.
PO June 9, 1909–; Pop. 22.

Victoria *(Limestone; Victoria)*

Founded in 1824 by Martín de León on the banks of the Guadalupe River, the town in Victoria County was originally called *Guadalupe Victoria* in honor of the first president of Mexico, Manuel Félix Fernández, who changed his name to Guadalupe Victoria in homage to the Virgin of Guadalupe. Later the name was shortened by dropping *Guadalupe.* The community of Victoria in Limestone County, established in the early 1900s, honors Queen Victoria through its name.
(Victoria Co.) PO May 22, 1846–; Pop. 44,842; Inc.

Victory City *(Bowie)*

The boomtown developing at the entrance to the Lone Star Defense Plan at the beginning of World War II was given a patriotic name to reflect its contribution to the war effort.

Vidor *(Orange)* ['vaɪ dər]

The town grew up around the Miller-Vidor Lumber company logging camp in 1907. It was named for C. S. Vidor, mill operator, whose son, King Vidor, became a director of motion pictures, including *The Champ* and *Northwest Passage.*
PO Feb. 1, 1909–July 31, 1911; Oct. 26, 1912–; Pop. 10,756; Inc.

Vinegarone *(Val Verde)* [vɪn ər gə 'ron]

The whip scorpion, which is common in the area of the community, emits a vinegarlike odor when alarmed and is called the *vinegarone.*
PO Jan. 27, 1926–June 15, 1926.

Voca *(McCulloch)* ['vo kə]

John Deans wanted to use *Avoca,* for the community in Arkansas, but upon being told that the name was already in use in Texas he dropped the *a-*.

Von Ormy *(Bexar)* [van 'ar mı]

Manns Crossing became *Von Ormy* in 1886 to honor Count Adolph von Ormy of Austria, who bought a 2,300-acre tract on the Medina River in 1885.
PO Jan. 14, 1879 (Manns Crossing)–Nov. 9, 1880; Sept. 18, 1886–Dec. 4, 1886 (Von Ormy)–; Pop. 264.

Waka *(Ochiltree)* ['wa kə]

The original name was *Wawaka* for the Indiana home-town of Mr. and Mrs. D. B. Stump, whose farm became the site of the first post office. The Indian meaning of the word was "wet or swampy ground." When the post office was moved to the Burnside railroad switch, it was dis-covered that *Burnside* duplicated another switch name, and the railroad accepted *Waka* as a shortening of *Wawaka*.
PO Sept. 7, 1902 (Wawaka)–July 31, 1917; June 14, 1920–May 1, 1929 (Waka)–; Pop. 145.

Wake Village *(Bowie)*

M. E. Melton suggested the name for the Texarkana sub-urb during World War II when the Battle of Wake Island was in the headlines. The community provided housing for defense plant workers, who lived on streets named with a World War II motif: Burns Road, McArthur Ave-nue, Victory Place, Midway Drive.
Pop. 3,600; Inc.

Walhalla *(Comal; Fayette)* [wal 'ha lə]

Fayette County settlers viewed the locale as such a heav-enly place that they chose the word for a Teutonic ver-sion of the ancient Norse Valhalla, a paradise for fallen warriors. The Comal County community that is now *Sattler* was also known as *Walhalla* in 1877, named for the Walhalla Singing Club.
(Fayette Co.) PO Sept. 29, 1886–Nov. 30, 1909; Pop. 37.

Wall Eye Creek *(Lee, Milam)*

A teamster was crossing the creek with his yoke of oxen when his wagon mired. Some passerby, interested in his predicament, foolishly asked, "What are you doing here?" "Just wauling my eye," the teamster replied. And from that time on, this creek has been Wall Eye Creek.

Wamba *(Bowie)* ['wam bɪ] ['wam bə]

The community was named between 1855 and 1860 at a time when Wamba was a popular brand of coffee.
Pop. 70.

Warsaw *(Kaufman)*

The community was founded near a water supply at Warsaw Creek. Friendly Indians directed White settlers to a spring-fed stream, which they called by a name interpreted as *Warsaw* by the settlers. The Indians were actually saying *water*, but their English was misunderstood. The name is also found in Harrison and San Augustine counties.
PO Dec. 23, 1847 (Warsaw Prairie)–Jan. 22, 1858; Apr. 24, 1858–Oct. 7, 1958; Pop. 58.

Wasp Creek *(McLennan)*

One of the Texas Rangers—with a fondness for honey, no doubt—mistook a wasp nest for a beehive. His mistake caused comrades to spin yarns and create a name for the nearby creek.

Waxahachie *(Ellis)* [wɔks ə 'hæ čı]

The Chamber of Commerce translates the Indian word as "cow creek," but outside historians believe a more accurate rendering would be "cow chips." The county seat is located on Waxahachie Creek, a name given by the Tonkawa Indians for the cows they found here. Other Indians inhabiting the area were the Kickapoos, Bidai, Anadarkos, and Wacos. The first White settler was Emory W. Rogers, who came upon the open expanses of prairie in 1846. His land grants for the town materially aided in the selection of Waxahachie as county seat in 1850. The famed Chisholm Trail once passed through what is now the center of town.
PO Aug. 13, 1850–; Pop. 13,785; Inc.

Wayland *(Stephens)*

In stage coach days, a popular way station developed here at a spot fifteen miles from Breckenridge, sixteen miles from Eastland, and seventeen miles from Ranger. It was "on the way" to several spots.
PO May 29, 1877–1945; Pop. 15.

Weches *(Houston)* ['wi čɪz]

After *Neches* was chosen as the name desired for the town because of the nearby river, postal officials discovered another town had been assigned that name. Local citizens then settled for changing the first letter to create *Weches*. T. J. Hennin had settled in the area before 1847 and provided its earlier name.
PO Aug. 9, 1887–; Pop. 26.

Weeping Mary *(Cherokee)*

A Bible-reading resident was responsible for the name when he recalled the scene in which Mary Magdalene wept at the tomb of Jesus.

Weesatche *(Goliad)* ['wi sæč]

The town was named for the huisache bush which grows abundantly in the area. The name was spelled as it was heard, rather than according to the Spanish-derived spell-

ing. An earlier name was *Middletown*, for its location midway between Goliad and Clinton.
PO Nov. 22, 1855 (Middletown)–Sept. 26, 1859; May 16, 1860 (Wesatch)–Nov. 5, 1866; May 16, 1870 (Wesatche)– Dec. 9, 1879; Jan. 5, 1880 (Weesatche)–; Pop. 516.

Welcome *(Austin)*

The name is attributed to J. F. Schmidt, who was impressed by the friendly hospitality shown by residents extending a vigorous welcome.
PO Nov. 20, 1871–; Pop. 150.

Wellington *(Collingsworth)*

Not far from *Aberdeen*, honoring the Duke of Aberdeen, Scotland, is this town named for the English Duke of Wellington.
PO Jan. 9, 1891–; Pop. 2,815; Inc.

Weslaco *(Hidalgo)* [ˈwɛs lə ko]

The town was laid out by the W. E. Stewart Land Company, promoted as a townsite in 1917, and incorporated in 1921. Its name is an abbreviation of the company name.
PO Mar. 17, 1920–; Pop. 20,007; Inc. 1921.

Wheat Oil Field *(Loving)*

The first oil field in the county was named for the wheat it ruined in a field near Mentone.

Whiskey Creek *(Young)*

On the bank stood a little shack where the widow of a man killed by Indians in the late 1850s sold her whiskey. One of the county's first saloons was opened near this stream.

White City *(San Augustine)*

A lumber company established a camp here using white tents as quarters for employees. The color of the tents supplied the descriptive name when it was time to submit one to the postal department. The same name is used for communities in Chambers, Gaines, and Wilbarger counties.
PO Jan. 13, 1910–discontinued 1931; Pop. 20.

White Deer *(Carson)*

The original name of *Whig* was changed to *White Deer,*
referring to White Deer Creek, where Indian tradition
maintained there was a white deer. The town moved a
half mile to its present location in 1908 to be on the
Santa Fe Railroad. A statue of a white deer was erected to
commemorate the town's namesake.
*PO Dec. 17, 1888 (Whig)–Jan. 7, 1889 (White Deer)–;
Pop. 1,054; Inc.*

Whiteface *(Cochran)*

When Colonel C. C. Slaughter brought the first Hereford
cattle to this area, he placed them in a special pasture,
known as the "whiteface pasture," since the Hereford has
the distinguishing feature of a white face with a red body.
PO Dec. 15, 1925–; Pop. 535; Inc.

Whiteland *(McCulloch)*

F. R. White, a rancher, donated land for the townsite,
making the area literally White land.
PO Apr. 26, 1912–discontinued before 1968.

White River *(Castro, Crosby, Floyd, Garza, Hale, Kent,
Lamb, Llano, Parmer)*

The Spanish name *blanco* was translated to provide a
name for the river. The intermittent stream heads in
New Mexico.

Whon *(Coleman)* [hwan]

A respected cowboy of Mexican ancestry named *Juan*
lived in the community. Mrs. Sam McCain, the first
postmaster, spelled his name phonetically in English and
submitted it as the post office name.
PO June 16, 1903–Apr. 30, 1909; Mar. 31, 1910–; Pop. 15.

Willimar *(Willacy)*

Will Harding and Lamar Gill were partners in the development of the town and partners in the name, which
combines Harding's first name and the last syllable of
Lamar's, adding the letter *i* to join the two syllables.

Wilymae *(Tyler)*

Despite the impression given that a woman had something to do with this name, it actually came from two

early male citizens, Wily Cunningham, a general store operator, and Mae Gore, a preacher.

Winedale *(Fayette, Washington)*

An earlier name was somewhat troublesome, and it was changed to *Winedale* because of the wine industry made possible by the excellent grape crops. The earlier name was *Truebsal,* meaning "trouble" in German. The founder of the settlement in 1870 was Charles Windewehen. Winedale, which is located on the county line, was a post office in Washington County April 1, 1879–May 2, 1881, but is now considered to be in Fayette County.

Wink *(Winkler)*

The town, nearby oil field, and airport took their name from the first syllable of Winkler County. The county was named for Judge C. M. Winkler (1821–1882), a colonel in the Confederate Army and a member of the Texas legislature. Stationery had already been printed with the town name of *Winkler* when the postal department disqualified it as duplication of another Texas office at that time; thus, the last syllable had to be eliminated. The name *Wink* is shared by settlements in Hunt and Wise counties.
PO July 1, 1927–; Pop. 1,200.

Winnsboro *(Franklin, Wood)*

The community derived its name from John E. Wynne, who settled here in 1854, but when the town was named the newspaper editor had run out of *y's* in his type case, and he altered the spelling. Some people unfamiliar with -*boro* as a shortened form of *borough* meaning "town" and who decided that perhaps Wynne had owned a burro have suggested that Wynn's burro had produced the name of *Winnsboro*. Such an explanation has no basis in fact.
PO March 6, 1855 (Winnsborough)–Feb. 7, 1868; June 25, 1874 (Winnsboro)–; Pop. 3,290; Inc.

Wizard Wells *(Jack)*

In the 1880s, George Washington Vineyard, who was afflicted with chronic leg sores and eye disease, found water on his land that was repulsive to the taste but miraculously curative to eyes and body. The community was known first as *Vineyard* and later as *Wizard Wells,* named for John Wizard, who developed the mineral wells into a health resort. Today Wizard Wells has no post

office, but the community receives mail service from the town of Vineyard, which developed a few miles to the south and took the original name of the Wizard Wells post office.
PO July 26, 1882 (Vineyard, first)—Oct. 2, 1914 (Wizard Wells)—May 29, 1889 (Sebree)—June 16, 1915 (Vineyard, second)—; Pop. 69.

Wobblety, Bobblety, Turnover, and Stop *(Trinity)*

The railroad was so named because it had so many wrecks. It was formerly the Waco, Beaumont, Trinity, and Sabine Railroad.

Woden *(Nacogdoches)* ['wod n̩]

The father of Germanic gods was suggested as the town name by Anna Dodds Green, second postmaster.
PO June 25, 1886—; Pop. 70.

Woodrow *(Lubbock)*

In the same county where New Deal and Roosevelt are located there is also a settlement named for Woodrow Wilson. The citizens had considerable trouble deciding on *Woodrow* or *Wilson* as the designation. A post office named *Woodrow* operated in Hardin County, 1913—1918. *Pop. 85.*

XIT Ranch *(Bailey, Castro, Cochran, Dallam, Deaf Smith, Hartley, Hockley, Lamb, Oldham, Parmer)* ['ɛks 'aɪ 'ti]

John V. and C. B. Farwell devised the brand for the ranch. Translated, it means *X*—"ten," *I*—"in," and *T*—"Texas," referring to the ten counties in which the ranch was located. The ranch was created in 1885 when the Capitol Syndicate of Chicago received 3,050,000 acres of land for building the Texas capitol in Austin.

Xmas Day Oil Field *(Titus)*

John B. Stephens, Jr., and his associates began drilling a well northeast of Talco in 1954. The well was declared a producer on Christmas Day, 1954.

X-Ray *(Erath)*

The ranching community was named for its location at a road intersection. A natural gas field discovered at this location in 1920 also took the name.
PO Dec. 1, 1897 (Exray)—Nov. 30, 1906.

Yankee Creek *(Rockwell)*

During the Civil War, according to an account passed down to oldtimers in the county, a Yankee was hanged here.

Yard *(Anderson)*

Bruce Gray, a merchant, was in his store writing a list of possible names to send to the post office department. While he was doing so, a customer came in and ordered a yard of cloth. Gray included the name *Yard* in his list, and when the post office chose a name for the town, *Yard* it was.
PO July 21, 1903–June 30, 1911; Pop. 18.

Yegua Creek *(Burleson, Lee, Milam, Washington, Williamson)* ['ye wɔ]

When foaling, the native white mares, Texas's famed mustangs, liked to stay along the screening banks of streams. In the Indian tongue, these streams became *yegua* or "mare" streams.

Yellow House Draw *(Cochran)*

The Indian cave dwellings in the yellowish bluff at Yellow House Lake gave the draw its name.

Yellowpine *(Sabine)*

The high quality of yellow pine lumber that was milled here provided the name.
PO June 17, 1902–discontinued; Pop. 75.

Yo-Lo-Digo Creek *(Frio, Zavala)* [yo lo 'di go]

Mexicans walking toward the creek in single file heard their leader make a noise that sounded like a splash. On being asked, "¿Es agua?" (Is it water?), the leader replied, "Yo lo digo" (I say it is), providing a name for the waterway.

Yorktown *(De Witt)*

The German community was founded in the 1840s by John York, who was slain in an Indian raid soon thereafter. When the community began to shift to the south toward the San Antonio and Aransas Pass Railroad, the

old location was called *Upper Town*, and the new town was called *Lower Town* until it took the name of *Yorktown*.
PO Mar. 10, 1851–; Pop. 2,302; Inc. 1871.

Yougeen *(Bee)* [yu 'jin]

The spelling is deceptive in light of the fact that Eugenia McGloin gave land for the railroad station in 1911 and named it for herself.

Zacaweista Ranch *(Wilbarger)* ['zæ kə ,wis tə]

Appropriately for a ranch, the name comes from an Indian word meaning "grassy" and is used for the home of Electra Waggoner Wharton on the Waggoner Ranch. Names around the ranch include *Whiskey Tank, Dead Man Tank,* and *Red Ass Pasture.*

Zapata *(Zapata)* [zə 'pa tə]

Emiliano Zapata, the Mexican revolutionary leader, had no influence on the naming of the county or of the county seat. The source is Antonio Zapata, a stockman who came from Mexico and supported creation of the Republic of the Rio Grande. An earlier name was *Carrizo*, Spanish for "reed, cane, or bamboo."
PO Jan. 16, 1854 (Carrizo)–Nov. 5, 1866; July 27, 1871 (San Bartolo)–Oct. 10, 1872; Nov. 19, 1872–Mar. 13, 1874 (Carrizo)–Mar. 5, 1880; Apr. 5, 1880–May 2, 1901 (Zapata)–; Pop. 3,500.

Zephyr *(Brown)* ['zɛf ər]

A party of surveyors plotting the original land grants in the winter of 1850 experienced a severe "blue norther." One surveyor remarked, "This is some zephyr we have run into." The name stuck and was chosen when application was made for a post office, although a zephyr is actually a west wind or gentle breeze.
PO Dec. 29, 1879–; Pop. 198.

Zigzag *(Medina)*

The road leading to the community had so many turns in it that many a zigzag was required to reach this destination.
PO Dec. 31, 1901–Aug. 31, 1911.

Zip City *(Dallas)*

According to a popular anecdote, the name was contributed by an elderly woman resident who passed the time
on her front porch watching the automobiles zip through
the town.

Zunkerville *(Karnes)*

One of the town's early Polish founders lent his surname
as the town name.

Texas County Map

Index of Counties

Diddy Waw Diddy or Ditty Waw Ditty, Freeport, Liverpool, Rosharon

BRAZOS: Boonville, College Station, Dinkins, Mudville, Reliance, Smetana

BREWSTER: Alpine, Calamity Creek, Christmas Mountain, Marathon, Study Butte, Terlingua, Tesnus

BRISCOE: Dinner Creek, Gasoline, Palo Duro Canyon, Quitaque

BROOKS: Encino, Falfurrias, Flowella

BROWN: Blanket, Cross Cut, May West Oil Field, Zephyr

BURLESON: Frenstat, Hogg, Hooker Creek, Snook, Yegua Creek

BURNET: Bachelor Peak, Dead Man's Well, Mahomet, Naruna, Oakalla, Oatmeal

CALDWELL: Black Ankle, Lockhart, Prairie Lea

CALHOUN: Chocolate Bay, Espiritu Santo Bay, Indianola, Long Mott

CALLAHAN: Admiral, Belle Plain, Deadman Creek, Three Aces Oil Field

CAMERON: Arroyo Colorado, Bluetown, Padre Island, Rangerville, Resaca del Rancho Viejo

CAMP: Elwood Lake, Leesburg

CARSON: Deal, Panhandle, Pantex, Skellytown, White Deer

CASS: Nickle Berry, St. Helena, Three States

CASTRO: Flagg, Nazareth, White River, XIT Ranch

CHAMBERS: Anahuac, Cherry Point Gully, Eminence, Fig Ridge, High Island, Lake Surprise, Needlepoint Road, Pine Island, Round Lake, Umbrella Point Oil Field

CHEROKEE: Alto, Angelina River, Battle Ridge, Beans Creek, Concord, Fastrill, Forest, Ironton, Java, Larissa, Maydelle, Neches River, One-Eye Creek, Ponta, Reklaw, Shorters Defeat, Troup, Weeping Mary

CHILDRESS: Carey, Loco, Tell

CLAY: Henrietta, Joy, Newport, New York, Petrolia, Prospect

COCHRAN: County Line, Whiteface, XIT Ranch, Yellow House Draw

COKE: Bronte, Nipple Mountain or Nipple Peak, Tennyson

COLEMAN: Bull Creek, Centennial, Echo, Mukewater, Rockwood, Trickham, Whon

COLLIN: Altoga, Culleoka, Desert, Frognot, Old Egypt, Pot Rack Creek

COLLINGSWORTH: Aberdeen, Samnorwood, Wellington

COLORADO: Altair, Bucksnag Creek, Eagle Lake, Mentz, Mohat, Nada, Peach Creek

COMAL: Comal, Devils Back Bone, Jacobs Creek, New Braunfels, Solms, Sour Creek, Walhalla

COMANCHE: Copperas Creek, Democrat, Duster, Energy, Potato Hill, Sipe Springs

CONCHO: Eola, Lowake, Paint Rock

COOKE: Custer, Dexter, Leo, Muenster

CORYELL: Clabber Creek, Cowhouse Creek, Ireland, Jack Mountain, Levita, Pancake
COTTLE: Cee Vee, Narcisso, Paducah, Tennessee Valley
CRANE: Crawar Oil Field, Soda Lake
CROCKETT: Devil's River, Ozona
CROSBY: Crawfish Creek, Estacado, Pansy, White River
CULBERSON: Diablo Mountains, El Capitan, Frijole, The Pass of the Camels
DALLAM: Dalhart, XIT Ranch, Texline
DALLAS: Dallas, Grand Prairie, La Reunion, Scyene, Zip City
DAWSON: Lamesa, Lost Draw, Sand
DEAF SMITH: Dawn Hereford, Tierra Blanca Creek, XIT Ranch
DELTA: Bloody Hollow, Cleveland, Doctors Creek, Eureka, Honest, Jot 'Em Down, Kensing, Long Taw, Old Granny's Neck, Race Track
DENTON: Aubrey, Drop, Flower Mound, Icarian, Innocent City, Pilot Knob, Pilot Point
DEWITT: Coleto Creek, Cuero, Five Mile, Irish Creek, Lost Creek, Pearl City, Yorktown
DICKENS: Afton, Espuela, Midway, Spur
DIMMIT: Espantosa Lake, Pilon or Pelon Creek, Soldier Lake
DONLEY: Clarendon, Jericho
DUVAL: Jaboncillos Creek, Sejita, Seven Sisters
EASTLAND: Ranger, Rising Star, Tiffin
ECTOR: Douro, Notrees, Odessa
EDWARDS: Bull Head Creek, Devil's Sinkhole, Painted Bluff, Pike's Peak or Pike Peak, Silver Lake
ELLIS: India, Italy, Maypearl, Ozro, Waxahachie
EL PASO: Anthony, El Paso, Franklin Mountains
ERATH: Duffau, Flag Creek, X-Ray
FALLS: Durango, Satin, Stranger, Union
FANNIN: Black Monk, Bug Tussle, Duplex, Edhube, Honey Grove, Ivanhoe, New Fulp, Orangeville, Sugar Bottom, Telephone, Three P
FAYETTE: Cistern, High Hill, Lost Pines of Texas, Muldoon, Nechanitz, Praha, Walhalla, Winedale
FISHER: Celotex, Eskota
FLOYD: Barwise, Floydada, White River
FOARD: Margaret, Paradise, Talking John Creek, Thalia
FORT BEND: Fresno, Katy, Missouri City, Needville, Rosenberg, Sugarland
FRANKLIN: Cobb Jones Creek, Friendship, Mount Vernon, Winnsboro
FREESTONE: Bi-Stone Oil Field, Dew, Donie, Fairfield, Israel, Tehuacana
FRIO: Big Foot, Derby Town, Dilley, Divot, San Miguel Creek, Yo-Lo-Digo Creek
GAINES: Arrow Oil Field, Loop, Seminole, Tex-Mex Oil Field
GALVESTON: Algoa, Dollar Point, Friendswood, Kemah, La Marque, Offatt Bayou, Pelican Island

GARZA: Justiceburg, Post, White River
GILLESPIE: Bankersmith, Contrary Creek, Flag Creek, Fredericksburg, Luckenbach, Mount Nebo, Pedernales River, Stonewall
GLASSCOCK: Fool Creek, Garden City, St. Lawrence
GOLIAD: Angel City, Berclair, Charco, Cologne, Goliad, Melon Creek, Mucorrera Creek, Weesatche
GONZALES: Bebe, Cheapside, Cost, Peach Creek
GRAY: Allenreed or Alanreed, Hoover, Pampa
GRAYSON: Bells, Bones Chapel, Dixie, Fink, Tioga, Tom Bean
GREGG: Bull Hide Slough, Hog Eye, Longview, Peatown, Rabbit Creek
GRIMES: Apolonia, Iola, Navasota
GUADALUPE: Barbarosa, Cibolo, Geronimo, New Berlin
HALE: Edenville, White River
HALL: Eli, Plaska, Turkey
HAMILTON: Cowhouse Creek, Fairy, Hico
HANSFORD: Hitchland, Oslo
HARDEMAN: Chillicothe, Medicine Mound, Quanah
HARDIN: Ariola, Concord, Grayburg, Hard Luck Creek, Neches River, Pigeon Roost Prairie, Sourlake, Thicket
HARRIS: Baytown, Buffalo Bayou, Genoa, Golden Acres, Humble, Katy, Missouri City, Moonshine Hill, Tomball
HARRISON: Darco, Elysian Fields, Five Notch, Karnack, Scratch Eye, Shoe String, Uncertain
HARTLEY: Dalhart, Romero, XIT Ranch
HASKELL: Red Paint Creek, Rule
HAYS: Buda, Niederwald, Pedernales River
HEMPHILL: Gem, Needmore
HENDERSON: Athens, Battle Creek, Fincastle, Koon Kreek Klub, Neches River, New York, Pattowatomie Creek, Science Hill
HIDALGO: Alamo, Bolsa Rancho, Citrus City, Mercedes, Relampago, Weslaco
HILL: Birome, Chatt, Itasca
HOCKLEY: Pep, Ropesville, Sundown, XIT Ranch
HOOD: Acton, Brandy Creek, Contrary Creek, Nubbin, Panter, Star Creek
HOPKINS: Addran, Buggy Whip Creek, Peerless, Pickton, Thermo, Tinrag, Tira
HOUSTON: Abe, Austonio, Fodice, Latexo, Neches River, Reynard, Weches
HOWARD: Alward, Big Spring, Coahoma, Elbow, Forsan
HUDSPETH: Acala, Arroyo River, Red Light
HUNT: Black Cat Thicket, Cash, Commerce, Concord, Cowskin Creek, Oyster Creek, Pleasant Valley, Scatter Branch
HUTCHINSON: Gewhitt, Starvation Creek
IRION: Bull Run Creek, Ketchum Mountains
JACK: Loving, Possum Kingdom Lake, Wizard Wells

JACKSON: Bacontown, Edna, Francitas, Ginville, La Salle, Lolita, Texana, Vanderbilt

JASPER: Angelina River, Beans Place, Bessmay, Browndell, Dryburg, Neches River, Remlig

JEFF DAVIS: Boracho Peak, Casket Mountain, Valentine

JEFFERSON: Beaumont, Concord, La Belle, Neches River, Nome, Providence, Spindle Top

JIM HOGG: Ramirito, Randado

JIM WELLS: Ben Bolt, Jaboncillos Creek, Palito Blanco

JOHNSON: Auburn, Bono, Dancl, Greenfield, Venus

JONES: Abilene, Avoca, Tuxedo

KARNES: Ecleto, Panna Maria, Zunkerville

KAUFMAN: Can't 'Cha Get Over Creek, Jiba, Lively, Mabank, Poetry, Styx, Warsaw

KENDALL: Bankersmith, Bergheim, Boerne, Comfort, Sisterdale

KENEDY: Padre Island, Sarita, Tres Marias Islands

KENT: Dry Duck Creek, Girard, White River

KERR: Legion, Silver Creek

KIMBLE: Contrary Creek, Johnson Creek, London, Pedernales River, Roosevelt, Segovia, Teacup, Telegraph

KING: Grow, Hollar Creek, Pen Branch

KINNEY: Anacacho Mountains, Laguna Plata, Tequesquite Creek

KLEBERG: Alazan Bay, Jaboncillos Creek, Padre Island, Riviera

KNOX: Knox City, Rhineland

LAMAR: Ambia, Atlas, Direct, Globe, Glory, Razor,

LAMB: Earth, Fieldton, Illusion Lake, Sacred Heart, White River, XIT Ranch

LAMPASAS: Izoro, Rumley

LA SALLE: Burks, Dull, Los Angeles

LAVACA: Moravia, Novohrad, Seclusion, Sublime, Sweet Home

LEE: Dime Box, Hranice, Wall Eye Creek, Yegua Creek

LEON: Bear Grass, Concord, Keechie, Leona, Nineveh, Normangee

LIBERTY: Beef Head Creek, Bledsoe Creek, Cleveland, Daisetta, Liberty, Macedonia, Milvid

LIMESTONE: Benhur, Bi-Stone Oil Field, Booker T. Washington Park, Box Car Center, Odds, Point Enterprise, Tehuacana, Victoria

LIPSCOMB: First, Second, Third, Fourth, Fifth Creeks; Sherlock

LIVE OAK: Dinero, Kittle, Lagarto, LaParra Creek, Three Rivers

LLANO: Baby Head, Enchanted Rock, Flag Creek, French John Creek, Hogholler Creek, Oxford, Smoothing Iron Mountain or Iron Mountain, Tan Tought Creek, White River

LOVING: Mentone, Wheat Oil Field
LUBBOCK: Heckville, Hurlwood, New Deal, Roosevelt,
Slide, Union, Woodrow
LYNN: Grassland, Lost Draw, Tahoka
MCCULLOCH: Fife, Katemcy Creek, Mercury, Voca, Whiteland
MCLENNAN: Bullhide Creek, Buttermilk Hill, Concord,
Crush, Ocaw, Stampede Creek, Wasp Creek
MCMULLEN: Cross Cut, Frio, San Miguel Creek, Nopal,
Tilden
MADISON: Jozye, Midway, Normangee, North Zulch
MARION: Gay Assembly, Lodi, Potters Point
MARTIN: Stanton, Tarzan
MASON: Art, Fly Gap, Grit, Pontotoc
MATAGORDA: Blessing, Buckeye, Elmaton, Peach Creek
MAVERICK: Indio Ranch, Quemado, Tequesquite Creek
MEDINA: Hog Wallow Creek, Hondo, Mico, Quihi, Zigzag
MENARD: Celery Creek, Scalp Creek
MIDLAND: Hi-Lonesome Oil Field, Midland, Sprayberry
Oil Field
MILAM: Cannonsnap Creek, San Gabriel River, Wall Eye
Creek, Yegua Creek
MILLS: Caradan, Cowhouse Creek, Center City, Ebony, Star
MITCHELL: Lone Wolf Mountain, Loraine
MONTAGUE: Illinois Bend, Jim Ned Lookout, Sunset
MONTGOMERY: Cut and Shoot, Peach Creek, Splendora,
Taminia
MOORE: Cactus, Excell, Four Way, Sunray
MORRIS: Daingerfield, Lone Star, Snow Hill
MOTLEY: Dutchman, Flomot, Teepee Creek
NACOGDOCHES: Angelina River, Etoile, Looneyville,
Naclina, Nacogdoches, Pisgah, Sacul, Terrapin, Woden
NAVARRO: Board, Cryer Creek, Emhouse, Eureka,
Mesmeriser Creek, Silver City
NEWTON: Adsul, Belgrade, Bon Wier, Mayflower,
Quicksand, Scrapping Valley, Swindler Creek, Toledo
NOLAN: Maryneal, Sweetwater
NUECES: Aransas Pass, Calallen, Flour Bluff, North Pole,
Padre Island, Robstown, Saxet Oil and Gas Field
OCHILTREE: Lord, Notla, Waka
OLDHAM: Gruhlkey, Vega, XIT Ranch, Tascosa
ORANGE: Neches River, Orange, Texla, Vidor
PALO PINTO: Bloodweed Island, Lover's Retreat, Mineral
Wells, Possum Kingdom Lake
PANOLA: Buncombe, Carthage, Clayton, Deadwood, Fair
Play, Snap
PARKER: Buck Naked, Dicey, Mineral Wells, Sanctuary,
Tin Top
PARMER: Bovina, Friona, Hub, Lariat, Lazbuddie, White
River, XIT Ranch
PECOS: Imperial, Iraan, Squaw Tit Peak

POLK: Barnum, Camp Ruby, Israel, Long Tom Creek, Moscow, Neches River, Pluck, Segno, Swartout
POTTER: Amarillo, Bushland, Excell, Pullman
PRESIDIO: Gettysburg Peak, Marfa
RAINS: Dougherty, Ginger, Pilgrim Rest
RANDALL: Amarillo, Nigger Arroyo, Palo Duro Canyon, Tierra Blana Creek
REAGAN: Best, Rita Santa, Teepee Draw, Texon
REAL: Con Can, Pole Cave Creek
RED RIVER: Bogata, Cuthand, Kiomatia, Shadowland
REEVES: Balmorhea, Barilla, Gozar
REFUGIO: Austwell, Cranell, Inari, Tivoli
ROBERTS: Coon Hollow, Miami, Sour Dough Creek
ROBERTSON: Bald Prairie, Government Creek, New Baden, Staggers Point
ROCKWALL: Fate, Rockwall, Spunkie Ridge, Yankee Creek
RUNNELS: Content, Rowena
RUSK: Angelina River, Concord, Glenfawn, Harmony Hill, New Salem, Reklaw, Shake Rag
SABINE: Geneva, Yellowpine
SAN AUGUSTINE: Angelina River, Black Ankle, Chinquapin, White City
SAN JACINTO: Byspot, Coldspring, Pointblank
SAN PATRICIO: Aransas Pass, Edroy, Papalote Creek, Saint Paul
SAN SABA: San Saba, Skeeterville
SCHLEICHER: Devils River, Eldorado, Kaffir, Toenail Oil Field
SCURRY: Fluvanna, Hermleigh
SHACKELFORD: Acampo, Ibex
SHELBY: Bobo, Bone Hill, Choice, Goober Hill, San Augustine, Teneha
SHERMAN: Stratford, Texhoma
SMITH: Joy, Neches River, Noonday, Omen, Troup
SOMERVELL: Mitchell Bend, Nemo, Rainbow, Shaky Springs
STARR: Delmita, Roma, Viboras
STEPHENS: Bass Hollow, Frankell, Gunsight, LaCasa, Necessity, Picketville, Possum Kingdom Lake, Steal Easy Mountain, Wayland
STERLING: Moon Chapel, Nanhattie
STONEWALL: Aspermont, Old Glory
SUTTON: Caverns of Sonora, Devil's River
SWISHER: Happy, Palo Duro Canyon, Sunnyslope, Tulia
TARRANT: Big Fossil Creek, Dido, Garden of Eden, Lonesome Dove
TAYLOR: Abilene, Cat Claw Creek, Impact
TERRELL: Eight Mile Canyon, Paint Mare Ranch
TERRY: Lost Draw, Needmore, Tokio
THROCKMORTON: Antelope Creek, Given Creek, Humble, Lambs Head Creek, Tonk Creek

TITUS: Dragoo Creek, Monticello, Panthers Chapel, Smackover Creek, Sugar Hill, Xmas Day Oil Field, Talco

TOM GREEN: Christoval, Kickapoo Creek, Knickerbocker, The Trap, Veribest

TRAVIS: Bull Creek, Creedmoor, Nameless, Pedernales River

TRINITY: Apple Springs, Dads Creek, Friday, Neches River, Nigton, Nogalus, Scrub Creek, Sebastopol; Wobblety, Bobblety, Turnover, and Stop

TYLER: Chester, Drunkards Branch, Spurger, Wilymae

UPSHUR: Coffeeville, Concord, Enon

UPTON: Crockett Oil Field, Pegasus Oil Field, Sweetie-Peck Oil Field

UVALDE: Concan, Utopia

VAL VERDE: California Creek, Devil's River, Juno, Langtry, Shumla, Vinegarone

VAN ZANDT: Canton, China Grove, Grand Saline, Neches River

VICTORIA: Julia Pens, Raisin, Victoria

WALKER: Chicken Creek, Dodge, Four Notch, Lake Raven, New Waverly, Patella, Pole Cat Branch, Sudan Lake

WALLER: Katy, Sunnyside, Threemile Creek

WARD: Pyote, Royalty

WASHINGTON: Berlin, Gay Hill, Independence, Yegua Creek

WEBB: Becerra Creek, Laredo .

WHARTON: Danevang, Egypt, Iago, Magnet, Peach Creek

WHEELER: Benonine, Magic City, Shamrock

WICHITA: Avon, Bare Butte, Burkburnett, Clara, Electra, Pumpkin Center, Tenth Cavalry Creek

WILBARGER: Grayback, Zacaweista Ranch

WILLACY: La Sal Viega, Lasara, Padre Island, Santa Monica, Willimar

WILLIAMSON: Bagdad, Circleville, Jollyville, Jonah; Matthew, Mark, Luke, and John; Round Rock, San Gabriel River, Yegua Creek

WILSON: Alum, Calaveras, Kosciusko, La Vernia, Lodi, Loire, Saspamco

WINKLER: Kermit, Wink

WISE: Balsora, Paradise

WOOD: Little Hope, Mutt and Jeff, Terrapin, Winnsboro

YOAKUM: Allred, Bronco, Denver City, Lost Draw

YOUNG: Gooseneck, Newcastle, Possum Kingdom Lake, True, Whiskey Creek

ZAPATA: Falcon Reservoir, Zapata

ZAVALA: Chaparrosa Creek, Cometa, Crystal City, Yo-Lo-Digo Creek